The Guide's Guide Augmented

A river journey with caring, well-trained guides is much more than just a physical movement from put-in to take-out, it is a journey from fear to confidence to joy; from being a stranger to being known and feeling bonded with one's boat mates; from feeling perhaps scattered and self-critical inside to feeling more self-accepting, more whole, more fully alive—and, as an extra plus, it is a journey from feeling cut off from the natural world to feeling connected with and truly amazed and delighted by the magic of our planet. In short, a well-guided river trip is a voyage into deep fun.

Also by William McGinnis: *Whitewater Rafting*
Class V Briefing
River Signals

To learn about Bill's upcoming books,
visit www.williammcginnis.com

by William McGinnis

THE GUIDE'S GUIDE AUGMENTED

REFLECTIONS ON GUIDING PROFESSIONAL RIVER TRIPS

WhitewaterVoyages.com

(800) 400-RAFT

fun@whitewatervoyages.com

www.whitewatervoyages.com

Illustration and design by Kate Czekala, Caitlin Berrigan,
Jim Gwin and Bill McGinnis
Typography by Gwin Graphics, San Francisco, California.
Jim Gwin
And Progressive Printing Agency, Hong Kong,
Kevin To
Production by Cynthia Gwin.
Index by J. Naomi Linzer Indexing Services
Second Printing 1987
Third Printing 2005
Printed in Hong Kong
ISBN 0-9772774-0-2

ACKNOWLEDGEMENTS

The original **Guide's Guide** and the expanded **Guide's Guide** *Augmented* were made possible by the generous help and encouragement of many, many wonderful souls who have made vital contributions to Whitewater Voyages and the universe, and have added immeasurable joy and meaning to my life! In particular I thank the entire Whitewater Voyages staff past, present and future and extend special extra thanks to the intrepid Brian Mauer, my beloved sweetheart Bev, my dad, my sister Mary and brother Neville, Jim Cassady, Barry Kruse, Toni Hall, Pete Angstadt, Dave Arnold, Ed Denson, Steve Givant, Harry Chest, Mark Kocina, Todd Brownell, Dan and Mike Grant, Sue Mooney, Wanda and Ray Coughlin, Sheri Cole, Kay Vallis, Stephen Messer, Gene Evans, Sherrin Lindsay Farley, Janet McGinnis Wortendyke, Pat and Clay Jensen, Bill and Polly Cross, Tim Hillmer, Sally Holstrom, Peter Moritz, Jennifer Gold, Alan McCreedy, Matt and Suzie Downing, all of the god-like Sullivan and Natter brothers, Jon Runnestrand, Kathy Meyer, Kim Mansoor, Greg Faddis, Jim Gwin the elder, Pat Crevelt, Susan Maida, Chuck Champe, John and Toby Silva, Orea Roussis, Judy Fox, Sandy MacFarland, Suzie Dodge, Jib Ellison, Juliet Wiscombe, Buck Beddie, Ronaldo Macedo, Buck Swashbuckler, Aaron Tippett, Laynne Cooley, Jesse Nichols, Greg Vose, Wendy Keller, Emily Norton, Alice Diesinger, Courtenay Cochran, Holly Bounell, Tracy Vietta, Ian Morris, Jasmine and Bessie Jackson, Joe Villasenor, Kelly Richards, MacDuff Everton, Kim Locklin, Greg Smith, Beth Rypins, Tom Logan, Trixie, Mike Gill, Tom Joyce, Richard Wright, Christine Kyckelhahn Wilkins, Don Logon, Toni Meurlott, Mary Ann Terry, Patrick and Diane Noonan, Amicaya Frediani, Josh Sher, Dr. Glenn Etter, Roland Stevenson, Kyle Noon, Diamond Dave Catechi, Velcro Annie Ellicott, Simon Saichek, Jamie Johnston, Brian and Graham Simpson, Lisa Hayes, Kari Krebs, Lisa Barros Brown, Heidi Hawkins, Bob Anderson, Art Fowler, Marc Goddard, Laurence Alvarez-Roos, Serina Tremayne, Steve Miller, Phil Boyer, Tom "Rooster" Campbell, Mac Stant, Cyrus Luciano, Gary Osberg, Mandy Bleeker, Mark Bayless, Kelly Wiglesworth, Bridget Crocker, Becca Foster, Doctor Dry, David Land, Jason Clements, Carly Furry, Mark Van Buskirk, Jim Hartinger, and Isabella and Spreck Salaverry-Rosekrans. For their sharing, support, openness, companionship, wise counsel and brilliant outfitting expertise, I thank and acknowledge my present and future Raftnet river running buddies Joe, Sue, Ben and Ethan Greiner; Bruce, Karen, Abby and Hannah Lessels; Peter, Betsy, Mariah and Jonah Grubb; Brian, Dena, Taylor, Dylan and Caden Merrill; Brandon, Melanie and Chandler Lake; and Paul and Jennifer Breuer; my Focusing friends Yishai Hope, Jill Woolums, Oak Freed, David and Joyce Curry, Diana Brooks, Elaine Hannah, John Maddox, and Ann Weiser Cornell; and all of my Lakeridge Club cronies including my fabulous trainer Vanessa Alvares, and Yacoub, Jack, Randy, Mario, Art, John, Ray, Al, Jay, Hoc, Earnest, Lloyd, Butch and Dragonman Chris. I thank my outfitting friends, whose dedication to outfitting and contributions to the rafting industry make this world a better place: John, Chantal and Sage McDermott, Dave Slover, Greg, Scott and George Armstrong, Nate Rangel, Bill Center, Marty McDonnell, Luther Stevens, Jim Ritter, Kenny Bushling, Bob Ferguson, Jeb Butchart, George Wendt, Dick Lindford, Joe Daly, Steve Welch, Bill Zell, Bryan Fogelman, Lannie Yeager, Chris Condon, Kevin Cassity, David Brown, Norm Schoenhoff, Don Hill, Bill Wing, Mike Martel, Roger Lee, Donny Dove, Bob Volpert, Jerry Ashburn, Mike Doyle, Dave Hammond, Betty Lopez and Steve Lyles, Lorraine Hall, Dan Buckley, John Munger, Noah Hague, Rick Demerest, Ken Streater, Tom Moore, John Stallone, Joe Chesney, Bill Parks, Beth Harper, Beth Rundquist and Doug Tims. In memorium, I would like to thank and pay tribute to my beloved mom and brother Gregor, and to my dear friends Steve Fairchild, Judy Hart, Bill Ward Hall and Jim Gwin the younger, may their spirits merge in joy with the great Oneness. Above all, I thank and acknowledge my son Will and daughter Alexandra, who, just by being themselves, are such an inspiration to me!

W.M.

To Will and Aly

Table of Contents

PART 4: *River Signals*

PART 5: *Rescue*

PART 6: *Specifics*

PART 7: *Expedition Food Planning Guide*

PART 8: *Entertainment and Interpretation*

PART 9: *Knots*

****

Poem: While Driving Home from the Kings River to El Sobrante

INTRODUCTION

Few undertakings require as many different skills as guiding people down whitewater rivers. Based on the combined wisdom of the Whitewater Voyages staff, this book assumes the reader knows the basics of guiding and goes beyond to deal with the subtleties of conducting safe, educational, professional and above all, enjoyable river trips. The underlying philosophy of this volume can be expressed quite simply: Enthusiastically dedicate yourself to guiding, and try with all your heart to make each trip the finest possible.

A note about this **Augmented** edition: It is deeply gratifying that **The Guide's Guide** is in wider use and greater demand than ever. In addition to the "classic" **Guide's Guide** contents, this **Augmented** edition, reflecting new developments in the art of guiding, includes a boatload of new material throughout (especially in Parts 3, 4, 5, 8 & 9) on signals, safety, rescue, evacuation, knots, guide training, entertainment and interpretation.

This volume is intented to be much more than just the staff manual of Whitewater Voyages. My hope is that it will also be helpful, even inspirational, to people in general, including private boaters, guides, trip leaders, outfitters, government agency river and recreation managers, and adventure travel companies of all sorts. Any individual, company or group which practices the philosophy and methods presented here is welcome to consider this book their own staff manual, and, wherever the name Whitewater Voyages appears, to mentally insert their own.

The safer and better all rafting trips and outdoor recreation experiences, the better for all. The more people who return home in one piece, thrilled and delighted with their river trip or outdoor outing, the more river rafting and outdoor recreation in general will be seen as a great thing to do and the more all outfitters, the recreating public and our recreation resources will benefit.

Although the myriad users of this book are independent, far flung adventurers, guides, outfitters, tour operators and recreation resource managers, at the very same time, ideally, we are all working together to enhance the quality of life on this planet! The highest purpose of this book is to contribute to this broad, growing, wonderful effort—which is, after all, an ongoing quest of planet-saving proportions.

It is not enough just to get people as safely as possible down the river, it is also paramount for guides to enhance the fun, camaraderie, learning and openness on river trips.

1: *THE BIG PICTURE*

GUIDING IN GENERAL

River guides devote themselves to developing their own skills. They strive to become thoroughly competent in all aspects of river running, including everything from rowing, paddle captaining, signalling, knot tying, rigging, packing, derigging and patching to menu planning, shopping, cooking, backing up trailers, setting up tents, interpreting nature, telling stories, etc., etc. Above all, they strive to maneuver their boats with precision and skill.

LEARN EVERYTHING

Insightful guides provide sensitive leadership. For example, someone climbs up onto a high diving rock, freezes up with fear, and cannot decide whether or not to jump. A guide can save the situation and take the onus of failure off the non-jumper by flatly telling him or her *not* to jump, but to climb down instead.

SENSITIVE LEADERSHIP

Whitewater guides use good judgement. Example: At put-in a guest climbs aboard a raft with a six-pack of beer and asks where it should be stowed. The tactful guide says politely, "Put it in the baggage boat so that it can be enjoyed in camp—or at the take-out."

GOOD JUDGEMENT

Guides conduct themselves with maturity and dignity. This is especially important near the beginning of trips when guests are usually nervous and need reassurance that they are in good hands. For example, mature guides don't throw things or waterfight at put-ins. Later on, conditions permitting, they waterfight with gusto!

MATURITY

Everything a guide says or does will become, quick as lightning, public knowledge. Experienced guides bear this in mind and act with circumspection. If a guide behaves in an honorable manner, the world will know—and if he or she does not, it will know also.

PUBLIC KNOWLEDGE

The wise guide is always safety conscious: When driving, when on the river, *caution* is the watch word. A good guide does not take unnecessary risks—and takes extra care when backing up vehicles.

CAUTION

**CLASS IV &
V RIVERS**

To raft class IV and, particularly, class V rapids and waterfalls is to incur inherent risk, and it is only through the continual exercise of utmost caution—an ongoing redoubling of our standard high level of safety consciousness—that we navigate these treacherous waterways in safety. In other words, *on class IV or V whitewater, be extremely careful and exercise every possible safety precaution.* Before conducting trips on class IV runs, seasoned guides do at least two familiarization trips, for class V a minimum of three familiarization trips is required.

**FIRST AID
AND CPR
TRAINING**

For the sake of the safety of our clients, not to mention insurance company and government regulations, it is vital that all Whitewater Voyages guides carry, as a minimum, current Standard First Aid and CPR cards from the American Red Cross or other accredited organizations. The Forest Service and other government agencies require that we supply them with copies of the up-to-date first aid, CPR, WFR, and EMT cards carried by our guides.

WFR

Wilderness first responder and/or emergency medical technician training are extremely desirable. Our regular company first aid kits with their air splints, compresses, antiseptics, etc. are complete. Nonetheless, it is recommended that WFR's and EMT's, particularly on class V rivers, carry their own supplementary kits with any additional items of special first aid equipment that they feel might be useful.

**KNIFE &
STUFF**

At all times while on the river, well-equipped guides carry a good sheath knife which can be quickly accessed with one hand. Also, they have a brightly colored yellow or orange life jacket—preferably a high-float with 22 or more pounds flotation and a quick-release rescue harnass; a micro shield or breathing mask for protection while doing emergency breathing, a wet suit, a watertight box such as a Pelican case; a flashlight; and, if possible, a pair of channel locks. Plus, for rescues: at least four carabiners; two pulleys; an 8-foot flip line of one-inch tubular webbing worn as a belt; one or two additional 15- or 20-foot lenghts of one-inch tubular webbing, prusik or French braid loops; a climbing chock; and a small personal toss bag. Guides wear clothing that does not let private parts hang out. Important note: Folding and sheath knives are for emergency and general use—but are *not* used on food. Dip such a knife in mayonnaise one day, perhaps forget to clean it thoroughly, use it to spread peanut butter the next day, and you have shigellosis, a type of dysentery causing severe abdominal cramps, fever, nausea and even death. For food, always use clean paring and kitchen knives from the lunch utensil bag or kitchen box.

**EXTRA
LENSES &
EYEGLASSES**

Guides who need eyeglasses or contact lenses always carry extra. They understand that their ability to guide must not hang on a single pair of fragile glasses or a single set of tiny, easily-lost lenses. In all crucial things, but especially with things that are easily lost or broken, always carry a back up, a spare.

GUIDING IN GENERAL

When cool or overcast weather is a possibility, it is a good idea for guides to take along a few extra windbreakers and wool sweaters to pass out to freezing people in their boats. Often, sweaters and windbreakers can be found in the lost & found boxes in the warehouse. Also, Goodwill always has a supply. **EXTRA SWEATERS & WIND BREAKERS**

Guides always follow through on their word: If they say they will do something, they do it. They can be relied on. **TRUST-WORTHINESS**

Guides do not use language that might be offensive to any member of the trip. **LANGUAGE**

Diplomatic guides avoid fruitless arguments with guests and staff. Interesting exchanges of differing views, though, are much sought after. Example of a fruitless argument: One person keeps saying, "Yes, it is!" while the other keeps insisting "No, it's not." In a situation like this, try to get the parties to "agree to disagree" and nudge them toward some new topic or activity. **ARGUMENTS**

Mature guides always speak well of others as much as honesty permits. They understand that the world will think the less of them if they think the less of it. Before judging anyone, wise river guides make sure they know all the facts. And even then they mute their criticism, remembering the ancient ritual of the Sioux Indians: A brave raises hands toward the sky and prays, "Great Spirit, help me never to judge another until I have walked fourteen days in his moccasins." **HESITATE TO PASS JUDGEMENT**

Whitewater Voyages strives to maintain warm, friendly relations with everyone. As much as possible we are friendly, honest, polite and helpful with all the people we come in contact with, including everyone from grocery store clerks to campground managers to the guides with other rafting companies to the personnel of government agencies. **GOOD RELATIONS**

Whitewater guides are aware of the importance of details: They don't lose keys, locks or other small items. They set sunglasses down with the lenses up so the glass won't be scratched. They put things back where they belong the moment they are finished using them. If they took something from a particular pouch or box, they return it to that same place—and reseal the pouch or box, When packing bread, cookies, lettuce, etc., in coolers, thoughtful guides seal these items in zip lock bags so they will not wind up in the icemelt—which *contaminates!* When cleaning the coolers after each trip, they scrub the cracks clean. When leaving the staff house or warehouse, they make sure *all* doors and windows are locked, and that the lights, stove and heater are *off*. Before leaving gas stations, they make sure the radiator and gas caps are back on. Seasoned guides know that if they make a habit of being careful about details, everything will go more smoothly. Example: Once, when leaving a gas station, we forgot to make sure the radiator cap had been replaced. The water boiled out of the radiator, overheating the engine— and the van had to be towed in for repairs. **DETAILS**

**THE SHOW
MUST GO ON**

Countless things can occur which seem to make continuing a trip impossible—such as a vehicle breakdown, a rip in an air chamber, etc. Within the limits of safety, it is up to the guides and trip leader to figure out a jury rig, some safe gap-step to allow the trip to proceed with a minimum delay. Of course, there are some situations, such as extreme high water, which can necessitate the cancellation of a trip. But most situations can be handled in such a way that the trip continues smoothly. Even in the event of a serious injury, one or two expert guides can float out with the victim (plus a few other guests to help) while the other guides stay with the group and continue the trip.

TIME

Experienced guides allow plenty of time to do what needs to be done. Most things take much longer than one thinks, so they start early! The ideal is to be ahead of schedule easily, without rush or strain.

The staff, particularly the chef or "morning person," gets up well before the guests and has hot coffee ready and breakfast underway when the guests wake up. This is an important element of the entire trip and reflects on the professionalism of the entire company.

Consider this situation: The morning person gets up late, starts the fire late; breakfast gets cooked late (with people standing around *waiting*—goal: minimize waiting); the rafts are packed late and start off late; the group eats lunch late (after all, who wants to eat at noon if they had breakfast at 10) and the group reaches camp late, leaving no time to relax for awhile before starting dinner; despite rushing into dinner the guides end up cooking in the twilight and eating and washing dishes in the dark! And what is worse, everyone stays up late and sleeps in—and the anxious cycle is carried over from day to day. All because the morning person got up late!

Veteran river guides, without feeling rushed, are aware of time and strive to be efficient and keep things moving. Clearly, there are times for relaxing and times for pushing forward with all due speed.

GROWTH

Thoughtful guides strive to understand and support and nourish one another—so that they may promote one another's growth. The whole point, after all, is growth—to learn about the world and one's self. To learn to handle both better. The ideal guide's goal: To learn, to grow and, in so doing, to provide the best trips possible.

**SPECIAL PEOPLE;
SPECIAL COMPANY**

The guides with Whitewater Voyages are, frankly, special, sensitive people. We are a special company, a family.

**BUILDING
SOMETHING**

Ideally, we are building something together which, if it succeeds, will benefit us all with more work, higher wages, more opportunity, and personal growth and satisfaction.

GUIDING IN GENERAL

Thoughts from Bill:
For me, one of the greatest ongoing challenges in guiding (and living) is being in each moment, being fully present and awake to each person, each group, each opportunity.

A sign of not being present is thinking about, yearning to be somewhere else other than where I am. More and more I'm training myself to notice when my thoughts are elsewhere—and gently invite my attention back into the moment.

One technique I use when I notice my awareness has strayed from the moment, is to say to myself: "What can I do right now to enhance my experience and the experience of the people I'm with?"

It's a sort of meditation. Human consciousness frequently wanders—and whenever I notice this, rather than kicking myself, I strive to simply bring my awareness back to the moment.

The key is inviting my attention into the present moment. When I am paying attention to my present situation with the intention of enhancing my experience and the experience of my companions—it seems the universe provides, often miraculously. Sometimes I'll check inside to see what I'm feeling—Maybe I notice I'm concerned how the people in my boat are feeling. Or maybe I realize I'm stumped as to what I can say to draw someone out—or what I can say to get an interesting conversation going in the raft. Then I sort of sit in a relaxed way with this awareness, this question. And miraculously, usually within minutes, but sometimes longer—somehow the very focusing of my awareness and asking of the question brings something which fills the request. Sometimes I think of something to say. Or the very person I want to reach out to reaches out to me. Or someone says something that I or others in the raft respond to—getting a great lively conversation flowing. Ask, and ye shall receive!

P.S. Does this resonate with you? I'd love to hear how others respond to what I've just written here—and how others cope with similar situations. Thanks—Bill

I always thought it was my unique personal challenge to struggle with shifting my thoughts and awareness away from thinking about and looking forward to the future and into the present moment, to think less about tomorrow and have more fun today. I feel a little bit better now knowing I am not alone in this. It works for me to just look around with my eyes wide open trying to see the beauty of ordinary things. When I give these ordinary things my time and attention, they can talk; they bring me back into reality. Being with people I am always asking myself, "what does this person know that I don't and what can I learn from him or her?"—Zdenek Skyvara

Somewhere along the way I noticed that if I really, really got into something, I had a lot of fun doing it, even if it was something simple and mundane, like washing the dishes or chopping wood or doing the laundry. So I always try to keep my attention on whatever's right in front of me so that it has the potential of becoming as rich and full and delicious as it can possibly be.—Susan Maida

CONSIDER THIS

Consider the possibility that your every thought, sensation, and emotion has its own perfect reason for being just exactly as it is/they are, right now. What we're talking about here is accepting and appreciating both ourselves and others.

🙐 🙐 🙐 🙐

GUIDES AND GUESTS

KINDNESS

A perceptive river guide is always considerate and understanding, and shows genuine concern for the clients' well being. For instance, considerate guides greet people with a big smile, make a point of learning names, and answer questions cheerfully and thoroughly. They are aware that the trip is the guests' big adventure. By identifying with the guests, the sensitive guide enters into their excitement, and thereby renews his or her own. Above all, the perceptive guide knows that sincere concern and gentleness are deeply reassuring to our guests.

THINK POSITIVELY ABOUT ONE ANOTHER & GUESTS

Whitewater Voyages guides project to our guests the feeling, "You're OK; You're welcome here." We are interested in and see good in the people who come on our trips; we care about them; we think and speak constructively about our guests and about one another.

REACH OUT TO BOATERS

A thoughtful river guide reaches out to the guests in a natural, comfortable way. She or he gently draws them out, finds out who they are, lets them know who he or she is, and shares freely. Ever so gently the guide gets the guests to let their hair down, open up, tell stories, sing, and act crazy.

MINGLE

At put-ins, lunch spots and camps, especially near the beginning of each trip, Whitewater Voyages guides do not clump together. Instead, they spread out and mingle with the boaters, the guests. Mealtimes in particular provide excellent opportunities to meet and talk with our guests. When eating, each guide generally sits down near a boater or two and starts up a conversation.* The importance of this cannot be overemphasized. When the guides mix with the group, the guests feel included, accepted, a part of the trip—and as a result they pitch in more, loosen up more, enjoy themselves more—and the trip is more enjoyable for everyone, guests and staff alike.

*If nothing else springs to mind, suitable conversation openers are: "Where are you from?" "How did you hear of Whitewater Voyages?" "Is everything OK?" "If you have any questions, I'll do my best to answer them." "Hi. My name is _____." Also see "Quiet Camaraderie" in "Part 8" below.

GUIDES AND GUESTS

At times, mingling with guests can be the most difficult—and important—part of guiding. River guides, especially those who both work and live together, day after day, trip after trip, tend to develop an intuitive rapport and closeness. It becomes so easy for guides to be with one another, that, by comparison, reaching out to the strangers who are our guests can seem difficult and require real effort. This sense of effort is all the greater if a guide has become tired or "burned out."

ON MINGLING, BURN OUT, & GROUP UNITY

So what is the solution? The answer boils down to this: Maintain an ongoing awareness of the need to mingle, and in each situation—at put-in, lunch, and camp—simply do the best you can to respond as an individual to our guests. Recognize that sometimes mixing with the trip members does take genuine effort, and sincerely extend yourself to mix and meet and interact with the guests.

Also, each guide must be careful to avoid burnout: Keep an honest inner eye on yourself. Keep your interest in meeting people alive and strong. Remain curious about life, the world and people. Look for and focus on the appealing qualities in the people you meet. As you get to know each boater ask yourself, "What can I learn from this person?" Get plenty of rest the night before each trip. Whenever possible, between trips take at least one day off and take time to read, be creative, and do things that are completely different from rafting. Above all, between trips give yourself enough time alone to recharge your batteries, to talk to yourself and absorb what is happening to and around you, to stay in touch with your heart and inner thoughts.

Of course, no one can be on stage all the time. Occasionally it is fine for guides to cluster together, but they should remain aware of what they are doing and not clump together too much. Especially at the first lunch and frequently throughout the rest of the trip, they should deliberately spread out and mingle, even if at times this takes a certain exercise of will. The effort is worth it. For when there is no division, no separation between the guides and guests, everyone feels a part of one group, pulling together to brave the river—and it is this experience of being accepted and belonging that is at the heart of a good river trip.

Guides do not play favorites. They divide their attention among all the people in the boat, and on land, among all the people sitting around them. Of course, they freely focus on people who are especially interesting, but they direct some attention toward everyone who wants to be included.

DON'T PLAY FAVORITES

A first-rate guide is aware of silent people; if they seem comfortable, that's fine. But if they show an inclination to participate, the guide helps them enter into things.

SILENT PEOPLE

Loud people are vexations to the spirit.

DON'T BRAG

PART 1: THE BIG PICTURE

BE SENSITIVE, NOT MACHO

Truly strong and able river guides are not tough, macho, or haughty. Often the greatest strength lies in the ability to be humble and sensitive, to care, to show affection, to be vulnerable.

ON LONG TRIPS DISCOURAGE SUBGROUPS

On longer trips of four days or more, aware guides seize every opportunity to unobtrusively break up subgroups. Subgroups fracture a trip, make for subtle ''in'' and ''out'' groups and rivalries, and undercut everyone's enjoyment and the group spirit. This is done by encouraging people to switch rafts each day, or, if the group is traveling a long distance in more than one vehicle, by encouraging people to switch back and forth among the vehicles. Also, on a trip that involves days or weeks on a bus, perceptive guides move all over the bus, sitting in a new seat each day, making contact with everyone—and they encourage others to do likewise. This counsel does not apply to shorter trips of three days or less.

ON SHORT TRIPS GENERALLY DO NOT SWITCH RAFTS

On trips of three days or less there usually is not enough time for everyone to thoroughly get to know everyone else. So, rather than encourage people to switch from boat to boat each day, where they will probably be with strangers, it is better to encourage people to stay in the same boat, where they can gradually come to feel at home with the crew and guide. A cozy voyage.

LET THEM SWITCH IF THEY WISH

If someone does wish to switch, fine, try to accommodate them. If the boat they want to switch to is full, suggest they find someone in it who would like to trade places.

ENTERTAIN & INSTILL RESPECT FOR RIVER

A river guide's responsibility goes beyond merely conducting a safe trip; the guide must also entertain and teach respect for the river. Much of this ''entertainment'' comes easily as one reaches out to the boaters; however, a portion usually has to be deliberate and each guide must come up with ways to provide it.

NATURE LORE

Whitewater Voyages guides study nature: They can identify and talk about trees, flowers, lichens, rocks, birds, animal tracks, stars, etc.

TEACH 'EM ABOUT RIVERS

They teach their crews something about rivers and river running: They explain river characteristics, such as haystacks, holes, eddies, and the basics of boat maneuvering.

PADDLE CHANTS

They invent paddle-tapping song chants for the sake of light-hearted fun—and for use as diversions when the crew is tired, cold, hungry or anxious.

GAMES

Companionable river guides, when appropriate, lead games like Pruee, Chinese Puzzle, Spiral (great for warming a group up), Amoeba Race, Hunker Houser, British Bulldog, The Mating Game, Nature Symphony, Emotional Symphony, Story-Story, Rock-Paper-Scissors Augmented, The Lap Game, Stand Up, etc., which minimize competition and bring people together. For more on games and interpretation, see Part 8, below, of this book. Also, see the *New Games Book*. Headlands Press Book, Doubleday-Dolphin (1976).

Guides invent ways to maximize everyone's enjoyment of and sensitivity to the river, the prime mover. Always keeping well within the limits of safety, they seek out the most exciting routes through rapids.

TEACH SENSITIVITY TO THE RIVER

On a rapid near the end of the run, the guide has everyone who wishes to do so close their eyes in the calm and quietly float toward and through the building roar and leaping waves. It is important that the crew understand beforehand that they will need to continue following commands—and that they should keep their eyes closed until told to open them (the guide has them open their eyes after the last big wave or hole). Also, they should know that the guide will tell them to lean in before the boat hits anything that could bounce them overboard.

BLIND RUN

Guides who play musical instruments often bring them along and devise ways to weave music into the trip. Flutes and trombones are beautiful in canyon calms and guitars add greatly to time spent around the campfire. Musicians, though, should be careful not to dominate things—and should stop frequently to allow room for conversation, stories, jokes.

MUSIC

Most guides commit a few stories and jokes to memory—tales they tell in the boat on long calms or at night around the fire. All guides should learn the jokes and yarns which accompany the names of the rapids and pertain to the river canyon.

STORIES & JOKES

Whitewater Voyages guides muster up something special, something creative. They pursue their own native talents. Maybe they give seminars in how to live off the land, how to tie knots, or on the life story of a rattlesnake. (See Nature Interpretation below and Part 8 of this book.) Or they juggle or perform magic tricks or work up a mock Houdini act or, with one guide sitting on another's knee, a ventriloquist dummy act.

SOMETHING SPECIAL

Above all, intelligent guides enjoy themselves. If the guides have a good, warm, friendly time, the chances are the guests will too.

ENJOY YOURSELF

All this does not mean guides should hound the boaters with entertainment. Silence is also an important part of the wilderness experience—time to be quiet, mull things over, dream. After all, a river trip is more than a carnival ride. Guides can make it fun—and at the same time instill a respect for the river.

SILENCE

**INSTILL
RESPECT
FOR RIVER**

To teach respect for the river, a guide must possess and display an appreciation and knowledge of the river and canyon—and show a genuine caution, an unwillingness to take unnecessary risks. This quality, by the way, also demonstrates respect for the people under the guide's care. Also, when appropriate, usually toward the end of a trip, guides may diplomatically urge boaters to support Friends of the River and help in the struggle to preserve our rivers.

**URGE BOATERS
TO HELP
PRESERVE
RIVERS**

**NATURE
INTERPRETATION
& YOUR
GUIDEBOOK
LIBRARY**

Each guide is encouraged to acquire a small library of interpretive guidebooks covering the geology, trees, plants, wildlife, history, etc., of the rivers we run. A guidebook library of this sort, which might contain anywhere from four to six to a dozen volumes and can be carried in a Pelican case, an ammo box or other watertight container, can be considered a basic tool of guiding, as essential as a belt knife and river shoes.

Not only is such a library useful as an educational resource to share with our guests, it is also valuable as a source of learning for the guide. By referring to these volumes often, a river guide can learn to identify geological formations, rocks, birds, trees, historical sites and so on. And, more importantly, the guide can learn more than just the names, but also the stories surrounding them—the history and causes of rock formations, the uses the Indians made of certain plants, the habits and characteristics of birds and other wildlife, the reason certain trees and plants grow where they do, the ways in which all living things adapt to their environment, and on and on.

When guides know the natural and human history of the river, lead nature walks, share their guidebooks with the guests, and generally, actively, often interpret the lore of the river and canyons, every trip is enriched. Let us hope that in our guests there will be awakened an appreciation, a fascination for what we have, for rivers, for our special natural and social heritage. Let us also hope that we win solid friends for the earth who will take care of and help save the rivers that remain.

**A BOAT LOAD OF
RIVER GAMES**

For more on entertaining and interpreting nature in the context of river trips, see Part 8 of this book!

**WHAT THE
OFFICE STAFF
TELLS THE
CLIENTS**

It's important we all know what information the clients receive both verbally from the office and in the paperwork we send them. This will help you better understand their requests and some of the miscommunication that at times happens at the river. Please read the brochure from cover to cover. Much of the time information that a client may claim they never got or weren't told is in print in the brochure or in the rendezvous and gear list information.

For the record, the office staff tells each and every client that wet suits are usually needed on all spring trips through May and possibly later depending on weather and water conditions and on all class IV+ and V rivers. They let them know that we rent wet suits, and if they don't end up using them they can call the office after the trip and get a refund. Since the office staff keeps in touch with the various areas, they should know what the conditions are at the river, and they can advise our guests accordingly. They also tell our clients that it is a good idea to wear a water-friendly fabric such as wool or capilene (not cotton) under their paddle jacket.

Although it's important to take care of your guests at the river, please remember that all of us at Whitewater Voyages are a team and it's equally important to support the office staff. The reservation staff tries to be consistent with the information they tell clients. Oftentimes, when guests say things like "nobody told me I needed a wet suit," or "I didn't know I was supposed to bring my own sleeping gear," it's because they didn't read their gear list or rendezvous information, or their trip organizer received the information but didn't give it to each person in his or her group.

If a client feels they were misinformed by the office staff, armed with the above information, a good response can start with "I'm sorry there was a misunderstanding, how can I help...?" This way you leave out the unnecessary blame that comes with statements like "you didn't..." or "they didn't..."

TURNING AWAY UNQUALIFIED CLIENTS: BE DIPLOMATIC

In the rare event that a client must be turned away—from a class V put-in for instance—it is best to discuss the matter with the client in private and to avoid uttering sweeping judgements. For example, instead of telling them that they are "out of shape," just say, "In my opinion you are not ready for this river."

WHEN CLIENTS DECIDE NOT TO RAFT

When clients decide not to raft, listen to them and support them. It's okay to present the positive reasons why one might go rafting, but always acknowledge there are inherent risks and it is a perfectly reasonable, okay, choice to decide not to raft. Similarly, make it clear to people that it is perfectly acceptable to walk around difficult stretches. Explain the risks of swimming, particularly in class IV and even more so in class V. Let them know that the reality of swimming really big rapids is that "you're on your own," that self-rescue is vital.

LIFE JACKETS AND OVERWEIGHT CLIENTS

Both common sense and our insurance carrier dictate that all trip participants must wear a Whitewater Voyages life jacket. If a client is too large to fit into and fasten all of the buckles on one of our extra-large jackets, the trip leader should gently and firmly inform him or her that they may not participate in the on-river portion of the trip. Of course, they would be more than welcome to join the trip in camp, if feasible. Refer all refund and credit requests to our main office, assuring them only of our ongoing commitment to fairness. In all situations where a refund may be requested—if you, as trip leader, have a recommendation for the office refund committee, please include it in your trip report. Do not share your recommendation directly with the client—leave this to the refund committee.

NON-ENGLISH SPEAKING GUESTS

In our brochure we say that clients on class IV and V must be able to understand the trip leader's safety talk and the guide's instructions in the boat. We also say that Spanish-, Japanese-, and Russian-speaking guides may be available by special arrangement. Plus, we say that all non-English speakers should, as the safest choice, come on a class III trip, and that they should bring an interpreter with them. If non-English speakers truly have prior rafting experience and fitness and desire to run class IV and V, then, in cooperation with all involved, we can schedule a suitable bilingual guide.

Because of the special scheduling and extra travel that this involves, we charge an additional $100 per bilingual guide, half of which goes to the guide, the other half to Whitewater Voyages for the extra time spent in organizing the whole thing. We are compiling a list of our bilingual guides. If you are truly fluent in another language, and want to be considered as a potential bilingual guide, then call the main office and have your name put on the list.

DISABLED PEOPLE ON WHITEWATER VOYAGES TRIPS

The following are some guidelines for both physically disabled people and developmentally delayed individuals joining Whitewater Voyages trips:

For people who don't have the use of their lower body: Wheelchair-bound folks must ride in an oar boat on rivers no more difficult than class III. (For safety reasons, no wheelchair folks on class IV or V.) They must be accompanied by at least two able-bodied assistants.

Here are some tips for making them more comfortable and safe: Rig a cooler in the oar frame so it sits tight up against the front thwart. Soften the front thwart so that it molds into a seat for the disabled person. Have the disabled person sit in the middle of the boat on the slightly deflated thwart, then have the able bodied assistants sit on either side of them. This enables the assistants to help keep the disabled individual in the boat. Also use the largest most stable boat possible with given water conditions.

Foot entrapment is a very serious concern for paraplegics. If someone who has no use of their legs should swim it is important that someone go in with them to help them keep their legs up and pointed downstream. Because of these constraints we will only be able to accommodate paraplegics on the Kings and South Fork of the American, where we are less likely to have swims.

GUIDES AND GUESTS

When we're booking special trips for groups of developmentally delayed people, we need to follow the guideline of four able minded paddlers per paddle boat. It is absolutely necessary that enough of the crew are able to respond to the paddle captain's commands. Both reservationists and trip leaders will need to keep this in mind.

DEVELOPMENTALLY DELAYED PEOPLE JOINING OUR TRIPS

With repeat clients, please be very careful regarding recommending guide school to them. Do this only if you feel it truly coincides with their personal goals or if you see them as a potential guide.

REFERRING REPEAT GUESTS TO GUIDE SCHOOL

On South Fork American, Kings, Upper Kern and Lower Kern trips we "talk up" other more challenging trips.

REFERRING GUESTS TO MORE CHALLENGING TRIPS

Cherry Creek is our only class V run which both has summer-long flow and is an easy drive from California's metropolitan areas. If you are guiding on a class V trip in the spring and you are aware of guests who either are, or might be, interested in Cherry Creek, and you consider them capable class V paddlers who are ready for Cherry Creek, consider referring these folks to Cherry Creek for a summer trip. These clients will be freshly experienced and excited about rafting and they may jump at the suggestion to paddle "The Creek."

REFERRING GUESTS TO CHERRY CREEK

Don't take possession of keys or valuables—advise clients to lock or hide them in a safe place. On the client gear list we recommend using a magnetic hide-a-key.

CLIENT'S KEYS AND VALUABLES

Supportive guides recognize that the end of a trip is a hectic time for everyone, and that personal belongings can be misplaced or lost. We have a great opportunity to show our support and caring at the end of a trip and well beyond by helping clients remember their personal belongings at trips' end, and by carefully following up on any lost items. Of course, Whitewater Voyages cannot assume responsibility for lost items, but we will pay reasonable shipping costs to return found belongings to their rightful owners. It is appropriate to inform clients of our lost and found policy in a positive way—and add, for example, "Thank you for coming with Whitewater Voyages, do you have everything you came with?" or "We care about you and we want you to have all your stuff. Did you double check the day bag, trailer, Klamath bags, etc?" It is not nurturing to announce our lost and found policy as "You leave it, we wear it." Also, remember that Whitewater Voyages and its guides cannot accept responsibility for keys, jewelry, cameras, or other valuables. If clients ask us to keep a valuable item, suggest that they find a good way to secure their stuff on their own, or offer some options that you would feel good about, such as locking valuables in their trunk. We should never promise people that their gear will be completely safe, or say that we have never had a problem with theft.

LOST AND FOUND

LOST AND FOUND (continued)

Sometimes guests who don't have their own camping gear borrow it from their friends. These people often don't know what the stuff they brought with them looks like, and on more than one incident, such guests have unintentionally gone home with guides' or other guests' gear. It is okay to let people know that this can happen and to ask them to please be extra careful when grabbing their stuff. Guides should take responsibility for separating their own gear out from a pile of trip gear so that it reduces the chance of confusion for the guests, and inconvenience for the guides.

ONE OPTION: GET THE BOATERS INVOLVED

When the boaters are standing around at the put-in or sitting around camp, wide-awake guides can ask for volunteers. Then they teach these volunteers to do whatever they are doing—or at least explain what they are doing. If the boaters show interest, the guides get them involved in the workings, the details of the expedition.

TEACH 'EM TO PACK BOATS

For example, at the put-in a guide calls out, "Who wants to become intimate with a tarp load?" or "Who wants to learn how to pack a raft?" or "Who wants to get their hands on some real river gear?" The guide tries to get two people for each tarp load, and tells them to pay close attention because they will unpack the load in the afternoon and repack it the next morning (and take care of it for the rest of the trip—if they wish). To simplify things the guide teaches them to pack the same number of bags the same way each day.

FOLLOW UP

Later, the guide follows up with these people. He or she checks on how they are doing with their tasks. Are they doing it correctly? Maybe the guide teaches them a new knot or some other way to improve their technique. The more people participate, the more they get out of the trip. By the way, if the boaters have good suggestions for improvements in our operation, listen carefully and pass them on to the trip leader.

DRINKING ALCOHOL

Discourage drinking (or pot smoking) before or while rafting by saying "This is a voyage down a wild, dangerous whitewater river and you will need all your wits about you. So, please, save the beer for camp!" If a client continues to insist, say, "You paid Whitewater Voyages to take you down this river because you wanted the benefit of our experience. Well, all of our experience tells us that alcohol, marijuana, and drugs should not be used on the river."

GUESTS & ALCOHOL IN CAMP: URGE MODERATION

In the evening in camp, it is okay to drink alcohol <u>in moderation.</u> <u>Absolutely do not drink excessive amounts.</u> It is essential that everyone be able to get up the next morning feeling good and able to tackle the river. <u>For clients to impair their ability with excessive alcohol, or with any chemical substance, endangers not only them, but the entire group!!</u>

Good river guides consider the feelings of the boaters. They *never* flirt with a boater's spouse or intimate companion.

BE CONSIDERATE

Mature river guides don't make overt, amorous advances toward our guests. If a guest is unattached, it is often alright to discretely show interest—provided the guide is careful not to play favorites and continues to mingle generally with the boaters. But it is usually best to save any serious or physical overtures until after the trip.

NO AMOROUS ADVANCES

This is not to say, of course, that guides should avoid showing affection to guests. Light, warm, playful displays of affection can be a very positive part of a river trip.

PLAYFUL AFFECTION

Two guides who are intimately involved with one another should be especially careful not to cluster together too much. Rather, they should spread out and mingle with others most of the time. Couples who find this difficult should guide on separate trips.

COUPLES

Guides should not make promises of full or partial refunds to boaters because of mix-ups or problems. The front office or area manager will make these decisions. Guides should be tactful and reassuring, however, saying that the company will be understanding and considerate in making these determinations.

REFUNDS

Unless there is a specific reason to do so, guides generally do not talk about past trips. It is important that the guests be allowed to feel that their trip is a special, unique adventure, and not just one of countless other shuttle runs down the rapids.

TALK ABOUT PRESENT TRIP, NOT PAST TRIPS

When guests ask guides what their favorite river is, discerning guides mention one which Whitewater Voyages runs—the boater is actually asking which trip he or she should take next.

FAVORITE RIVER

After a trip, far-seeing guides occasionally send letters to a few of the boaters thanking them for coming with Whitewater Voyages. This is not only great for the company, it is also good for the guide—because it subtly but significantly reinforces the guide's name in the minds of the boaters. Later, if the guide should happen to use a boater as a reference or contact him or her for a job in the "real" world, the boater will remember the guide as a bright, mature, young soul going places.

WRITE LETTERS

It is important that our guides do first-class work in three areas: 1) running the river; 2) making the trip enjoyable for the boaters; and, 3) giving the boaters the feeling that they have come on the river with a unique and certainly the best river company. A company set up by an expert ("the man who wrote the book"), with excellent equipment and top flight guides. Our guides give the impression that we are more than just a bunch of people who run rivers: *We are a special company.*

IMPART THE FEELING THAT WE ARE A SPECIAL COMPANY

STAFF RELATIONS

SUPPORT ONE ANOTHER

Good feelings among the staff are important. When the guides support and respect one another, everyone enjoys the trip more.

LOVE THE LEADER

A good staff fully, warmly, lovingly supports the trip leader. Compassionate guides make a point of identifying with the leader, of seeing things from her or his perspective, of checking out perceptions, of talking about how things seem to the leader. An insightful leader, likewise places him- or herself in the position of each guide and shares perceptions.

TAKE RESPONSIBILITY

Each staff member takes responsibility for creating the trip, for doing everything from packing beforehand to unpacking, cleaning the coolers and jugs, and repairing damaged gear afterwards.

FILL-IN FOR LEADER

When the leader is occupied, as is often the case at put-ins and take-outs, with greeting and looking after the boaters, the other staff fill in for him or her.

PITCH IN

Alert guides pitch in eagerly and early. For instance, they prepare meals early—and do not wait until the sun approaches the horizon to start dinner.

SEE LARGER PICTURE

River guides try to see not just their particular role, but also the larger picture, and do whatever needs doing without being asked. For instance, when packing their rafts, able guides occasionally look around the river beach for odds and ends that others have overlooked and add these things to their own loads. Also, the guides usually ask a trustworthy boater to carefully check the camp for litter and overlooked gear.

ASK

When guides can't think of anything that needs doing, they ask the trip leader or another guide how they can help: They just say, "What needs doing?" or "How can I help?"

BE THERE

Seasoned guides place the work of the trip above all else. They do not disappear. Instead, they anticipate things, and make a point of *being there* when they are needed. Conscientious guides get an OK from the leader before sleeping in an out of the way place. When something needs doing, a good guide does it then and there.

DO MORE THAN YOUR SHARE

If this whole venture is to work, everyone has to be willing to do more than their share. Only in this way, as each of us now and then takes time out for our own personal needs, will everything balance out.

STAFF RELATIONS

The ideal is for everything to be done correctly and smoothly without anyone having to tell anyone else what to do. But when something is not being done correctly, or is not being done at all, it is up to the other staff members, particularly the leader, to explain the matter to whoever is making the error.

EXPLAIN THE MATTER

When guides are asked to do something, a quick and cheerful "OK" is much appreciated—with this response they give much needed support to the person requesting help. In situations where a guide is about to do something else, she or he does not say, "Oh, I am going to wash my hair." Instead, if possible, the guide temporarily puts aside what he or she is doing—or, if this is impossible, *asks* something like "Would I have time to spread my sleeping bag out to dry first?"

SAY "OK"

If guides are in doubt about doing something, they check with the trip leader. When a guide has an idea to help things along, he or she mentions it to the leader—and if the word is yes, the guide does it.

CHECK WITH LEADER

Guides strictly follow the leader's directions. If they don't understand the directions, they get clarification then and there. But if they don't understand the reasons behind the directions, or disagree with them or have what might be a better idea, they talk with the leader, aside, at the earliest *convenient* moment. Sometimes, when things are thick and busy, it may be best to just do what the leader says and ask questions later.

FOLLOW DIRECTIONS

When a guide has a complaint or negative feeling toward another staff member it is vital that, at an appropriate time in private away from the boaters, he or she express these feelings directly to the person concerned. Good guides do not bottle up their feelings and *never* grumble to others behind the person's back. Bad feelings are usually caused by a lack of communication—and the sooner talk is opened up the better.

COMMUNICATE

Likewise, when a guide feels good about someone, he or she blows them a kiss, gives them a hug, squeezes their big toe. When guides feel someone did a particularly good job with something, they let them know, they shower them with compliments. Anytime is a good time.

EXPRESS APPROVAL

My deepest hope is that we will develop a wild affection for one another that will carry us through rocky times. When people truly like and respect one another, it is easy to resolve differences.

WILD RESPECT

When guides are with the boaters, they always speak well of everyone in the company. River guides are on stage. Everything they say will be repeated and passed round. Even if a guide is having problems with another staff member, when she or he is with the boaters, differences are buried and the positive is emphasized. The guide taxes his mind a bit and thinks good thoughts

SPEAK WELL OF FELLOW GUIDES

about the other. Interestingly enough, this often helps resolve the problem.

LET OTHERS KNOW HOW YOU FEEL: SHARE, LISTEN, GROW, BECOME WHOLE

For us to succeed as individuals and as a team, it is vital that we communicate directly—at an appropriate time <u>away from clients</u>—with anyone we have a problem with. Here are a few tips from the Community Board of San Francisco regarding managing conflict with friends, neighbors, and strangers:

— Talk directly to the person involved.
— Choose a good time where you can both be comfortable and undisturbed.
— Plan ahead what you want to say.
— Don't blame or name-call.
— Give information about your own feelings and perspective. Don't judge or interpret the other person's behavior.
— Listen and try to learn how the other person feels.
— Show that you are listening, even if you don't necessarily agree with what's being said.
— Talk it all through. Don't leave out parts that seem too difficult to discuss.
— Work on a joint solution.
— Follow through by checking with each other to make sure the agreement is still working.

One tool for effective listening and communication is to use the following format: "I see, I feel, I imagine." In this way, you begin by stating what you observe, without imposing any judgement on it. This is akin to acknowledging what you are taking in from the situation. Then, you follow with how you feel, as opposed to how the other person makes you feel. This is akin to revealing how you are responding to what you've taken in. Finally, you conclude with what you imagine the situation to be, which is not necessarily the same as how it actually is. This is basically your unique interpretation of how things are, and by presenting it as what you are imagining, you are not forcing your perception on anyone else as "the truth about how it is."

Another tool for working out conflict is called active listening. Here, one person says what they need to say and the other person repeats back what they think they heard. This allows the speaker to make any corrections in the listener's interpretation so that they are accurately heard.

SHARE, COMMUNICATE WITH MANAGERS, TOO!

The Whitewater Voyages management staff welcomes your communication and feedback on things important to you—including your evaluations of how we are doing as managers. As a company, we strive to run safe, high quality, fun trips, and we care about our staff. We really value and welcome your feedback, constructive criticism, and ideas—feel free to communicate them to your area manager or Bill. We encourage everyone to complete Manager Evaluation forms whenever issues deserving special attention arise, for both high praise and constructive critcism. In general, whenever you witness circumstances that strongly affect our ability—positively or negatively—to provide our clients with the highest quality trips possible, please communicate your thoughts on the matter. It is communication of this sort which is the very life blood of our personal, organizational, and spiritual growth.

OUR COMMON GOAL

Through thick and thin remember we are all part of one company with a common goal: The finest, safest, most enjoyable trips possible.

Cultivate an appreciation for the possibilities of human groups: Human groups, such as the circle of human souls in a raft or around a campfire, are capable of amazing quantum-leap magnifications of energy and aliveness. When a charismatic guide receives the energy flowing from the group and channels it back out to everyone present with the implicit message, "Everyone is cool and appreciated," everyone, including the guide, tends to experience, to put it mildly, an improved sense of well being, a heightened awareness (colors become more vivid, etc.) and a greatly increased flow of energy and aliveness! An amazingly wonderful aspect of all this is that everyone, including the guide, gets to experience the god-like pleasure of hanging out with cool, god-like people.

2: *THE TRIP*

THE TRIP LEADER

Trip leaders are expected to assume full responsibility for staging their trips. Beginning well before and continuing throughout each trip, the leader simultaneously makes sure the myriad details are handled correctly while keeping in view the overall quality, safety and progress of the trip. Leaders are aware that each trip is the boaters' grand adventure, and do their utmost to make each and every trip safe, professional, educational, exciting and, above all, enjoyable.

LEADER CREATES TRIP

Trip leaders anticipate and prepare for problems. Before each trip, leaders mentally go step by step through the entire trip, picturing each situation, imagining possible problems, deciding how they will handle them, realizing what equipment they will need. For example, a leader might, with eyes closed, say to him- or herself, "OK, we're at the put-in, it's morning, we're inflating the rafts. What do we need? The electric blower, a few foot pumps, gear to rig boats—frames and decks, short line bag, etc. OK, I'm greeting the guests, what do I need? Let's see, trip file and roster, release forms, pens, clip boards, and waterproof bags." And so on for each phase of the trip: The drive up, put-in, greeting the guests, dealing with shuttle drivers and rangers and campground managers, on the river, at lunch, doing a portage, in camp, at take-out. When imagining her- or himself in each phase of the trip, the leader realizes things like: "I'll need tickets or money for the ranger at the Marshall Gold Discovery State Historic Park." "I'll need keys for the gate or stash box." "We'll need a chain & padlock to lock up the rafts." "We'll need extra line for the portage. And I'll want gloves to keep the line from burning my hands." "There may be fluctuations in weather requiring a day bag for extra clothes." "Oh yeah, when the boaters are packing their bags, I should tell them to put their sweaters and rain gear in the day bag." "That's right, it will be hot, I'll remind the chef to put extra ice in the coolers and large drink jugs." "The river will be high; the lead boat may flip and need an emergency beaching line for a self rescue." In this way the leader anticipates the unusual, maps out ways of coping with difficulties,

ANTICIPATE & PREPARE FOR PROBLEMS

and remembers to bring unusual pieces of gear that may not be on the standard Whitewater Voyages packing list.

DESIGNATE CHEF

Well before the trip, the leader, in cooperation with the operations or area manager, designates a chef and sees that this designation is indicated on the operations calendar. Occasionally this is done by the manager, but in any case the leader checks to see whether or not a chef has been selected. If not, the leader, in concert with the manager, sees that one is chosen and that the person selected accepts the role.

LEADER DOES NOT CHEF

Generally, when the guides on a trip are relatively equal in experience, the trip leader lets one of the other guides chef. This spreads the wealth and experience of chefing and frees the leader to concentrate on other details, seeing the overall picture, and, most important, reaching out to the boaters.

GUIDES MEET AT WAREHOUSE EARLY

Trip leaders contact their guides well before each trip to arrange an early staff rendezvous at the warehouse. This rendezvous time should allow plenty of time to pack, travel, and arrive at the river early.

BE THERE IN PERSON

Whenever possible trip leaders should *personally* see each trip through from pre-trip file inspection and packing to post-trip unpacking and cleaning and repairs. On those occasions when a trip leader cannot personally arrive *early* to read the file and supervise the packing, he or she should delegate this responsibility to one of the other guides on the trip, preferrably someone with considerable guiding experience. As always, leaders ride to the river and back with the staff and gear, both to give the group cohesion and to make certain that they are present to cope with any difficulties.

STUDY TRIP FILE & PREPARE PACKING LIST

Before packing, the trip leader carefully examines the trip file, noting the total number of people, the number of children, special requests, preferences for oar or paddle rafts, unusual medical conditions, wet suit rentals, and so on. On the basis of this information the leader prepares a detailed packing list—see our standard packing list in ''Specifics'' on page 109.

PACKING LIST VITAL

A thorough packing list is vital—especially when the river is a great distance from the warehouse and there will be no opportunity to go back for forgotten items. As each item is loaded it is checked off the list. In this manner many people can help pack simultaneously without confusion, duplication, or omission. The importance of a complete packing list is particularly apparent when one considers the possible consequences of forgetting any of the dozens of crucial pieces of gear—pumps, life jackets, repair kits, first aid kits, etc., etc.

Carefully check the contents of the first aid and repair kits to make absolutely sure they are fully stocked and ready to go. If they are not, note the previous user's name in the trip report. See below: "Restock, Seal and Sign Repair Kit," " . . . First Aid Kit."

CHECK & RESEAL FIRST AID & REPAIR KITS

Trip leaders arrive at the trip rendezvous point to meet the guests at least ten to fifteen minutes early!! Preferably earlier! To be late or barely on time is unprofessional and starts the trip off on entirely the wrong note. To accomplish this, trip leaders must make sure the guides get up on time.

BE EARLY TO GREET BOATERS

Trip leaders should carry a compact traveller's alarm clock. Also, a waterproof watch is a good idea.

ALARM CLOCK

At the put-in trip leaders generally focus on the guests and delegate other tasks to the guides. Occasionally, however, a leader may delegate the role of greeting the boaters to a guide who is diplomatic and personable—and able to answer all the boaters' questions.

LEADER CONCENTRATES ON GUESTS

Before starting a trip, the leader must have in hand a signed release form from each and every trip member. Even when boaters say they have mailed their releases, if those releases are not in the file the leader asks the folks to sign another.

RELEASES FROM EVERYONE

When two or more trips are meeting at one rendezvous site, each of the trip leaders should have a copy of the other trips' roster(s)—as well as the original copy of her or his own roster. This reduces confusion.

HAVE TRIP ROSTERS

For our guests, one of the special opportunities of a river trip is the chance to ease off of worrying about time. Basically, during the trip we take care of any time concerns so they don't have to. However, in order to get everyone to show up to the rendezvous on time, we do put some time pressure on them. By necessity, we remind them in their rendezvous information to "please be a bit early... don't be late!" So folks tend to show up at the rendezvous feeling a little time stressed. In light of this, it might be appropriate for trip leaders, shortly after the rendezvous, to invite the group as a whole to let go of time worries. We can say something like: "It is very much the norm in our culture to be stressed about time—and to be so concerned about the future that we forget to appreciate where we are right now. Let's all take a deep breath and look around. We're in the world of the river. It's okay here to let go of any preoccupation with time we may have brought with us and ease into the easier, looser, flow of river time, where we can take things one step, one paddle stroke, one flip, at a time." Of course, we as guides, and particularly as trip leaders, need to remain aware of, but hopefully not stressed by, time! Our reservation staff routinely emphasizes going by "river time"—relax, don't make any tight plans, and allow for unexpected delays.

SUGGEST FOLKS LET GO OF TIME WORRIES AND ENTER "RIVER TIME"

SAFETY TALK At the beginning of each trip, the trip leader gives the safety talk.

THOUGHTS ON BEGINNING AND ENDING A TRIP Something to think about at the beginning of a trip is how to best encourage people to connect and come together as a cohesive group. When all the people on a trip, guides and guests alike, are able to feel that this is their collective trip rather than each of them seeing it only through the eyes of their own individual experience, then the trip is enhanced for all.

The gathering of trip participants for the put-in talk provides a good opportunity for the trip leader to create an opening for the trip, to set the stage for the trip, address any questions or concerns, and to allow trip members to meet each other. One possibility is to have an opening circle in order to introduce people to each other and set the stage for "group bonding." On a soul level, this can both enhance the trip and heighten awareness. This opening circle can happen naturally with the welcome and the put-in talk. It's not at all necessary to make a big deal about it, and in fact, being too explicit about it can make some people uncomfortable. By doing it casually within the context of the welcome and put-in talk, people may not even be aware that they are "bonding." Of course it seems wise to evaluate each trip to determine if it's appropriate—sometimes it might work and other times it clearly won't fit or be appropriate. Overnight trips certainly seem to lend themselves to this type of opening more than half-day trips.

However, often no such natural coming-together exists at the end of a trip and so some trips tend to fizzle at their completion as participants wander off to their individual cars and go home. Announce that you had a really good time; acknowledge your paddlers, guides, chef, and driver. One suggestion, if it feels appropriate, is to have a closing circle at the end of good trips to provide an opportunity for thanks and acknowledgment. Thank our guests for coming with Whitewater Voyages, acknowledge their courage in showing up, their grace under pressure, their strong paddling and teamwork, cheerfulness in the face of hardship, etc., etc. Share briefly your feelings about the trip and invite anyone who wants to share to do so. Conclude with another heartfelt thanks for choosing Whitewater Voyages, for being a part of our "family" of adventure, friendship, and growth. Follow it up with a wish that everyone have a safe trip home, and a hope that we'll get to share a river with them again soon.

SET MATURE EXAMPLE Whitewater Voyages trip leaders set a wise, mature tone and are a reassuring presence. A trip leader's very manner, actions and speech inspire trust, and, beneath the joking and warmth, communicate that this is someone who can cope with whatever might happen. For example, leaders do not perform dangerous high dives. A trip leader's concern and caution in regard to his or her own safety reassures our clients that he or she has the same concern for theirs.

THE TRIP LEADER

The trip leader shepherds her or his group of rafts down the river, keeping them together and seeing them safely through the difficult rapids. Often the leader runs the more challenging rapids first and waits in rescue position as the other boats come through.

LOOK AFTER GROUP

Leaders generally stay with the main group and delegate errands, shuttles, and other side trips to others.

STAY WITH GROUP

Particularly with large groups, leaders repeatedly announce ahead of time when meals, shuttles, evening entertainment, etc. will take place.

ANNOUNCE EVENTS

When people will be adding or dropping off on the second day of a twp-day trip (or at any time in the middle of a multi-day trip), it is very important that we prepare people—on the morning of day one—for the shifting and re-sorting of people and boats that this sometimes entails. By preparing folks at the outset for these necessary changes in boat and crew arrangements, we can prevent these changes from being a big negative surprise—and help them be seen instead as simply a necessary, inherent part of this sort of trip.

PREPARE GROUP WHEN FOLKS ADD OR LEAVE MID-TRIP

Under extreme circumstances, when continuing would be unsafe and no other solution or alternative is feasible, a trip leader has the authority to cancel a trip.

CANCELLATIONS

In addition to orchestrating a safe and fun trip, the trip leader also acts as a role model and mentor—teaching, inspiring, and bringing out the best in our newer guides.

TRIP LEADER AS MENTOR

As a part of assuming primary responsibility for the quality of a trip, the trip leader confers, in a tactful way, with guides who are doing things that are detrimental to the trip's quality. Whenever possible, these conferences are held in private with no one else within hearing distance.

LEADER CORRECTS MISCONDUCT

A Key Trip Leader Responsibility: The End-of-Trip Energizing Thank You Talk: Just before the very end of every trip, perhaps as the return shuttle bus approaches the parking lot, it is important that trip leaders give a warm, upbeat, thank-you-for-rafting-with-us talk. This talk should energize folks, thank them, and end the trip on a high note. In it the trip leader might: Recap some of the special pleasures of the trip just ending. Remind folks to recycle their bottles and cans in the specially marked bins as they get off the bus. Ask folks to be sure to say good bye before they leave. Point out the availability of photos/videos of the trip. Mention that "by a stroke of incredible luck" we just happen to have wonderful Whitewater Voyages souvenir t-shirts, hats and visors available. In a light, upbeat, humorous way mention that, if they feel moved to do so, it is definitely OK to tip their guides–who, contrary to appearances, all have

END-OF-TRIP ENERGIZING THANK YOU TALK

starving grand mothers in need of aid. Sincerely thank them for choosing Whitewater Voyages, and warmly invite them to come raft with us again–either on the same river or on one of the many other wonderful rivers in the Whitewater Voyages family of rivers. And definitely mention that one of our goals is to send each of them home delighted with their trip–with a Whitewater Voyages catalogue in their hand–eager to come back and bring their friends. "So please take a brochure or two or three, and give them to friends." And point out the locations of brochure racks and stacks. Also, urge them to drive safely–and be extra careful on the windy roads leaving the river canyon.

EMERGENCY CASH

The trip leader spends emergency cash only on things *essential* to the trip, and under no circumstances ever uses company funds for loans, treats, guides' meals, or other nonessentials.

RESTOCK, SEAL & SIGN REPAIR KIT

Upon returning to the warehouse the leader makes sure the repair kit is thoroughly checked and restocked. This includes refilling or replacing glue and toluene containers, replacing any patch fabric used, etc. When the repair kit is fully ready for the next trip, the leader seals the box closed with a piece of tape and then legibly signs and dates the tape, certifying the kit is ready. The sweep-boat guide sometimes assists the trip leader in carrying out this responsibility.

RESTOCK, SEAL & SIGN FIRST AID KIT

Likewise, the leader makes sure that each item in the first aid kit is carefully checked and replaced if necessary. As with the repair kit, to certify the first aid kit is completely ready for the next trip, the leader seals the box with a piece of tape and signs and dates it. The trip WFR, EMT or sweep-guide occasionally assist the leader in this duty.

TRIP REPORT

During and after each trip, the leader thoroughly and accurately fills out a trip report, which includes the river and trip dates, the number of boaters, a detailed record of all expenses (including check numbers and amounts), a frank evaluation of all guides and trainees, gear needing repair, vehicle status report, wages, camps and lunch stops used, and so on. All wages are fully calculated, including chef, naturalist, and other extra pay. (See latest staff briefing for current pay scale.)

RETURN REPORT TO OFFICE FAST

The completed report together with all annotated receipts including the *food* receipt (these are vital tax documents), remaining emergency cash, keys, credit cards, etc., are returned straightaway to the office. If possible, each trip file folder is returned to its proper place in the main file, and the complete trip reports with receipts, cards and cash are placed in the box labeled: "Trip Reports—Just In."

URGENT VEHICLE PROBLEMS

Urgent vehicle problems are described on a separate note, which is placed in the vehicle manager's box. Because our mechanic often comes in *early* in the morning, turn these reports in the night the trip returns.

The leader also assists the chef in reporting permanent-camp stash-box needs and supplies. (See special clip boards.)

STASH BOX UPDATE

THE HEAD CHEF

The head chef takes responsibility for the trip's food. Note: Nowadays, most of our areas of operation have their own food rooms with walk-in refrigerators and freezers, etc. Some of the material in this section applies only to areas without food rooms.

CHEF HANDLES FOOD

First the chef examines the trip file for special requests. Then, keeping in mind both the food budget and the importance of having plenty of good, hearty, tasty food, the head chef prepares a menu and a detailed shopping list specifying quantities.

CHECK FILE, PREPARE MENU & SHOPPING LIST

Before shopping, chefs check the warehouse for food, beverages, and supplies left over from previous trips. Items that fit into the menu are set aside, perhaps in a cooler, and labeled with the chef's name and trip, so chefs for other trips will know they are spoken for. Also, the ice and frozen-water-jug supplies are assessed: If there is not enough ice for all the trips departing that day, the various chefs coordinate among themselves the purchase of more ice. In some cases, a chef may label or set aside (in a cooler) the ice he or she plans to use, so the other chefs will not count on using it.

BEFORE SHOPPING CHECK FOOD & ICE ON HAND

The food budget for a trip is based on the current price of food, the number of meals, and the number of people counting both guests and guides—plus a little extra money for the take-out beverages. The formula follows:

Current cost of one meal for one person × number of people × number of meals + a little extra for take-out beverages = food budget

The amount allowed per person per meal is sufficiently high that a chef can with reasonable care purchase abundant amounts of good food.

THE FOOD BUDGET

Before going shopping, it is a good idea for chefs to call the store; they'll pre-slice meats and cheeses and have them ready to go!

CALL STORE TO HAVE MEATS & CHEESE PRE-SLICED

While shopping, the chef continues to maintain both a close eye on the budget and a keen awareness of the very special nature of the trip to the guests—and the importance of having an abundance of good food. Guides who consistently go over budget or run short of food will not be asked to chef.

GET PLENTY, BUT STAY UNDER BUDGET!

Occasionally there is a good reason for going over budget. Perhaps extra kitchen-box spices or warehouse supplies are needed. In such cases, a prominent note of explanation verified and initialed by the trip leader is included in the trip leader's report.

EXPLAIN IF GOOD REASON OVER BUDGET

SEEK ADVICE WHEN JUDGING FOOD QUANTITIES

Judging food quantities is a subtle art. Every group is different, and learning to predict how much food a group will eat requires much sound advice and considerable experience. Novice chefs should consult their more experienced colleagues when they are unsure of quantities. Also, they should consult the "Expedition Food Planning Guide" beginning on page 213.

EXTRA FOOD IN COLD WEATHER

Athough no two groups are identical, there are a few general rules of thumb for determining quantities. For example, groups of active younger people in cold weather (such as the spring white-water school) will tend to eat half again as much as the average group in warm weather.

EXTRA FOOD FOR LARGER GROUPS

With larger groups it is vital that the first meal be extra plentiful and presented in a big display. Spread the food out on lunch boards (keeping cut and unwrapped items on the plastic cutting boards and tablecloths) so that everyone can see there is plenty for all. Otherwise, large groups tend to adopt a greedy, needy policy of, "I better get lots now because there won't be any left for seconds." This anticipation of scarcity tends to be self-fulfilling; for, when everyone takes more than they want or need, sure enough, the food runs out. When, God forbid, the first couple of meals run short, this psychology of scarcity usually becomes entrenched for the rest of the trip, however long that might be. If, however, the first couple of meals are truly abundant in both appearance and fact, most of the guests relax, eat only as much as they actually want, and there is plenty for all, even though later meals are not so over-abundant.

HORS D'OEUVRES

A happy hour with hors d'oeuvres, such as chips, dips, cheese, celery, fruit and carrots, plus drink, such as a zesty cooler, is generally a good idea.

TURN IN ANNOTATED FOOD RECEIPTS WITH LEADER'S REPORT

Always turn in the receipt for the trip food with the trip leader's report. On the back of each receipt write:
1) "Trip Food" for river and trip's date
2) chef's name
3) date
4) check number and amount. If cash was used, write "cash."

BUY MAYO IN SMALL JARS

Buy mayonnaise in smallish jars. Large jars (that is, jars which can not be emptied in one meal) may allow the mayonnaise to spoil—and spoiled mayonnaise is extremely dangerous.

PACK FOOD IN ORDERLY WAY WITH FIRST LUNCH SEPARATE

The chef packs the food into ice chests and metal boxes in an orderly manner. The first lunch is packed in a separate cooler with: Serving spoons, knives and forks, a can opener, paper or metal cups, plastic garbage bags, paper towels, an extra long spoon for mixing the drink, and plenty of paring knives. Note: It is important to have plenty of paring and kitchen knives in the lunch utensil bag and kitchen box, because the guide's belt knives should *not* be used for food.

THE HEAD CHEF

On class IV and V rivers and during high water on class III, it is often wise to waterproof the lunch bread and cookies in a sealed plastic bag. Otherwise, because the coolers are not watertight, these items may be reduced to a soggy pulp.

WATERPROOF LUNCH

When packing coolers, use plenty of ziplock plastic bags. These keep bread, cookies, lettuce, etc. out of the ice melt—which contaminates.

PROTECT FOOD

During hot weather, use twice the normal amount of ice and, each morning, put ice in the lunch drink jug so the drink will be ice cold by lunch time. Use lots of frozen water bottles because they serve two purposes: they cool the food and they provide extra drinking water. For example, when a group empties the lunch drink jug, these bottles can refill it.

WHEN HOT USE EXTRA ICE

Don't drop blocks of ice directly from the freezer trays into the fragile plastic coolers. Instead empty the trays onto a clean, sturdy table. Then gently place the blocks into the coolers.

LOAD COOLERS GENTLY

Remember to refill the ice trays immediately! Otherwise, the trips leaving in the next day or two will not have enough ice. Note: It is easiest to refill freezer trays *inside* the freezers using the hose.

REFILL TRAYS

The head chef makes sure the meals are served at a good time. For instance, whenever possible, dinners should be served well before dark! This means rounding up the guides and beginning preparations plenty early. For lunches, of course, this means preparing the lunch cooler in the morning right after—or during —breakfast.

START FIXING MEALS EARLY

During meal preparation, the chef plays an overseeing, coordinating role. By delegating specific tasks to the other guides and to guests who offer to help, the chef stays free to see the overall picture. This allows time to ensure the various parts of the meal are ready at the proper time and to anticipate important details—like seeing that the handwash with liquid soap is ready, seeing that serving utensils, spices, condiments, drinks, dishwater and rinses are all ready when needed.

CHEF COORDINATES MEAL PREPARATION

This is our company policy as dictated by our insurance carrier. Due to dram shop liability law, if we give our guests alcohol and they later get in a car wreck, we can be held responsible for the wreck. Please continue to fill the take-out coolers with plenty of ice-cold juice, water and soda to quench the thirst of our paddlers. It is still okay to provide alcoholic beverages for guests that are staying with us in camp so long as we model and advocate moderation. Of course, we are not to provide any alcohol to minors.

NO BEER OR ALCOHOLIC BEVERAGES OF ANY SORT IN TAKE-OUT COOLERS!!!

IMPORTANT NOTE

Please be understanding when and if some clients are disappointed that we no longer provide take-out beer. People will probably understand this policy if you tell them about dram shop liability law and how it makes us responsible if we give them beer and they later get in an auto wreck.

SHIFTING BEVERAGE EMPHASIS FOR CHEFS

Happy hour coolers should contain more juice and sodas and less beer and wine. Similarly, plan more turkey and white meat and less beef, especially for the deli lunches.

COFFEE

Please be sure to offer coffee and tea after dinner, and perhaps even with happy hour. On smaller trips, guides can ask if anyone wants any; on larger trips we just put it on with a friendly announcement.

AVOID POULTRY POISONING

Processing of commercial chicken includes blasting the carcasses with high pressure water to remove the feathers, the water then washes down into a big storage tank where it is sucked up and shot at the chicken again. In this process skin, bone, feathers, and chicken feces are washed off the chicken into the tank and then shot with high pressure back into the chicken. The result is that all raw chicken is contaminated with potentially fatal bacteria. **But be reassured, if handled properly and thoroughly cooked, chicken can be completely healthy and wholesome.**

PROPER HANDLING OF CHICKEN

Raw chicken must be handled properly!!! Here are some guidelines:

— Pack chicken in well sealed ziplock bags in coolers so that juice does not leak out and contaminate other cooler contents.
— Anything that comes in contact with raw chicken must be cleaned with hot soapy water before it can be used again. For example: After cutting raw chicken, be absolutely sure to wash the cutting board and knife (and your hands!) before they come in contact with anything else.

It is absolutely essential that we be worthy of our clients' trust, and treat this issue as a vitally important matter.

AFTER DINNER CLEANUP

After the meal, the chef is responsible for getting the kitchen area cleaned. This involves closing the kitchen box so that supplies aren't damaged by rodents or rain. It includes cleaning, oiling and putting away the D.O. so it doesn't rust. Also put away all food and secure all rocket boxes so they don't attract skunks, bears, raccoons, etc.

SELECT MORNING PERSON

In cooperation with the trip leader, the chef designates the "Morning Person." It's best if this is someone who rises early by nature. This person gets up *extra* early, even earlier than the other guides, to start the fire and start the coffee and dishwash water.

After each trip, the chef's responsibilities include:

POST TRIP FOLLOW-THROUGH

—Washing and putting away any dirty utensils and cooking gear.

—Putting all food that will keep for a future trip (this includes all unopened containers) in the "Save for Future Trips" shelves and refrigerator.

—Refilling and refreezing the ice/water bottles.

—Notifying the office of supplies needed in stash boxes (see special clip boards).

—Thoroughly cleaning the kitchen box if it needs it.

Above all, each chef should try to delight our guests with the finest food possible. Do it for love! Really put your heart into providing great food!

PUT YOUR HEART INTO IT

BEFORE THE TRIP

When guides have been out of touch for a long time, it's a good idea for them to call both the area manager and the trip leader about a week before the trip to confirm their arrival and discuss last minute details.

CALL IN

Before a trip, the guides show up at the area base with everything needed for the trip. It slows things down significantly if staff members are always saying things like, "Well, gee, I forgot my wet suit booties. Can we stop somewhere so I can get some."

SHOW UP WITH EVERYTHING

All guides arrive at the warehouse at the prearranged time to help pack. Under special circumstances some guides may arrive later, after getting approval from the trip leader beforehand.

ARRIVE EARLY

Experienced guides understand the need to begin preparations early. To get the trip off to a good start, they allow, in concert with their trip leader, enough time to pack properly, drive safely to the river, and, on far flung trips, still have time for a good night's sleep—so they wake up refreshed.

ALLOW TIME

In preparing for each trip the guides and shuttle driver do a variety of things, including: Packing, making wood runs, checking out equipment, last minute stenciling, repairs, riveting loose paddle handles, filling vehicles with gas, refilling ice trays in freezers, helping the chef, sweeping and organizing the warehouse and staff lounge, carefully locking up, etc.

PREPARING FOR TRIP

The equipment checklist filled out by the trip leader is followed closely, to ensure that nothing is left behind. As each item is packed, it is checked off the list. See "The Trip Leader" and "Equipment Packing List."

PACKING CHECKLIST

BOATS LOOK ALIKE

If possible, all of the boats on each trip should be made by the same manufacturer. When all the boats look alike, we look more professional. Same with life jackets, paddles, etc.

LUNCH BOARD/ BACKBOARDS ON CLASS IV & V

For trips on class IV & V rivers pack at least four of our special lunch boards which combine to form an emergency backboard for immobilizing neck and spine injuries.

PACK PLENTY OF WATER

Because the water in most of our wild rivers is no longer drinkable, we either carry a water filter or we pack 20 to 30 gallons of water for most two-day trips. A typical two-day trip of 20 to 25 people needs:
  —five full one-gallon canteens
  —one five-gallon jug for the first lunch
  —five to 10 gallons for camp drinking
  —five gallons for morning juice and general drinking
  —five gallons for second day's lunch drink.

WET SUIT RENTALS

The entire staff takes extra care to make absolutely sure no one's wet suit is left behind. Extreme misery or even hypothermia could result. Each complete wet suit and bootie outfit is placed in a blue bag—and labeled with the renter's name.

BRING ALONG EXTRA SPLASH JACKETS AND WET SUITS

When weather is questionable, it's okay to take along extra splash jackets and wet suits for clients to use. Always clear it with the area manager so you're not taking wetsuits or splash jackets already reserved for other trips. Ideally, collect the rental fee—either by cash, check, or Visa, MasterCard or Discover number with expiration date—at put-in and note the transaction in the trip report. Generally, a client will appreciate your foresight and money will not be an issue. If it is, however, let their safety and comfort be the deciding factor. It is better to keep our trips as safe as possible and preserve good will than collect a few dollars. Do make clear, however, that on future trips requiring wet suits or splash jackets, they should not count on us having extras, but must reserve one ahead of time—or bring their own.

SWEEP AND TIDY WAREHOUSE

After packing and before departure, the staff takes 15 minutes to sweep and tidy up the warehouse, tool room, lounge and surrounding area. In the hustle and bustle of pre-trip preparations, the warehouse sometimes comes to look like a disaster area. To fight the chaos, paper bags are folded and put away (or packed up and taken along for use in starting fires), stray tools and pieces of equipment are returned to their proper places, the floor is swept when needed, clip boards are not left lying around but are returned to their proper place in the office, and order is generally restored. The goal: Make the warehouse an uplifting place to come back to.

LOCK WAREHOUSE

The last trip to leave locks the warehouse up tight. The heater, stoves, air conditioner, lights and other appliances are all turned off. All windows and doors are carefully closed and locked.

ON THE HIGHWAY AND CARE OF VEHICLES

The most dangerous part of any trip is that spent on the highway. So Whitewater Voyages guides drive with utmost care. If a guide feels tired, if he or she is having even the slightest trouble keeping the eyes open, it's best to pull over, rest and let someone else drive.

DRIVE CAREFULLY

Sensible guides and drivers accelerate easily, slowly and gently. They take corners slowly and, when possible, brake gently, coming to a gradual stop. They try to make the vehicle last forever.

EASY DOES IT

River guides are extra careful when backing up vehicles—they always have someone behind the vehicle to give warning in case something is in the way. When backing up alone, shrewd drivers walk back to see that the way is clear whenever there is the slightest doubt.

BE EXTRA CAREFUL BACKING UP

Our drivers are aware that our vehicles are quite long—and take care not to swing the sides into things when turning. Also, they are careful to not slam the tires into curbs when parking because this throws the wheels out of alignment, causes rapid tire wear and nerve-shattering shimmies.

TAKE CARE WHEN TURNING AND PARKING

When driving vehicles with roof racks, don't attempt to drive under awnings, low garages or other low places. That high rack out of sight overhead is easy to forget—so make a special mental note to keep it in mind.

BE AWARE OF HIGH ROOF RACKS

At all of our facilities, treat the trees like delicate, precious babies. Swing extra wide to miss them by a broad margin when turning. Don't hit 'em with trailers and don't back into the graceful darlings.

LOVE THE TREES

Remember: Many of the people who sign up for our trips show up at the put-in nervous and afraid. They need reassurance. Good-looking vehicles and gear suggest a careful, professional company—run by people you can trust your life to. Battered, damaged equipment suggests the opposite and makes the boaters, or guests, wonder if they are with the right company.

WELL KEPT VEHICLES ARE REASSURING

At the beginning of every long trip, the guides check the radiator, the battery, automatic transmission fluid, oil, trailer and hitch locks, all lights, and tire pressure, including spares. Van tires, when cold, should be inflated to 35 psi (pounds per square inch) in the front and 42 to 50 psi (depending on load) in the rear. Trailer tires should be at 35 psi. Note: When a vehicle will not be used to carry heavy loads for a long period, the rear tire pressure is reduced to about 35 psi. Later, before resuming heavy use, the pressure is increased to 45 psi again.

CHECK VEHICLE REGULARLY

CHECK OIL AND WATER

The oil is checked every time gas is bought. The water is checked regularly and frequently, preferably when the engine is cold. Most of our vehicles use 20-50w or 10-40w oil.

LOOK FOR LIQUID SPOTS UNDER VEHICLES

From time to time, before getting into a vehicle, kneel down and look underneath for liquid spots on the ground. Large spots or puddles could mean trouble and should be mentioned to our mechanic as soon as possible. In reporting a puddle, the important thing is not so much the type of liquid as it is its location, such as near the rear left tire, under the transmission, under the crankcase, etc.

STARTING

When starting a cold engine, first press the gas pedal to the floor and release it. Then turn on the starter/ignition for short two- or three-second spurts with one- or two-second intervals between bursts. The *combination* of short bursts interspersed with momentary pauses usually starts cold engines faster than long grindings of the starter—and avoids draining the battery. If the engine becomes flooded, however, hold the accelerator to the floor and turn the engine over until it starts. Many of our vehicles, particularly the Dodge vans, should be warmed up for several minutes before being driven. Just sit there peacefully for a few minutes, relax, let your mind wander and savor the moment.

WHEN DRIVING

When driving, guides always maintain a safe speed, don't sway and, because a heavily loaded vehicle takes a long time to stop, maintain an enormous, galactic, 100-yard following distance. They keep an eye on the gauges and stop as soon as possible to check out any sign of malfunction.

CARAVAN

Whenever possible, vehicles headed for the same destination should travel together. In this way they can assist one another in the event of difficulties. Stay together all the way to your destination. A while back, there was a two-vehicle trip that split up when they were *almost* home—it was late and everyone wanted to get back so they left the driver of the slower vehicle behind. When the slower vehicle unexpectedly broke down, the driver was alone—stranded. Please, stay together!

REPORT UNUSUAL NOISES, SMELLS AND VIBRATIONS TO MECHANIC

When riding in a vehicle, make note of *unusual* noises, smells and vibrations. Notice particularly:
—high-pitched or very low-pitched sounds
—metallic sounds (like two pieces of metal hitting each other)
—unusual vibrations, slippages and hesitations (as when the vehicle hesitates before accelerating from a stop)
—burning smells, etc.
If an unusual sound seems to be coming from a wheel, stop, get out, place your hand on the tire: A certain amount of heat is normal, but if the rubber is uncomfortably hot or burning hot, someting is wrong. Also, take note if at night the headlights gradually grow dim, then brighter when you rev the engine.

ON THE HIGHWAY AND CARE OF VEHICLES

Unless the problem seems to require immediate attention, you often won't need to figure out exactly what's wrong. The important thing is that you notice and report these unusual noises, etc. to our mechanic as soon as possible. In your report, as accurately as you can, describe each unusual sound, smell or vibration and try to indicate its point of origin. These reports are crucial because they help us fix problems before they cause breakdowns on the highway.

When descending steep grades, such as the Hwy 193 grade from Placerville to Chile Bar, use both brakes and low gears and go very, very slowly. On downhill compression *never* rev an engine over 3,000 RPM—or the engine is likely to throw a rod. (When this happens the engine must be completely replaced! So please keep an eye on the tachometer!)

USE GEARS & BRAKES & GO SLOW DOWN STEEP GRADES BUT DON'T REV MOTOR OVER 3,000

Because of legal, health and insurance company considerations, no alcohol (including beer) or drugs whatsoever are partaken in the company vehicles.

PROHIBITED

Please do not smoke in any of our vehicles. Even a brief smoking session creates a stench that takes months to go away.

NO SMOKING IN VEHICLES

When a vehicle is in motion, the passengers should never open the back windows. This sucks in exhaust. Also, whenever opening or closing the latch windows in the Ford vans, one must push in the latch button—and drivers must caution passengers to do the same. It is a poor design: The window opens even when the button isn't pressed, but the latch breaks off.

WINDOWS

On long hauls, rational drivers don't leave the main highway to search back roads and little towns for open gas stations. Open stations tend to be lit up right next to the main highway.

MOST GAS STATIONS ARE NEXT TO HIGHWAY

Each vehicle carries a driver's log in which are recorded all repairs and vehicle related expenses. The name, date, odometer reading, location, description and cost of each item is noted. The driver's log together with the complete vehicle record book kept in the office allows our mechanic to carry on a thorough program of preventive maintenance for each vehicle.

DRIVER'S LOG

As always, whenever spending company money, receipts must be saved and four things must be written on the back of each: Date, name of item purchased, whether cash, check or credit card, and purchaser's name.

A REMINDER

Every company vehicle should carry a set of heavy duty jumper cables—plus, of course, a good spare tire and jack. Also, on extremely long trips, Whitewater Voyages vehicles often carry spares for everything likely to need replacement: Fuses, bulbs, fan belts, radiator hoses. When a spare part is used or lost, it is replaced. The river guide's motto: Always have a backup.

SPARES

PLEASE Company gas and vehicles are used only for company business.

GAS CARDS Always sign out for gas credit cards and return them immediately after use. Don't latch onto them without specific, explicit permission.

LOCK VEHICLE, COVER CONTENTS When leaving a vehicle unattended, even if only for a short period, our guides lock all windows and doors. When parking a vehicle for long periods, blankets or tarps are used to completely cover the equipment left inside. Gear mounted on the vehicle's exterior, such as gas cans, is placed inside and also covered. Company gear must never be left in the back of unattended pickups or open trucks. When actually on the river, credit cards are kept in the guide's bag, not in the parked vehicle.

CAREFULLY TIE LOADS IN We don't lose gear out of the back of vehicles. Make absolutely certain the van doors are securely closed and, when carrying gear in our open trucks, carefully tie in each load.

HIGHWAY MEALS On the highway, the staff members pay for their own meals.

CLOSE DOOR IF COLD By the way, when thoughtful people climb out of a vehicle at night or in cold weather, they close the door behind them so people remaining inside don't freeze.

PASSENGERS Generally, only the staff rides to and from trips in company vehicles (except shuttles, of course). Occasionally, there might be room for the friend of a guide, but this will be only on a space available basis, with no reservations possible. (Clearly, staff must have priority and guides might be added at the last minute.)

NO HITCHHIKERS In general, we do not pick up hitchhikers. This saves our psychic energy for our fellow guides and the boaters. Big exception: When near the river, we forget this rule. If someone asks for a ride, say, upriver, and we're going that way anyway and have room, we give them a ride.

BUSES ARRIVE EARLY Whitewater Voyages drivers make a point of arriving at rendezvous plenty early, to be ready and waiting when the group arrives.

DRIVERS DO NOT DRINK Bus and shuttle drivers don't drink alcohol before or while driving. Because the bus shuttle is probably the most dangerous part of the trip, this guideline is strictly adhered to.

DRIVE LOADED VANS WITH UTMOST CAUTION! Loaded vans are susceptible to rolling over, especially if the driver simultaneously slams on the brakes and turns suddenly. So drive loaded vans with focused attention and great caution: Maintain moderate speed and ample following distance, brake smoothly and gradually, and at all costs avoid sudden swerves.

SAVE THE BATTERY In general, do not play the radio when the engine is off. This drains the battery.

When leading a long line of cars on a shuttle, drivers take care not to lose any following cars. They wait and take a car count at each corner, and, if possible, they ask someone who knows the route to bring up the rear. **BIG SHUTTLES**

Shuttle drivers may share in the extra pay for packing and unpacking before and after each trip. **SHUTTLE DRIVERS**

A part of the responsibility of a shuttle driver is to at times help cope with vehicle problems in such a way that they have a minimum impact on the trip. **SHUTTLE PROBLEMS**

If possible, fill the gas tanks of company vehicles just before returning to the warehouse. This ensures that vehicles will be ready to go for the next trip. **RETURN WITH FULL TANK**

During the off-season spread use among all the vehicles so each is driven at least once per week. Vehicles stored for the winter should have their batteries disconnected and fuel stabilized with a fuel stabilizer such as "STA – BIL." **WINTER ROTATION**

AT THE PUT-IN

When ever possible, the guides arrive at the put-in well before the boaters. Whenever feasible, they inflate and rig the boats well beforehand. They arrange the life jackets, paddles, black bags, etc. neatly on the river beach, knowing people are reassured by a sense of order. **ARRIVE EARLY**

Seasoned guides make sure they get a good, long night's sleep the night before a trip. **DON'T STAY UP ALL NIGHT**

Obviously, guides, like boaters, do not drink alcoholic beverages, including beer, on the morning of a trip. **NO BEER**

At certain rendezvous points, it is wise to advise boaters to lock valuables in their trunks. A guide might say, "We've never had a car broken into, but better safe than sorry." **LOCK VALUABLES IN TRUNK**

The guides treat our gear with care. Although they might seem incredibly tough, our rafts and other equipment are, in many ways, extremely delicate and vulnerable. **HANDLE GEAR CAREFULLY**

To avoid strain on diaphragms, take care to inflate all air chambers equally. Do not top off any chamber until all have been inflated, and when topping off the boats later in the trip, distribute the air to keep the chambers equal. **INFLATING RAFTS**

A tip: When there is a crease at a diaphragm, the pressure in the two adjacent chambers is *not* equal; when the diaphragm is smooth, the chambers are equal. Inflate all Whitewater Voyages **ELIMINATE CREASES** rafts to 21 psi (pounds per square inch), which is drum tight.

STEP AROUND   Avoid stepping on rafts spread out on dry land. A boat's fabric could be punctured if pinched between a shoe and a piece of glass, metal or sharp stone.

LIFT & CARRY RAFTS   Careful guides avoid dragging boats across the ground. I've seen holes put in brand new boats this way—it is enough to make a strong person weep.

RENTED BOATS   With boats rented from other companies, government regulations dictate that, over their company markings, we tape a piece of cloth or opaque plastic, such as one of our medium-sized decals, printed with our company name. All boats must bear our company name.

GENTLY PUT DOWN GEAR   Mature guides set things down gently. I remember being flabbergasted years ago upon seeing a boatman with a Rocky Mountain outfitter actually throw oars onto rocky ground.

WATCH GEAR   When the gear is not locked up, at least one guide always stays to watch it. For instance, if the crew needs to go someplace when the gear is sitting out on the put-in beach, a guide stays there to watch it. Whenever possible, we avoid entrusting this responsibility to people outside the company.

RIGGING   All gear is closely, tightly tied to the rafts to minimize injury, loss, and entanglement risk. When loading our boats, maintain 180° clearance for both oar handles.

OAR SAFETY LINES   *Always* secure *all* oars with safety lines!

AMMO BOXES   Ammo boxes tied to cross thwarts should always have a life jacket covering the corners, which are sharp and might otherwise do serious injury. By the way, when securing ammo boxes to cross thwarts, use a rafter's (modified trucker's) hitch to cinch box tight. See sketches.

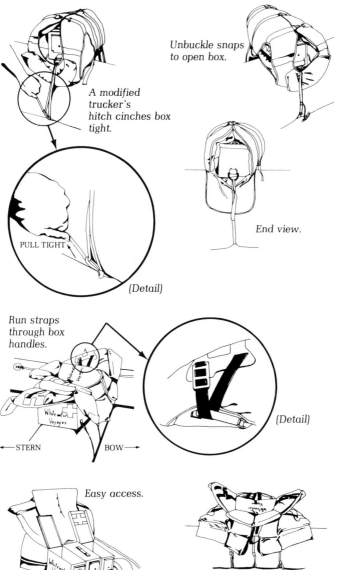

PADDING A SINGLE AMMO BOX WITH A LIFE JACKET

Unbuckle snaps to open box.

A modified trucker's hitch cinches box tight.

PULL TIGHT

(Detail)

End view.

PADDING THREE AMMO BOXES WITH TWO LIFE JACKETS

Run straps through box handles.

(Detail)

←—STERN   BOW—→

Easy access.

Boxes should be concealed when viewed from stern.

At least one spare paddle is carried for each paddle boat. Whenever an oar boat is along, spare paddles are tied into it. In a paddle boat, spares flat on the floor get bent and paddles with one end down and the other up are dangerous to both boat and crew. When a spare paddle must be carried in a paddle raft, it is tied to a cross thwart. See sketch.

SPARE PADDLES

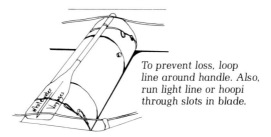

To prevent loss, loop line around handle. Also, run light line or hoopi through slots in blade.

HANDHOLDS IN BIG WATER

In big or technical water it is crucial to keep people in the boat. So, when the river is high or especially difficult, rig handholds on the cross thwarts by securing two lines around the center of each thwart. This is particularly vital in paddle boats. See sketch.

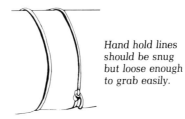

Hand hold lines should be snug but loose enough to grab easily.

EXTRA CORD

Thoughtful guides carry a few yards of string to cut up and pass out to boaters as chin and head straps for hats and eyeglasses.

UNNECESSARY ITEMS

Gently discourage boaters from carrying unnecessary items on the river. Inexperienced boaters sometimes think they should take onto the boat things that are not needed and often just get wet, lost or in the way.

CHECK BEACH

Before leaving put-ins and take-outs, carefully check the river beach for overlooked items, such as lengths of short line, personal gear, etc.

ON THE RIVER

LEAVING PUT-IN

Guides often finish their put-in talks and launch preparations at different times. At most put-ins those ready to head downriver before others, may, after notifying the trip leader, float down to the first big eddy to escape the congestion of the put-in and experience the psychological lift of getting underway, if only for a short distance. When all the boats have arrived at the eddy, the entire group continues downstream together with proper boat spacing, with each boat keeping the one behind continuously in view.

Occasionally it is necessary for the entire group to leave a put-in or eddy tightly and together, in one, two, three fashion. This is the case, for instance, on extremely swift, difficult rivers where there are no good eddies just downstream from the put-in. Also, on crowded rivers, unless the *entire* group pulls out together in one, two, three succession, our boats are likely to become mixed up with those of another group. To pull out in unison, all of the boats must first be "ready:" That is, each guide must have her or his crew briefed and set to go. Each boat is untied completely, all lines are tucked away, and all gear is tied in. (Note: Guides with gear in their boats start packing well beforehand, so they are "ready" when the other boats are.) Each boat is off the beach or river bottom, floating completely. Either the guide or the "agile line person" stands in the water ready to push off and jump in—or someone sitting in the boat holds onto a branch or rock. The crew is in their proper places, life jackets strapped on, with paddles in hand. And all of the guides keep an eye on the trip leader. When all of these conditions are met, the group is "ready." (Note: If a line is still uncoiled or a boat is still a bit up on the beach, the group is not "ready.") When the lead guide points to each guide with a questioning look, a responding nod or OK signal means "ready," while a shake of the head means "we need more time"—a number of fingers held up indicates the number of minutes needed to get "ready."

SPECIAL TECHNIQUE FOR PULLING OUT IN UNISON

Once all the boats are "ready," the lead boat pulls out into the current, and all of the boats follow, one after another, quickly and together, allowing just enough distance between boats for safety. The sweep boat pulls out last, yet stays within view—except, perhaps, on tight bends—of the lead boat. We stop and push off many times in the course of every trip—and it is important that we do it smoothly, professionally.

PULL OUT TOGETHER

As the group moves downriver the boats stay together, stopping or rowing or paddling hard if necessary. If the lead boat seems difficult to keep up with, it is probably because the lead guide feels the group should move more quickly downstream. All the more reason to work to keep up.

STAY TOGETHER; KEEP UP

The reasons for staying together are many. The boats stay together for safety—so they can help one another in the event problems arise. On the straightaways, being able to see all the boats is reassuring to the trip leader—when the leader loses track of a boat, he or she becomes anxious and concerned.

IMPORTANCE OF STAYING TOGETHER

No boat passes the lead boat and the sweep passes no other boat. This order is maintained even on short hops. If other boats go ahead, the leader's options are eliminated. But if all the boats are in formation, the leader can choose a different landing point, etc.

LEAD & SWEEP

that might be advantageous on that day. Also, injuries and difficulties can occur on easy as well as difficult stretches, so it is important that the sweep boat bring up the rear every foot of the way from put-in to take-out—except when it goes first through rapids to get into rescue/picture-taking position.

STOP NEAR LEADER

An exception to the above guideline: If the lead boat is stopped in a swift section of river with no good eddies nearby, following boats float past and catch the next good eddy. In general, the other boats make every effort to catch an eddy within sight and signalling range of the leader. This is particularly important with large groups on crowded rivers, where the possibilities for confusion and separation are increased.

DON'T COLLIDE WHEN STOPPING

When pulling in to the bank near other rafts, adept guides do not crash into the other boats, driving them against the rocks.

RIVER ETIQUETTE

Each group of rafts stays together and tries not to get mixed up with other groups. Each group waits its turn to proceed. If one group does wish to pass another group, the lead boat of the following group first asks permission from the sweep boat of the preceeding group. See "River Etiquette" in River Signals below.

WHEN PASSING PEOPLE FISHING

When passing people fishing, it is usually best to stay as far away as possible, remain quiet, and keep moving. A friendly smile and wave of the hand is usually appreciated. However, pausing in the eddy right in front of a fisherman to ask how many he's caught is not the way to improve relations.

POSITION OF KAYAKS

The inflatable kayaks are kept behind the second raft and in front of the second to last raft. Kayaks must be cautioned to stay well clear of the rafts in rapids—for if they get too close they could interfere with the rafts' ability to maneuver, get clobbered by a paddle or an oar, and, worst of all, get entrapped under a hung-up raft!

ENFORCE SAFETY GUIDELINES & SET GOOD EXAMPLE

River guides teach more by example than by precept. As a result, wide-awake guides always follow all safety guidelines themselves. For instance, if the boaters are expected to wear their lifejackets, the guides wear theirs also. Whitewater Voyages guides enforce all safety rules in a gentle but firm manner. They are especially alert about not letting lines dangle in the boat. And they make sure that everyone wears tennis shoes or some other type of safe footwear at all times while on the river.

JUMP FEET FIRST

Safety-minded guides caution all swimmers to jump into the river feet first, regardless of whether they are swimming from the raft or from shore.

DISCOURAGE HIGH JUMPING

Responsible guides generally discourage diving or jumping from above ten feet. They explain that high jumping can injure kidneys, dislocate shoulders, and cause other serious injuries. If guests insist on doing a high jump anyway, the guide makes it clear that they do so at their own risk. Clearly, some people can handle this risk better than others, so modulate cautioning remarks accordingly. The situation to avoid above all is that in which everyone—uncoordinated and adept people alike—suddenly decide to join in a high jump. Except when with especially physical, rugged groups, whitewater guides usually avoid high jumping themselves, as this sets a risk-taking example and encourages others—perhaps people poorly suited to the challenge—to toss caution and their fragile necks to the wind. We do make one exception to this guideline at the jump rock on the Lower Kern, where our guides very carefully supervise and monitor the jumping—and have done so safely for over twenty years.

STAY CLOSE WHEN SWIMMING IN CALMS

Before guests jump out of the boat to swim in calms, thoughtful guides advise them to stay close to the boat—say, within 50 feet in long calms, closer if a rapid is looming in the distance. And the guides are careful to have everyone back in the boat at least 100 yards above the rapid.

NON-SWIMMERS FLOAT IN CALM

Depending on the weather, the water temperature, and the willingness of the person involved, it is sometimes good for non-swimmers to float briefly in their life jackets beside the boat in calm water early in the trip. Sensitive guides often suggest but never insist on this. This demonstration tends to calm guests who might be nervous about getting tossed out of the raft. It shows that the life jacket will keep them afloat even if they can't swim.

ON LETTING BOATERS CAPTAIN AND ROW

Each guide is totally responsible for what happens to and in his or her boat. Boaters may captain or row only at the guide's discretion. Intelligent guides do not take chances. They let boaters take over only on rapids they are sure the boaters can handle—and they are *certain* to step in whenever there is any chance of injury to people or equipment. To a large extent the boaters do not know their limits and look to the guides to tell them what those limits are. We are responsible. When we let boaters attempt things they are not ready to handle, we betray their trust. Good guides are not afraid to be stern: They are polite, but firm. Our motto: Err on the side of caution, never on the side of danger.

OAR CLEARANCE

Even as they float down the river, guides in oar boats are careful to maintain 180° clearance for the oars—and particularly to seat people where they are out of range of the oar handles.

GET 'EM DOWN FOR BIG ONES

Before hitting big waves and strong reversals where people might be sucked off the tubes, oar guides tell their crews to, "Hold on, lean in, and get down." Depending on the situation, paddle guides may say the same—or may have their crews, "Paddle hard forward!" and "Dig, dig, dig!" through big holes.

**CLASS IV
& V RAPIDS**

When running class IV and V rapids and waterfalls, it is wise to secure all hard baggage and equipment completely out of range of the boaters—so no one falls on a hard object and gets injured.

NO BOOZE

We insist that people not drink alcohol on the river. This policy is based on liability considerations, river permit regulations, and, above all, common sense. Veteran guides are tactful but firm on this point, saying, "This is a wild, whitewater river. To raft it safely, you need all your wits about you." And, if necessary, a guide can say, "You paid Whitewater Voyages to take you down the river because you want the benefit of our experience and expertise. Well, everything we know about rafting tells us that it is not safe to drink on the river. Please, save your (beer, etc.) for camp. Thanks."

**DRINKING
WATER**

Unfortunately, due to giardia spread by beaver, all surface water is not safe to drink without filtering or treatment. To ignore this fact can lead to diarrhea, stomach cramps, and even poisoning. Advise all guests accordingly. Except in an emergency do not use chlorinated river water for drinking. We carry a canteen in each raft and approximately 25 to 30 gallons of additional water per trip in 5 gallon containers. This supply is used for all drinks. (For typical groups of 25 we allow: 5 gallons for the first lunch, 5 to 10 gallons for evening camps, 5 gallons for morning orange, grape or apple juice, 5 gallons to refill the canteens on the second morning, and 5 gallons for the second day's lunch. Total: 25-30 gallons.)

**CARRY PLENTY
OF DRINKING
WATER ON THE
RAFT AND
CLEAN HANDS
AT EVERY MEAL**

It is easy to become dehydrated on river trips, in hot <u>and</u> cold weather, without knowing it. In hot weather, dehydration can lead to heat exhaustion or heat stroke, and in cold weather, dehydration can contribute to hypothermia. We as guides have a responsibility to make sure that our guests are drinking enough water. Also, use a hand sanitizer or set up a handwash at every meal, including soap, and make a show of cleaning hands before preparing food.

**NON-COMMUNAL
DRINKING
WATER SYSTEM
ON RAFTS**

To create a non-communal drinking water system which reduces the spread of germs and diseases, we are asking all guests to show up at the put-in with their own filled water bottles. See the Gear List in the Whitewater Voyages brochure. To hold these bottles in our boats, we have "thwart ditty bags" which secure with a cam strap onto thwarts. These bags are easy to access during the trip, whenever someone wants a drink of water. It is important that each boat have one or more filled gallon water jugs aboard to refill these bottles, and it is a good idea for each guide to have a few extra, filled, clean bike bottles for the folks who forget theirs.

LANOLIN

Pure lanolin, the natural lubricant of wool, prevents the drying, cracking and splitting of skin caused by the repeated wetting and drying of hands. Because lanolin does block skin pores, use it only on the hands.

SUNBURN

When someone starts to turn red with sunburn, the alert guide will strongly advise them to put on a long sleeved shirt and long pants. Beyond a certain point, sunburn is more than just uncomfortable, it can be a medical problem.

NO NUDITY

On popular rivers where other groups are present, we discourage nudity on our trips.

NO PETS

No dogs or other pets are allowed on our rafts.

LIBRARY BOXES

When guidebook library boxes are along, the guides usually encourage people to make use of them. But they make a point of asking the guests to return the books whenever *they are not actually reading them*, saying something like, "Please don't set the book down someplace or put it in your bag—put it back in the library box so someone else can find and use it."

PHOTOGRAPHY RAFT

When there are people with cameras along, it is often good to designate one boat—oar boats are best—as the photography raft. This boat runs spectacular rapids first, in order to get into position to photograph the other boats coming through. Sweep boats serve as good camera boats: They can power past the other boats just above the photogenic rapids to get into camera position (which is also, usually, a good rescue position), and later they can fall in behind in sweep position after the other boats have come through.

URGE SAFETY

Of course, we explain in our release/assumption of risk forms, web site, brochures and safety talks that rafting involves an inherent element of risk. With this understood, we never encourage clients to take additional, unnecessary risks. Be a voice of caution. Urge safety. If someone insists on taking an unnecessary risk anyway, explain that they do so at their own risk.

WATERFIGHTING

REPEAT RULES EARLY

On trips where waterfighting is a possibility, the rules of waterfighting are explained in the trip leader's talk and repeated to each crew early in the voyage:

NOT JUST ABOVE RAPIDS

—No waterfighting when approaching or running rapids. To allow adequate time to calm down and refocus, all waterfighting should stop at least 200 feet above rapids.

NO BOARDING

—No boarding or pulling people overboard. Once, after three weeks in Canada, I returned to find that it had become standard practice for the big people to climb aboard enemy rafts and throw all the small people into the river! Sensitive guides do not teach people to be bullies.

CAREFUL WHEN CLOSE

—Use caution at close range: Do not throw water super hard, and be careful not to clobber someone with a paddle or a bucket.

CAREFUL WITH WATER CANNONS

—Do not shoot water cannons and powerful squirt guns straight into people's eyes or faces. Instead, shoot up and rain down on the enemy.

NO BILGE WATER

—Do not throw bilge water—it tends to be dirty.

ABIDE SCRUPULOUSLY

Sure, there are times when it might seem safe to ignore a rule, and, say, initiate a waterfight just above an easy rapid. But this sets a poor precedent and a novice boater may not be able to so distinguish. So, sharp guides abide by these rules scrupulously.

NEVER ABUSE SIGNALS

Reliable river guides never use signals to lure another raft into a waterfight. Signals are to be used only in earnest—and are to be taken seriously.

DON'T HOG THE ACTION

Guides do not hog the action in waterfights. After all, it is the boaters' trip—and they should be encouraged to participate.

COLD

When it's just too cold, considerate guides discourage water-fighting.

BE CONSIDERATE

Of course, guides think of the guests first. If someone is being made miserable by a waterfight, the guide tries to tone down the fray—or removes the boat from it.

BE LIGHT & GALLANT

Professional guides waterfight in a light-hearted, fun-loving manner. They throw water with gusto but are careful not to become so serious about a waterfight that they forget to be generous and gallant—and think of the guests' safety and enjoyment above all else.

THE ART OF WATER-FIGHTING

When energetic guides explain the rules, they often also offer a few pointers on the art of waterfighting: If you use buckets, don't overfill them. Keep a tight grip so the bucket doesn't go sailing out of your hands. Don't throw wildly, but take careful aim and soak the entire enemy crew with each bucketful. An upwind (usually downriver) raft, by the way, has a delicious advantage.

HIGH WATER SAFETY GUIDELINES

EMPHASIZE SAFETY

High water can dramatically change our rivers, and requires that we redouble our ongoing emphasis on safety: The following high water safety guidelines reflect state-of-the-art expert and professional boating practices now used throughout the world:

Even if you are familiar with a run at lower flows, before taking clients on high flows new to you, consider "retraining" on the high flows with one or more practice runs.

RETRAIN ON HIGH FLOWS

Holes and lines which are runnable at moderate flows may become too dangerous, while new safer routes—sometimes along the sides, sometimes down the middle—often open up. Avoid waves and holes which might flip your boat, and take great care to hit big runnable waves and holes square—straight bow on—with forward momentum.

LEARN NEW LINES

Keep your boat right side up and keep your people in the boat. Give extra thorough safety talks and in-boat training. Because mishaps and the resultant pandemonium can occur any time, including the instant you leave the put-in eddy, take extra time right at put-in to provide super thorough in-boat trainings— teach people how to: paddle well, stay in the boat, dig through holes, avoid entanglement (keep lines coiled, etc.), and, if swimming, avoid and cope with holes and strainers.

RE-EMPHASIZE THE BASICS

Keys to keeping people in the boat: Teach them how to sit and how to brace their feet. Teach them how to gain stability from their paddle in the water and how to "Paddle hard forward!" and "Dig, dig deep, dig!" through runnable big waves and holes. And, when appropriate, especially with less strong paddlers, teach, practice and use the "lean in", the "lean in, get down", and the "hold on, lean in, get down" commands.

KEEP EVERYONE IN THE BOAT

Err on the side of caution. Look far ahead and start super early to miss obstacles—which come at you much, much faster in high water.

START MOVES EARLY!

To keep swims short, tighten boat spacing—often down to two to five boat lengths. With this tight boat spacing, emphasize that swimmers should immediately swim as fast as they can to the nearest right-side-up boat.

TIGHTEN BOAT SPACING

During extreme high water, to prevent swimmers from getting away downstream, maintain a downstream safety net by placing either the strongest crews and guides (possibly with oar/paddle rigs) or dedicated safety boats (16-foot safety cats and kayaks) in the lead positions.

LEAD BOATS ARE DOWNSTREAM SAFETY NET!

High water rigging and gear: Rig a flip line across the bottom of your boat. Rig grab lines around the perimeter or at least along the straight sides of your boat. Dress yourself and your crew for a swim. Wear a brightly colored high-float life jacket with 22 lbs or more of buoyancy.

RIGGING & GEAR

STRAINERS OFTEN LINE BANKS

Remember that with high flows the banks are often lined with strainers, and stopping may require spotting a large eddy far downstream and starting early to develop momentum into it.

For more on high water technique, see the **The Class V Briefing**.

KNOW SIGNALS

Know all standard signals, which are explained in PART 4 of **The Guide's Guide *Augmented***.

BE EXTRA ALERT, EXTRA PREPARED

Above all, do not be complacent or laid back. Realize that high water increases the risks for all rivers, including class III. Know and practice these high water safety guidelines. Be alert. Really, thoroughly prepare yourself and your crews for the increased risks and heightened pandemonium that high water can trigger. With your fellow and sister guides, talk about, think about and practice rescue scenarios, including ways to rescue swimmers and other boats without getting your own boat into trouble! Realize that in some scenarios you may have to be very active— for example, if there is trouble upstream, some guides may need to hustle fast up the bank to provide help in a hurry, while others stay with, communicate with and divert, entertain and reassure <u>all</u> of the downstream clients. Of course, if there is a serious injury, we must provide care all the way to the hospital or until the patient is turned over to trained medical professionals.

REMEMBER TO INSPIRE FUN

Another big thing: As much as possible, even as you emphasize safety, remember to have and inspire good humor and fun, and focus on the positive. Even if a secret (to the clients) part of you feels gripped with fear, also cultivate and stay in touch with— and give voice to—other genuine parts of yourself: Parts which might be excited, intensely alive, energized, deeply appreciative of life itself, calm, thankful for your crew, awe-struck by the sheer beauty of the canyon, etc.

USE ONLY GUIDES WHO ARE READY

Ultimately, it is essential that each trip leader set a tone of <u>Safety First</u>, and make sure that all of the guides on each trip create a safe and enjoyable experience for the guests. If a guide is not providing a safe, enjoyable experience for his or her guests, the trip leader should speak with the particular guide and also inform the area manager or company owner.

IN CAMP

When tying up the boats at camp, our guides tie all the boats to one another, end to end if possible. When end to end, the boats are sideways to the beach and easy to load and unload. Those boats with the greatest loads are placed where the landing is best for loading and unloading. In order to hold the entire string of boats snug against the river bank, at least one line is run ashore from each boat. When there are no solid tie-up points near the boats, at least one long line—consisting, if necessary, of several shorter lines strung together—is extended to an absolutely secure tie-up point, such as a tree or big, grippable rock. The other lines can be tied to deadmen, bushes, medium-sized rocks or cairns. Consistently tying up the boats in this manner not only insures against losing a raft and makes for easy loading and unloading, it also lends a professional touch to the trip and a homey sameness to each camp.

TIE UP BOATS IN A LINE

Careful rafters never tie up their boats where they will buck, bounce, rub or chafe against rocks, roots, or anything hard or sharp. Even mild rubbing, when continued for an entire night, can wear a hole through the toughest raft. In places where the river works the boats up and down even slightly, it is best to pull the boats entirely out of the water to prevent chafing.

BOATS MUST NOT CHAFE

To prevent loose, light-weight items, such as inflatable kayaks, from being blown away in a strong wind, experienced guides tie these things down for the night, every night. A line strung through the bow loops of a row of inflatable kayaks and tied at each end to, say, a tree or rock secures them nicely.

TIE LIGHT THINGS DOWN

Toward the end of the unloading process, when the heavy stuff—the coolers, rocket boxes, kitchen box and grills—are being brought ashore, one of the guides, with an eye to safety, aesthetics, and traffic patterns, supervises the arrangement of the camp. The fire is located in a safe place, preferably an existing fire spot. The kitchen box, its tray, the coolers and rocket boxes are, if possible, placed in a circle around the fire. They should be at least five or so feet back from the fire, with walkways between each so as to avoid traffic bottlenecks, in such a way that people can later either sit on them or sit on the ground and lean back on them with their feet close to, but not in, the fire. If feasible, the dishwashing pails are placed out of the way in a row with the rinse near a big flat rock, a table of some sort, or the kitchen box lid. A few minutes of careful thought arranging the camp can prevent inefficiency, frustration, traffic jams—and truly contribute to the comfort and convenience of a camp.

CAMP ARRANGEMENTS

The toilet is set up right after unloading. Lime cans are lined with at least *two* plastic garbage bags, toilet paper is kept in a plastic bag, and, most important, everyone is instructed to keep the lid tightly fitted to the can between uses. This last step—keeping the lid on between uses—is vital to prevent possible cross-contami-

SET UP TOILET RIGHT AWAY

nation from fecal matter to food via flies, a potentially grave health hazard.

TEACH BOATERS TO HANDLE D.O. CAREFULLY
Careful guides teach the boaters to handle cast iron Dutch ovens with great care. If dropped, a D.O. can crack easily, and once cracked it is useless.

RETURN HOT COALS TO FIRE
Be extra careful with Dutch oven coals. When the D.O. is done, put all the hot coals back in the fire, and either cover or soak the hot spot where the D.O. was.

OIL D.O. AFTER EACH USE
Whenever possible, do not use soap to clean a Dutch oven. Wash it out with a scrub brush and hot water, dry it thoroughly—preferably over the fire—and lightly oil the D.O.'s entire inside: bottom, sides and top. See page 157 of *Whitewater Rafting* for more on the use and care of Dutch ovens.

RENTAL TENTS
Guides should show guests how to put up the tents they rent from us. It takes very little time to do so, but if not properly informed, folks can spend a lot of time trying to figure it out and often end up breaking them in the process.

RAIN SHELTERS
In the event of heavy or persistent rain, Whitewater Voyages guides customarily erect a large, high tarp shelter over the campfire area. Using oars, lines and the best tarps on the trip, and selecting water-shedding, wind-resistant designs, we make these shelters plenty high and extra big so the group can move about underneath with ease and comfort, without traffic bottlenecks, without stooping. If some of the guests do not have tents, sleeping shelters must be made. These are designed to be quite low, so rain will not blow in under them, and often consist of raft lean-tos or tarp and paddle tents. Sipping a hot drink beside a cozy campfire under a well-built tarp shelter while looking out at a downpour is one of the coziest, most triumphant feelings available to homo sapiens. The cave man in control of his universe.

A large, high shelter over a campfire.

A low sleeping shelter.

Set up a handwash with running water from a spigot jug and liquid soap at every meal and encourage boaters to use it. The guides, of course, always wash their hands before food preparation. This is not only common sanitary practice, it also, by setting a correct example, teaches the guests to do the same. One case of dysentery will ruin someone's long anticipated vacation. **HAND WASH**

To start a full cooking fire efficiently, first fill up the space under the grills with wood, thoroughly soak the wood with lighter fluid, put on the first pails of dishwater, pot of coffee water, etc., then light. Using a full spread of wood from the start and soaking it with lighter fluid quickly creates a broad, hot fire that will last a relatively long time. This gets things cracking and is a huge help in serving meals on time. Because it ignites more gradually, more subtly, lighter fluid is preferable to white gas, which ignites with a dangerous explosion. **LIGHTER FLUID**

For larger groups, expand the circle of seats and build a bigger fire. This way more people, perhaps everyone, can sit in the warm front row. **BIG GROUP, BIG CIRCLE**

Children often enjoy taking responsibility for keeping the fire going. **LITTLE FIRE PERSON**

Caution guests not to burn plastic in the campfire. It creates toxic fumes. **DON'T BURN PLASTIC**

Whenever mixing alcoholic drink, guides make absolutely sure everyone on the trip understands the drink contains alcohol. Some people take medication that, when combined with alcohol, can produce severe reactions! If necessary put a sign on the container stating, "Booze" or "Wine Cooler." In general, by the way, do not spike wine coolers with hard liquor. **ALCOHOL**

SUPPORT CHEF In the same enthusiastic way they help the trip leader, all guides are aware of the head chef's responsibilities and whole-heartedly support him or her. Whenever possible, they *anticipate* the chef's requests and take care of things before the chef thinks of them. A small example: Steaks will soon go on the fire. A guide foresees the need for spices and sauces, and places them close by the campfire without waiting for the chef to ask.

MEALS Ideally, river meals are served at a reasonably early hour, with enough daylight remaining to eat and wash all pots and dishes before dark. The various parts of the main meal, such as the chicken, rice, and salad, are ready at the same time and are presented attractively. The guides serve during the first big rush for food. Shortly thereafter, when the onslaught becomes a trickle, the guides serve themselves. Still, though, the guides keep an eye out for stragglers—and as latecomers arrive, the guides tell them what there is and where to find it, including a few words on the beverages and spices available. Generally, the guides or volunteer boaters do the cooking. The coffee pot and water for hot chocolate and tea are put on the heat as the food is cooking, if possible, timed so that they will be piping hot and ready to go a bit before folks finish eating. Likewise, the tea, hot chocolate, sugar, and cream are placed out a little while before the meal is finished.

DISHWASH & TWO RINSES The dishwashing area is customarily prepared before the meal is served. It includes: A hot, soapy dishwash with scrub brushes. A hot clear rinse. A cool chlorine rinse. And a clean, spacious drying area, preferably covered. The intermediate clear rinse is essential because soap destroys chlorine's purification ability. The wash and first rinse are kept *hot* with hot coals under the pails—or, with the stainless steel dishwashing units, by means of special propane burners. If the wash or rinse water becomes dirty or scummy, it is replaced with fresh. Wash and rinse pails, basins, and special dishwashing units are kept extra clean through regular, thorough scrubbing.

STRAINER & SUMP HOLE Waste liquids such as left over coffee, the wash and rinse water, etc. are poured out through a strainer into a sump hole at least 100 feet from the river, and the solid bits are disposed of in the garbage. Nature can purify liquids, but has difficulty with solids. Also, liquid-waste holes with bits of floating food attract trash-seeking vermin: rats, crow, etc. to a campsite. Sump holes in permanent camps should be covered completely; garbage can lids work well.

SHOES IN CAMP Because the risk of foot injury is high, experienced guides always wear foot protection on the river and give serious consideration to wearing say, tennis shoes, in camp. In the old days, before foot protection became standard practice, the most common guide injury resulted from stepping on dropped Dutch oven coals.

IN CAMP

Because strange people wandering in disrupt group closeness and unity, guides usually avoid dropping in on the camps of trips they are not working. However, if a guide does visit an overnite camp, she or he is careful to mingle with the guests, help with the chores, and in general make a positive contribution to the trip. Above all, a guide *never* just drops in, eats and leaves.

GUIDE'S VISITING CAMP

The evening campfire can be a special time. If handled with warmth, sensitivity and enthusiasm, the time spent around the fire can put an extra sparkle, an extra glow into the trip. Of course, every group is different and there are no guaranteed recipes for a successful campfire. Nonetheless, here are a few things to consider:

MAKING THE CAMPFIRE SPECIAL

> Our goal is to create a sense of closeness
> and belonging, a relaxed feeling that
> everyone is welcome and OK. Holy
> Reversal! The folks in our camp are more
> than OK, they're jolly fine!

EVERYONE BELONGS

Generally speaking, no one person should dominate the whole time. Musicians, for instance should not play constantly, on and on, leaving no openings for anyone or anything else. Rather, a guitarist might play for a while, then stop to let others tell a few stories, do magic, interpret nature, or play a game. Later, the guitarist can play again.

NO ONE DOMINATES

The guides have a tremendous influence on the tone of a trip. If the guides seem competitive, macho, arrogant or indifferent, the group—though no one might admit it—will tend to be tense, distant and guarded. However, by being warm, friendly, cooperative and supportive both among themselves and with the guests, the guides can create an atmosphere in which people can let down their guard and express themselves more freely, act out a bit, be open or goofy or tender. Our goal is to put people at ease.

BE WARM, FRIENDLY, SUPPORTIVE

Games that exclude or cause serious torment are to be avoided. Games that create lasting "in" and "out" groups, such as "Who has the hat?" divide rather than unify a group. Activities and games that are non-competitive and *include* people, such as "Nature Symphony" and joke-telling are to be favored. Of course, guides should avoid ethnic and graphically pornographic jokes. See "Guides & Guests" section on page 6.

PLAY GAMES THAT INCLUDE RATHER THAN EXCLUDE

One way to create a positive atmosphere and help people relax and open up is to play games. See PART 7: Entertainment and Interpretation below.

GAMES

Be yourself. In your own way, put your heart into each campfire experience and try to spark life into the group.

PUT HEART INTO IT

DRINK

Intelligent guides drink wine and spirits in moderation. They never drink so much that they cannot get up early the next morning feeling good.

ILLEGAL DRUGS PROHIBITED

The use of marijuana or any illegal drug by guides on trips negates our insurance, jeopardizes our permits, and, most important, adversely affects trip safety and quality. Any guide who uses illegal drugs on trips will be fired.

SQUARE AWAY CAMP FOR NIGHT

The last two or three guides to go to bed square away the camp for the night. They put away all paper stuff—otherwise toilet paper and paper towels soak up dew during the night and become useless. They assist the chef in closing up the kitchen box, putting the tray inside and locking the latch to keep out insects. They fold over the flaps of watertight food bags to drain off dew and rain. They clamp the lids on rocket boxes. And they put away or place a weight on any light things, such as tin plates, which might be blown away.

EARLY BIRD

In the morning, the guides rise before the boaters and prepare breakfast early. Often, one staff member in particular, the morning person, gets up extra early, even before the other guides, and builds the fire *big*, puts coffee and dishwashing water on to heat and starts breakfast.

MORNING IDEA

When feeling inspired, guides may sometimes make their way around to the guests waking up in their sleeping bags and pour each a cup of hot coffee, tea or hot chocolate. A further possibility is to tell everyone the night before to set their cup out within reach of their sleeping bag.

LUNCH CHEF

Just after breakfast, the lunch chef prepares for lunch, making sure the appropriate utensils, liquid hand soap, cups, can opener, paring knives, plastic garbage bags, and food are in the lunch cooler. Also, on hot days, he or she mixes the lunch drink and adds lots of ice to the jugs, so the drink will be ice cold when the group reaches the lunch stop.

STREAMLINE PERSONAL ROUTINE

Seasoned river guides streamline their personal routine to their own comfortable minimum. For instance, upon getting up on a cold morning a guide might climb straight into a pair of shorts plus a parka. Later, when the sun warms the world up, the guide simply takes off the parka and is ready for the river.

LOCK UP EVERYTHING

When leaving a camp with a permanent storage box, our guides lock all company gear inside the box. They do not leave out so much as a duffle bag or a black bag of charcoal, for things left out look junky and are very likely to be stolen.

CHECK FOR LITTER

Just before leaving a camp (or for that matter, a take-out or lunch site), experienced guides, while they concentrate on loading the boats, ask a few conscientious guests to comb the camp for litter and forgotten items.

AT THE TAKE-OUT

Just before reaching the take-out, each guide thanks folks for rafting with us, and asks his or her crew to help unload and carry the rafts and gear to the vehicle. Depending on the take-out and the amount of gear, a guide might say something like, "That beach up ahead on the right is the take-out. We would like to thank you for coming with us. And we'd like to make one last request: We would really appreciate your help carrying the boats and gear up the bank. If all of us pitch in, we can probably get everything up to the truck in one trip."

GET CREW INVOLVED WITH TAKE-OUT

In the course of rallying the support of the boaters, each guide points out that other groups are taking out here also and emphasizes the need to keep all of our stuff together. Often, the first guide to land selects a spot for the gear, points the spot out to each crew as it comes in, and has someone stand on the place or on the path leading to it to direct traffic and see that everything gets to the right place.

KEEP GEAR TOGETHER

After all the gear has been carried to the vehicle, one of the guides goes back down to the take-out beach and checks for any items that may have been overlooked, such as Pelican boxes, paddles, lengths of short line, etc.

CHECK TAKE-OUT BEACH

Boats, tarps, duffle bags and waterproof bags are dried thoroughly, for if stored when damp they will rot. If, due to rain or frenzy at the take-out, the gear must be rolled up wet, the staff dries everything upon returning to the base house.

DRY RAFTS & TARPS

Inflated rafts set out to dry or placed on roofracks or flatbed trailers should be bled. Release air evenly, simultaneously from all air chambers until the boat is slightly soft. If this is not done, the air will expand in the hot sun and strain or even rupture the seams.

BLEED BOATS OUT OF CONTACT WITH WATER

When deflating boats, we avoid blowing diaphragms by deflating all air chambers simultaneously.

OPEN ALL VALVES AT THE SAME INSTANT

While the boats are drying, the guides say their goodbyes—and again thank the boaters for coming with us. For example, a guide might say something like, "We are glad you came with us; it was a great trip. Keep us in mind when you want to go again." The key words here, aside from the statements, are "we" and "us."

THANK THEM AGAIN FOR COMING WITH US

Roll up rafts so that any wet bow or stern lines—these are usually coiled—hang to the outside to dry.

KEEP WET COILS OUT

ROLLING A RAFT

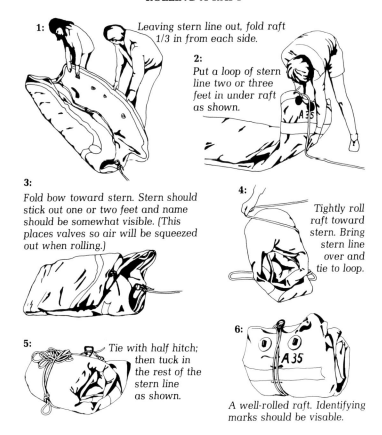

1: Leaving stern line out, fold raft 1/3 in from each side.

2: Put a loop of stern line two or three feet in under raft as shown.

3: Fold bow toward stern. Stern should stick out one or two feet and name should be somewhat visible. (This places valves so air will be squeezed out when rolling.)

4: Tightly roll raft toward stern. Bring stern line over and tie to loop.

5: Tie with half hitch; then tuck in the rest of the stern line as shown.

6: A well-rolled raft. Identifying marks should be visable.

END-OF-TRIP FOLLOW THROUGH

HEAD STRAIGHT HOME

Unless a prior plan has been worked out with the manager, all company vehicles and gear head straight back to their base after each trip. Guides don't take our vehicles on unauthorized side trips or mini-vacations.

END-OF-TRIP RESPONSIBILI-TIES

A trip isn't over until everything is unpacked, cleaned, dried and put away. In general, because it is an important part of the trip and the job, the members of the staff pitch straight in and perform this end-of-trip follow through as soon as they return to the warehouse (before climbing into the hot-tub spa), or, if they return in the middle of the night, first thing next morning.

PUT STUFF AWAY

All gear is returned to its proper place in the warehouse.

Damaged gear, which should be tagged describing the problem, is set aside and repaired at the earliest opportunity. **DAMAGED GEAR**

Most of the line returning from trips is still somewhat wet. To dry it: hang the longer, coiled lines on pegs; remove the short line from its bag and spread it out on the short-line shelves and net hammocks. **DRY DAMP LINE**

The rental wet suits and booties are washed and hung up to dry. **WET SUITS**

The garbage is dumped either in the dumpster at the warehouse or, preferably, at an appropriate place en route home. **GARBAGE**

The potty cans are emptied (not at homebase) and scrubbed. **POTTY EMPTIED**

The coolers and jugs—and any food storage bags or boxes that need it—are thoroughly scrubbed inside and out, rinsed and propped to dry with lids open. **SCRUB COOLERS AND JUGS**

The staff helps the chef reorganize, restock and clean the kitchen box. This often includes refilling or replacing soap and clorox bottles. **CLEAN KITCHEN BOX**

The staff helps the chef wash and put away in the warehouse all utensils from the lunch cooler, etc. **WASH UTENSILS**

The guides help the chef store all the food that will keep on the shelves labeled: "Food for Future Trips." Perishable food and opened packages go to the staff kitchen. **SAVE FOOD**

Put all leftover beer in the warehouse refrigerator. Beer returning from trips is to be saved for future trips! **SAVE BEER**

The dishwashing unit is scrubbed and its propane bottle checked and, if necessary, refilled or replaced. **DISHWASHING UNIT**

In order to avoid stinky life jackets, all life jackets need to be cleaned after each trip, if feasible, or at least every couple of weeks. Set up 4 plastic garbage cans. The first has a soap solution, the second is a clear rinse, the third contains a dilute solution of vinegar and Clorox (about 2 cups of vinegar and 1 cup of Clorox for a garbage can that is about 2/3 full), and the fourth has a solution of about 1 cup of 303 Protectant per gallon or so of water. One-by-one submerge each jacket in each of the 4 dips, in succession, then hang them up to dry, out of any direct sunlight. The addition of the 303 dip is an attempt to prolong the life of the jackets by soaking them in a UV Protectant. **CLEANING LIFE JACKETS**

Dry bleach is not effective for cleaning coolers, or even for deodorizing porta-potties. Liquid bleach, in approximately 10% strength, will sterilize clean coolers, Gott jugs and lunch boards—this is actually the way hospitals and restaurants sterilize some **AVOID DRY BLEACH**

surfaces. Get some powdered agricultural lime from the local hardware store or agricultural supply store for use in our traditional plastic-bag-style porta-potties.

SCRUB PAILS　Buckets and chickie pails with scummy rims are scrubbed.

RELEASE HOSE PRESSURE　After everything is washed and rinsed, the water is turned off and the pressure in the hose is released by squeezing the pistol nozzle.

LIGHTER FLUID　Lighter fluid containers are refilled or replaced.

RESTOCK FIRST AID AND REPAIR KITS　The staff, particularly the sweep boat and WFR/EMT guides, help the leader completely check, restock, seal, sign and date the first aid and repair kits.

CLEAN VEHICLE　The vehicle is swept out; its driver's log is brought up to date; and the vehicle is parked in its customary place.

REPORT VEHICLE NOISES　The staff should call to the leader's attention any vehicle problems or unusual noises or vibrations that should be mentioned in the trip report.

TAG UNSAFE VEHICLES　If the vehicle has a serious problem that must be corrected before it can be safely used again, a tag describing the problem is attached to the steering wheel. Also, of course, the problem is described in the trip report.

RESTORE ORDER　After everything is unpacked, cleaned and put away, the staff takes a few minutes to straighten up and generally restore order in the warehouse and staff lounge.

KEYS　All guides not specifically assigned a set of keys, return all keys.

EXCEPTION　If the same gear (excluding coolers and jugs) is to be used on the next trip with the same vehicle, and it is safe to leave the equipment in the vehicle, the staff generally does not unpack.

DEBRIEFING　Plan and allow time to debrief, as soon as possible after saying goodbye to the people. Things to include in a post-trip debriefing are:
— Opening appreciation.
— Discuss things well done.
— Discuss areas needing improvement. Maybe go around in-turn and invite guides to offer their point of view.
— Create the opportunity for each person to share high points and low points, pluses and minuses of the trip, from their experience.
— Focus on solutions. Mistakes happen, but let's learn from them. This way, we can avoid making the same mistakes in the future.

END-OF TRIP FOLLOW THROUGH

After a trip, far-seeing guides occasionally send letters to a few of the boaters thanking them for coming with Whitewater Voyages. This is not only great for the company, it is also good for the guide—because it subtly but significantly reinforces the guide's name in the minds of the boaters. Later, if the guide should happen to use a boater as a reference, or contact him or her for a job in the real world, the boater will remember the guide as a bright, mature young soul who is going places.

WRITE LETTERS

Answer all question with thoroughness, care and appreciation. Realize that your caring answers can turn any question into a good question and can send the message that here, in this boat, it is okay and safe to know what you know, okay and safe to not know what you do not know, and okay and safe to be open and unguarded.

Earn the group's trust and support: In the beginning of each trip you are laying a foundation of seriousness that must underlie heartfelt silliness. Give an extra thorough safety talk with humor and supportiveness, and extra thorough in-boat training with a blend of humor, lots of positive strokes, nurturing and firmness. Thoroughly teach your crew everything they need to know to paddle well, stay in the boat, and cope with emergencies. It is only when everyone feels reassured that they are in good hands and knows how to play their part that they can completely relax and really be silly— and, in a sense, build an edifice of silliness on this foundation of seriousness.

3: *SAFETY TALKS*

CLASSIC TRIP LEADER'S SAFETY TALK

All guides know the trip leader's put-in safety talk and review it at the start of the trip with the boaters in their rafts. They repeat the crucial points, and add and embellish wherever they think necessary.

KNOW SAFETY TALK

As the trip leader gives the put-in safety talk to the group, the other guides continue packing and preparing to push off, but all the while keep an ear tuned to the talk. This way they can, with their own crews, fill in anything left out—and follow through on any things predicted or promised by the leader. Above all, the staff avoids chatting during the talk, as this encourages inattention among the boaters.

DURING SAFETY TALK

It is often best to have the guests put on their life jackets before the talk. This gives them something to do while they are waiting for the talk to begin, and allows the leader and other guides to make sure the jackets are snug and properly fastened.

LIFE JACKETS

The important thing is that each trip leader, while covering all of the main points, strike a balance between humor and seriousness. Keep the talk warm and lively and funny, and at the same time set a serious tone that encourages caution and respect for the river.

BLEND HUMOR & SERIOUSNESS

CLASSIC LEADER'S TALK: MAIN POINTS

Presented here is a bare-bones outline of the trip leader's talk. For further detail and possible embellishments refer to the long version on page 64, and the modular safety talk below on pages 75 to 104.

INTRODUCTION

I. INTRODUCTION
—Introduce self, guides, & boats
—Point out lead and sweep boats
—Explain difference between oar and paddle boats
    —Oar: Hold on, relax, take pictures

—Paddle: Everyone paddles
Follow captain's commands
Later, the guides will give an instruction session
in each boat

II. MISTAKES TO AVOID

**TERRIBLE
MISTAKES
TO AVOID**

—Avoid entanglement: Keep bow and stern lines in pouches or coiled and tucked away
—Do not tie yourself to raft
—Wear foot protection: tennis shoes or wet suit booties
—Keep life jacket securely fastened

III. EMERGENCIES

**COLLISION
WITH ROCK**

—When raft collides with a rock, jump toward the side of the raft against the rock
—Do this when guide yells, ''High side''
—This lifts upstream tube, allows current to flow under rather than into boat, and can prevent a wrap, that is, a pasting of boat flat around upstream face of rock

**PERSON
OVERBOARD**

—Don't jump in to save 'em, stay in boat
—Follow guide's directions, boat will maneuver to swimmer ASAP
—To pull swimmers in, grab them at the shoulders by the life jacket, slide 'em belly over the tube

**IF YOU
YOURSELF GO
OVERBOARD**

—Relax, hang onto paddle, you'll bob to surface
—It is normal to experience a moment of disorientation and have difficulty breathing in cold water
—Head passes through crests of waves; breathe in troughs between waves
—Often you'll pop up near the raft and be pulled right back in

**IF YOU SEE
YOU WILL NOT
BE PULLED IN
SOON—SELF
RESCUE NOW
OR LATER**

—Get away from the downstream side of the raft, so you won't get crunched between raft and rock
—Keep feet up to avoid foot entrapment
—Key decision: Self rescue now or later:
—If self rescuing immediately: Swim hard for nearest boat or shore
—If self rescuing later: Ride out turbulent water in sitting postion facing downstream with toes at the surface, using your feet to bounce off rocks, using a backstroke to move toward raft or shore
—Avoid places where swift current sweeps through half submerged brush and trees; called strainers, these obstacles can be deadly traps
—Hold onto your paddle, enjoy yourself
—Follow your guide's instructions

RAFT FLIP

—Relax, hang onto paddle, bob to surface
—If you bob up under raft, pop up on upstream side

—Unless there is a serious hazard downstream, stay with the boat. On downstream side you can get crushed, and on upstream side you can't see what is coming, so hang at sides (in relation to river) so you can see downstream

—Toss any loose stuff (paddles, etc.) onto bottom of raft

—A rescue boat will come ASAP; this is why we keep the group together

—Follow guide's directions; generally the boat will be righted mid river; sometimes the crew can paddle or swim upside-down boat to shore

—If separated from boat, swim in same manner as person overboard, i.e., in sitting position facing downstream with toes at surface, using feet to bounce off rocks

—Explain holes, reversals **ON CLASS IV &**
V RIVERS

—If caught (tumbled around and around in a hole) kick off bottom and swim hard to get out downstream. Also, a person sometimes can swim out to side

—Flatten yourself onto the bottom of the boat below the level of **LOW BRANCHES:**
the tubes **DUCK**

—When overboard, avoid all branches and trees (strainers)

IV. ECOLOGY TALK

In order for us to leave the canyon as it now is for those who follow, we must be very careful with four things:

—Cigarette butts, matches, bits of paper, seeds, foil, food, in- **LITTER**
cluding lettuce, orange peels, etc., *are litter!*

—Please pick 'em up, put 'em in your pocket or the trash

—Let's try to leave the river as clean as—or cleaner than—we find it

(Discuss one) **HUMAN WASTE**
—Lime can:

    —Metal can with toilet seat will be set up in secluded location near camp

    —Solid waste, No. 2 only

    —When finished, sprinkle lime in can to cut smell

    —Return toilet paper to plastic bag and fold opening closed so dew or rain won't soak it

    —Keep lid fitted tightly to can between uses; this is vital to prevent possible cross contamination from fecal matter to food via flies, which can result in serious disease

—(On rivers where a porta-potty is carried ready for use) A porta-potty is available on request during the day. So please do not go No. 2 in the bushes, instead use the potty (Also mention the location of toilets, if any, at put-in, rest stops, take-out, etc.)

—All soap causes suds **SOAP**
—Never use soap directly in river or in a side stream

—Instead, fill a pot or bucket with water, carry it well away from the river, wash, and dump the sudsy water at least 100 feet from the river or side stream

FIRE

—Wild fire is a grave danger
—At camp we will have only the main campfire, no private fires
—If you smoke, do so near campfire, inside cleared area or fire break, not off in your sleeping bag (Put butts and matches in the fire, not on the ground)
—(Choose one)
    —We will use a fire pan and carry out all ash
    —We will use an established fire pit and make sure the ashes are cold to the touch before leaving

V. VITAL DETAILS

VITAL DETAILS

—Drinking river water is dangerous. Use the canteens; each boat has one (Omit on rivers with potable water: Forks of the Kern, North Fork of the American, etc.)
—Eyeglasses without headstraps will probably be lost; we have cord for headstraps if you need it
—Keep everything tied tight to the raft (except yourself)
—Hold on in big waves
—Dip feet in water to wash off sand and mud before climbing into boats
—Please mention any special medical condition to your guide
—On land avoid poison oak (the guides will point this out) and watch out for rattlesnakes

A WORD ABOUT WATERFIGHTS

—No boarding of other rafts or pulling people into water
—No waterfighting just above rapids
—Be careful not to hit anyone when throwing and splashing water
—Do not aim water squirt cannons into people's faces, instead shoot up and rain down

VI. CONCLUSION

FOCUS ON RIVER

—Discuss flow
—Describe events in store that day, including evening entertainment
—Tell the group what rapids to expect
—Tell how far and how much time to lunch

SO LONG & GOOD LUCK

—Ask 'em to be careful and follow their guide's instructions
—Invite guests to pick up a paddle and choose a boat

CLASSIC TRIP LEADER'S SAFETY TALK: THE LONG VERSION

The following talk is thorough and quite long. Most trip leaders choose to give a shorter, more condensed talk, and leave some of the embellishments and details to the individual guides. This long version is included here as a source, a mother lode, from which to mine material for shorter talks—and as an example of one way to flesh out the preceding barebones outline. Be sure to also see the modular safety talk later in this section.

CLASSIC TRIP LEADER'S SAFETY TALK: THE LONG VERSION

I. INTRODUCTION

The trip leader introduces him- or herself, the other guides and the boats. As each guide is introduced, the leader indicates which raft he or she will be handling. Mention is made, in passing, of the unique characteristics of each boat. Example: "And the ingenious fellow in the biege sportcap is John (John tips his cap) who will be captaining Certain Death, the third raft from the left. Certain Death is a small, lively, tipsy paddle boat; if you ride in it, your chances of survival are nil."

INTRODUCTION

The leader points out the lead and sweep boats, and designates the boat order. She or he mentions also that the sweep boat carries the repair and first aid supplies.

LEAD & SWEEP

If inflatable kayaks are along, the leader announces that the kayaks should stay behind the second raft and in front of the second-to-last raft.

INFLATABLE KAYAKS

If both oar and paddle rafts are on the trip, the leader points them out and explains the difference: "In an oar boat, the guide controls the boat with 10-ft. oars, so you can sit back, relax, take photographs, think and grow.

OAR & PADDLE

"In a paddle boat, on the other hand, the guide has little direct control, so he or she depends upon you, the crew, to paddle to provide the power to maneuver the boat. Remember, your paddle captain depends on everyone, big and small. Even though you might feel overwhelmed by the waves and speed and flying spume, don't give up—keep trying to follow the commands. Also, sit with both feet inside the raft. Otherwise, if you straddle the tube, your outboard leg can get badly scraped or even broken when the boat slides closely past rocks. Later, the guides will give an instructional talk in each boat."

(pause)

II. MISTAKES TO AVOID

"Rafting is a relatively safe thing to do provided you don't make any number of terrible mistakes:

TERRIBLE MISTAKES

"For instance, never tie yourself to or allow yourself to become entangled with the raft—because if the boat flips you want to come free and float to the surface. So, to avoid entanglement, never wedge your legs in under a tube or frame. And, above all, never let the bow or stern lines dangle loosely in the bottom of the boat where they could wrap around someone's foot. Rather, keep all lines either stuffed in the special pouches, or neatly coiled and wedged under gear tie-down straps, or slung through the large, outboard bow and stern D-rings.

AVOID ENTANGLEMENTS

"To prevent foot injuries—the most common type of river accident—keep tennis shoes tightly laced on at all times on the river or wear wet suit booties.

FOOTWEAR

LIFE JACKETS   "And wear your life jacket—making sure to fasten all snaps—at all times when on the river, unless your guide specifically says it's alright to take it off."

(pause)

III. EMERGENCIES

EMERGENCIES   *"Emergencies. There are a number of emergency situations which you should know how to handle:*

COLLISION WITH ROCK   "If the raft collides with a rock, move quickly to the side of the raft nearest the rock. The command for this is 'High side!' If you don't move quickly, or, worse, if you don't move at all, the upstream tube may be sucked down, water will very likely start pouring into the boat, and within seconds, the boat can be wrapped flat around the rock, pinned there by tons of force." (Illustrate this by wrapping one hand, representing the raft, around your other hand closed into a fist, representing the rock. You can also represent the raft with a hat, and the rock with a child's head.) "So remember, when your guide's eyes get as big as saucers and he or she yells, 'High side,' jump toward the side of the raft that's against the rock. This lifts the upstream tube, and allows the current to flow under rather than into the boat. (Illustrate with hands.) And the crew often winds up sitting in a little row with their backs against the rock. At this point, lean back and relax. Savor the sudden contrast between the tumult of the rapid and the tranquility of the rock. If you have any interesting or, for that matter, boring thoughts, share them with your companions. A midstream rock is a fine place for new perceptions and for getting to know people. Later, your guide will figure out a way to free the raft—this is usually done by shifting everyone's weight to one end of the raft in such a way that the current twirls you off—and back you go into the mainstream once again.

PERSON OVERBOARD   "Now, let's talk about what to do if someone falls overboard: First of all, don't jump in after them, because this more than doubles the problem. Your guide will maneuver the boat toward the swimmer as soon as it is safe to do so. As you approach, extend your paddle handle first, so the swimmer can grab it and be pulled toward the boat. To haul someone up into the boat, grab them at the shoulders by the life jacket, slide them belly over the tube, and tumble them into the bottom of the boat like a gaffed salmon (demonstrate this with appropriate gestures). Don't waste time gingerly setting them back up into their spot. (Gestures.) Instead, get back to your own position as soon as possible and resume following commands. It follows that in the sort of water where people get washed overboard, the boat needs all the power it can get.

IF YOU YOURSELF GO OVERBOARD   "Now, let's say you yourself are washed overboard. At first, submerged, you will probably experience a few seconds of total disorientation. It is common to wonder: 'Where am I? How did I get here?' Then you realize, 'Oh yeah, I signed up for a trip with Whitewater Voyages and just got washed out of the boat.' Also, the sudden shock of the cold water may make it difficult to breathe at first. (Delete on warm-water rivers.) Bear in mind, too, that no lifejacket will float your head over the crests of the waves. Instead, your head will pass *through* the crests; so you must breathe in the troughs, and hold your breath in the crests. This comes naturally after a few waves. Anyway, throughout all this hold onto your paddle and relax and enjoy yourself.

"Most of the time you will find yourself floating right next to the raft and you'll be pulled in lickety split. However, it is possible that you may be separated from the raft or see that you will not be pulled in right away. In this case, first, get away from the downstream side of the raft—so you won't be crushed between the raft and a rock. And keep your feet up to avoid foot entrapment.

"Next, make your key swimmer's decision: Do I self rescue now or later? If you self rescue immediately, swim hard for the nearest boat or shore. If you self rescue later, ride out turbulent rapids in a sitting position, facing downstream, with your feet out in front of you, toes at the surface, and use your feet to bounce off the rocks. Use your paddle or an elementary backstroke (demonstrate) to maintain this orientation to the current and to move either toward your raft or toward shore, whichever seems best. Don't do what seems worst—after all, what's the point in that? To repeat a key point: As you swim it is vital to keep your feet up at the surface; or a leg could become jammed between rocks—and the force of the current could prevent escape.

SELF RESCUE NOW OR LATER

"Also, avoid places where swift current sweeps through half submerged brush and trees. Called strainers, these obstacles can be deadly traps.

AVOID STRAINERS

Throughout all this, continue to listen to and follow your guide's instructions, which might be: "Swim to the boat!", "Swim left!", "Swim right!" or something else depending on the situation.

FOLLOW GUIDE'S INSTRUCTIONS

"Next, what do you do if the raft flips? Basically, hang on to your paddle, relax, and enjoy yourself. If you bob up under the raft, come out from under immediately. After flips, the first thing the guides do is count heads—and if we don't see enough heads, we start checking under the boat. So come out quickly—preferably on the upstream side of the boat. If you pop up just downstream from the raft, quickly move to one side—so you won't get crushed between the flipped raft and a rock—but so you can still see downriver.

RAFT FLIP

"Once you are at the surface, have your feet up and see you will not be crushed between the raft and a rock, look around and decide whether to swim for the nearest right-side- up raft, stay with the flipped raft or swim for shore. Swimming for the nearest right-side-up raft is often best. Also, provided there is not a big rapid or some other serious hazard immediately downstream, staying with the flipped boat can be a good choice. This way the crew doesn't get strung out along a half mile of river, and if one of the other boats isn't able to come to the rescue fast enough, you can help your guide right the boat in mid river or help paddle the upside-down boat to shore. By the way, put paddles and anything floating loose up on the bottom of the overturned boat.

(pause)

ON CLASS IV & V RIVERS
"Now a word about reversals, which are also called holes. One of the most dangerous of river obstacles, reversals are often found at the bases of waterfalls and just downstream from where the river pours over a submerged rock. The falling water pouring over the rock or down the face of the waterfall plunges to the river bottom where it stays for a good distance as it flows on downstream. (Demonstrate with hand motions.) This leaves a gap or low pressure zone at the surface just below the waterfall or rock. This gap is filled in by white, aerated foam rising and flowing upstream, forming a treacherous mouth where the two currents meet.

"Large reversals can swamp or flip a raft or stop it dead. Most reversals will flush swimmers on through. Occasionally, however, swimmers are caught and tumbled around and around. If you find yourself in this pickle, try to kick off the bottom and swim hard to get out downstream. Also, a person can sometimes swim sideways out the end of the reversal wave.

LOW BRANCHES: DUCK
"And for our last emergency: If your boat is swept under branches hanging low over the water, dive into the bottom of the boat—especially if it is your side of the boat which is being driven under the tree."

(pause)

IV. ECOLOGY TALK

ECOLOGY TALK
"We are earth people. This is our planet and our river. We belong here, and what we are about to do is natural and good. But along with the appropriateness of this voyage comes a responsibility not to consume the river, but to leave it as it now is for those who follow. Now, a raft, by its very nature, leaves no trace of its passage down a river. But in those temporary toeholds, lunch and campsites, every one of us—if we are to leave the river unscathed—must be careful with four things: litter, human waste, soap, and fire.

LITTER
"Litter: We will pack out all unburnable garbage. On this trip and whenever you are out in nature, devote a pocket to litter. Pull tabs from cans, cigarette butts, matches, orange peels, watermelon seeds, bits of lettuce, paper and foil—all of these things are litter. Whenever you have any or see any on the ground,

please pick it up and put it in your pocket. If you don't have a pocket, give it to someone who does. Later, burn everything flammable—except plastic—in the campfire and put everything else in the garbage bags which the guides will set up. Let's all try to leave the river as clean—or, if possible, cleaner than—we find it.

Depending on the particular river, give one of the following: **HUMAN WASTE**

A. (If the lime can is used.)   **LIME CAN**
"We will carry out all solid human waste in a big, tight-sealing, metal lime can about so big (gesture to indicate size of can). In a secluded spot near each camp the can will be set up with a toilet seat and a bag of lime close by. After you've made your contribution—and please remember: No. 2 solid waste only—sprinkle a bit of lime into the can with the scoop provided. Then take the toilet seat off and carefully replace the lid, making sure it fits tightly. This is vital to prevent possible cross-contamination via flies from fecal matter to food, which could result in serious disease. So remember, keep the lid on the can between uses." (Optional: "By the way, along the approach to the lime can there will be a paddle—when the paddle is up, the can is occupied. When the paddle is down, the can is free.")

B. (If the porta-potty is used.)   **PORTA-POTTY**
"A porta-potty in its own little tent will be set up near each camp. Once inside the cozy tent be sure to read the instructions hanging there on a board." (The rest is optional.) "The crucial thing is: The potty is for No. 2 solid waste only. So try not to pee in the potty. Also, don't put toilet paper in the potty—instead burn it in the campfire or, if the fire has been doused, put it in the garbage. Because the waste tends to pile up in the center of the holding tank, the potty may appear to be full before it actually is. Closing the trap door and rocking the potty from side to side will generally open things up. But, when the potty actually is full, and before it overflows, please tell one of the guides. We'd appreciate your help on this point more than we can say."

C. (If the waste is buried.)   **SHOVEL**
"The elements which cause most rapid decomposition of human   **TECHNIQUE**
waste are in the top six inches of soil. So, when you feel the urge, take one of our shovels which you will find in camp and head out into the woods. Take your time, pick a spot well above and away from the river—a nice spot with a good view of the canyon. Dig a six inch hole, get comfortable, take your time, and savor the experience. Then, fill in the hole. But, because paper decomposes very slowly, don't bury your toilet paper. Instead, wrap it up in a bit of extra paper, bring it into camp, and burn it in the campfire, or, if the fire has been doused, put it in the garbage. When you bring your bundle of toilet paper into camp, don't hold it low and sort of sneak along. Instead, hold it high, like a badge of achievement, and step proudly. And, by the way, try to remember to tuck

the end of the toilet paper roll into the hole as you slide it over the shovel handle. Otherwise the roll unravels all over the place."

POTTY AVAILABLE

(On rivers where a porta-potty or lime can is carried ready for use.) "During the day a potty is available on request. For No. 2 please use the potty, not the bushes." (Also mention the location of toilets, if any, at put-in, rest-stops, take-out, etc.)

SOAP

"Soap: You may be interested to know that all of the soap manufactured in North America and most of Europe (except Turkey) is biodegradable. But even biodegradable soap takes time to decompose and a small amount can create lots of suds. So never use soap directly in the river or in a side stream. Instead, whenever you want to wash, brush your teeth, shave or whatever, take a pot or bucket, scoop up some water, and carry it well back from the river. Then, after washing, dump the water well above and at least 100 feet back from the river. This way the land will act as a filter to purify the water as it seeps down to once again merge with the majestic river.

FIRE

"Wild fire is a serious danger. At camp we will have only the one, main campfire—no private fires. If you smoke, please do so near the campfire inside the cleared area or fire break, not off in your sleeping bag. Also, please put butts and matches into the fire, not on the ground."

(Give one of the following, depending on the river.)

A. (If established campfire sites are to be used:)
"We will build our campfires in established sites approved by the U.S. Forest Service (or Bureau of Land Management, depending on the river) and, before leaving each camp, will thoroughly douse and stir the coals until they are cold to the touch."

B. (If a fire pan is to be used:)
"In order to avoid leaving ash and fire scars in our camp(s), we will build our fire(s) in a fire pan and carry out the ash."

V. VITAL DETAILS

IMPORTANT DETAILS

"A few final words. (Optional, the trip leader can leave these to the individual guides.) On the river, details are important:

DON'T DRINK RIVER WATER

"Drinking river water is dangerous. Use the canteens—each boat has one.

EYEGLASSES

"All eyeglasses should be secured with headstraps. If you don't use a headstrap, you will probably lose your glasses. And if you don't *have* a headstrap, ask a guide to cut you a piece of string.

SECURE LOOSE ITEMS

"Keep everything, such as ditty bags and loose clothing, secured to the rafts. Loose things may be washed overboard.

HOLD ON

"When the raft crashes through holes and large waves—and whenever you feel yourself starting to fall overboard, hold on!

"If you have a special medical condition, such as allergies, or take prescription drugs, please mention this to your guide.

MEDICAL CONDITION

"Be sure to wash off your feet as you climb into the raft, or else you'll have to sit in a muddy boat.

WASH FEET

"When stepping from the raft to shore try not to step on sloping or slippery rocks at the water's edge.

SLIPPERY ROCKS

"On land avoid poison oak—a plant with three-leaf clusters which the guides will point out. Also, be careful not to step on rattlesnakes.

POISON OAK

"When it's hot, waterfighting can be great fun. However, to keep it safe, we ask that everyone keep in mind these rules:

A WORD ABOUT WATERFIGHTS

—No boarding of other rafts or pulling people into the water.
—No waterfighting just above or in rapids.
—Be careful not to clobber anyone when waterfighting at close range.
—Do not squirt water cannons directly into people's faces. Instead, squirt up and rain down.

VI. CONCLUSION

"Always be alert and somewhat cautious. Use good judgement. Follow your guide's instructions." This is all part of setting a cautious, professional tone, a tone which discourages people from taking foolhardy risks.

BE CAREFUL; FOLLOW INSTRUCTIONS

Next, the trip leader focuses on the river and the events immediately in store. The flow and anticipated weather is discussed. The group is told what to expect in the way of rapids before lunch and after lunch. Also, the leader estimates the number of miles and hours before the group stops for lunch.

FOCUS ON RIVER

Last, the leader wishes the group luck. He or she tries to talk them out of going. If this fails, the leader invites them to pick up a paddle and choose a boat—and says goodbye.

SO LONG & GOOD LUCK

CLASSIC PADDLE-BOAT TALK

(To be given by paddle captains at or near the put-in)

The guide introduces her- or himself and the boat.

INTRODUCE SELF & BOAT

The guide clearly and carefully explains and demonstrates all strokes and commands. He or she demonstrates the correct and incorrect way to do the forward and backpaddle strokes. When demonstrating the backpaddle stroke, the guide emphasizes the need to use the entire torso and shows the crew how to fulcrum the paddle shaft off the hip and how to really lean back into

EXPLAIN STROKES & COMMANDS

each backstroke. The turn commands are reviewed—the crew practices the turns repeatedly right at the put-in. Seasoned guides spend plenty of time on this, especially when launching just above rapids.

EXPLAINING THE COMMANDS

A way to explain the commands: "In order to maneuver the boat down through the rapids, I will use four commands: The first two 'Forward' and 'Backpaddle' are easily understood. But the other two, it has been scientifically proven, have never been done exactly right: They are 'Right turn' and 'Left turn.' For a right turn, the right side backpaddles while the left side paddles forward. And for a left turn vice versa, that is, the left side backpaddles while the right side paddles forward. One way to remember this is, if you hear your side in a turn command, back paddle. And for all other turn commands, paddle forward. OK, let's practice. . . ."

ENCOURAGE-MENT

Throughout all this, the guide gives the crew a good deal of support and encouragement, saying things like "Good," "That's it," or, perhaps, "That's better," and "You are a good crew; we may even survive—but don't get your hopes up yet. First, let's practice the turns again and try to do them perfectly." Of course, when a crew member is doing something incorrectly, the guide gently but firmly tells him or her so—and sees to it that she or he gets it right. But at every opportunity, especially in the beginning, the guide expresses approval and encouragement.

THE STROKES

The guide designates the two people in the bow as the "strokes," and emphasizes the need for everyone to paddle in unison, saying something like, "When everyone's blades flash through the air together, hit the water in unison, and drive through the water at once, we do not bang paddles, everyone's strokes are more effective, the boat lunges into motion with each stroke, a powerful oneness develops, and, most important, we look sharp." The guide reinforces this by every so often speaking directly to the "strokes" when giving a command. For example, when the boat is about to cross a long calm, the guide might say, "OK Bob and Betty, set an easy, slow but powerful stroke we can all follow to move across this pool."

EVERYONE MATTERS

The guide reminds the crew that everyone, even small people, matters, and even when crewmembers feel overwhelmed, they should keep trying to follow the commands. The guide makes it clear that he or she depends on them.

REVIEW MAIN POINTS OF LEADER'S TALK

The main points of the leader's put-in safety talk are briefly reviewed: What to do in case of collisions with rocks, people overboard, flips. If there is a strong possibility of the crew going high side, needing to draw downstream out of a hole, or ducking under a low branch, the guide has everyone, when he or she gives the appropriate command, rehearse the actual motions in the raft. This practice can be invaluable, for it trains the crew members' limbs and muscles as well as their minds. Go over the techniques for proper care of the environment: Pick up litter; smoke only near the campfire; don't use soap in the river, etc. Describe poison oak; and alert people to be careful not to step on rattlesnakes. Also, the guide covers all details of the put-in safety talk omitted by the trip leader.

The safety guidelines are reviewed: **SAFETY**
—Keep bailing buckets stowed.   **GUIDELINES**
—Keep both feet inboard.
—Keep tennis shoes laced on or wear booties.
—Keep lifejackets on with all buckles fastened!
—Attention! Keep all lines neatly coiled (the guide shows them how) and hung through outboard D-rings or wedged under straps.
—Lean inboard when the boat is about to hit big waves and holes—but continue paddling as requested. This way if anyone does fall, they will tumble into the boat rather than out of it.

Emphasizing the need to stay in the boat (especially in high or   **HOLD ON &**
difficult water), the captain teaches the crewmembers, at the   **LEAN IN**
sound of the command, "Hold on and lean in," to hold on, lean way in over the boat, and point their *shoulders*, not their heads, toward the person opposite—this avoids the cracking of heads. Paddlers are cautioned not to flail their paddle handles around in the air when holding them in one hand. Instead, handles should be held where they will not chip teeth, bop heads, or hit eyes. Teach 'em to hold the blade vertical to avoid being pulled overboard by a paddle caught in a downpouring current. Also, teach 'em to grab others being washed overboard—and pull 'em in.

In high and tough water the crew is taught to grab, with the   **HOLDING ON**
inboard hand, handholds tied around the center of the cross thwarts. (See sketch, page 40.) On milder runs paddlers may be taught to hold the perimeter safety line with the outboard hand (and, hence, the paddle with the inboard hand). When seizing a hand hold that is on the raft's main perimeter tube, it is important to use the *outboard* hand: I once had a big, strong, agile fellow in my raft who, much to my amazement, kept getting washed overboard. I was baffled—until I noticed that he was grabbing the perimeter safety line with his inboard hand. This prevented him from getting his body well in over the raft, and so he got flushed out by every big wave.

Paddle guides also prepare their crews to respond to the   **HOLD ON,**
commands, "Hold on, lean in and get down." Crews are taught   **LEAN IN &**
that before hitting big holes and formidable turbulence, these   **GET DOWN**
words will warn them not only to hold on and lean in, but also to slide their fannies somewhat down into the boat, to really get their weight down inside the boat.

AGILE BOW PERSON

The guide places a strong, *agile* person in the bow to be the "agile bow person." This person is in charge of keeping the bow line coiled, up off the floor and ready for instant use. The guide teaches the "agile bow person" to first stow their paddle, next grab the line and then jump ashore. The guide also teaches them how and when to jump ashore: With one foot on the tube, the other foot is launched forward through the air—as the boat first sweeps into the bank, not after it bounces.

WHEN CHANGING SPOTS

Paddle captains teach the crew members to leave their paddles in their old spots when changing places.

CLASSIC OAR-BOAT TALK

This talk is given on oar boats at or near the put-in.

INTRODUCE SELF & BOAT

The guide introduces him- or herself and the boat.

REVIEW

The guide reviews the main points of the leader's put-in talk and the safety guidelines as they apply to oar boats (see above).

HOLD ON

The guide tells all aboard to hold on tight in the rapids—and explains that if they don't they could be washed overboard. Also, when teaching the crew to hold on and get down for big waves and holes, the guides emphasize the need to point the shoulder, not the head, toward any person opposite—to avoid cracking skulls.

SIT CLEAR OF OARS

People in the bow are cautioned not to sit where they could get struck by an oar.

AGILE LINE PERSON

An agile person is designated as line person and put in charge of keeping the bow or stern line neatly coiled (show 'em how) and ready for instant use. The guide teaches this person how to jump ashore with the line.

Trip Leader's Checklist for **MODULAR SAFETY TALK**
By William McGinnis with Holly Cochran and Susan Maida

River _____ Date _____ Trip Leader_____

Trip Length (Days)_____ No. of Release Forms Attached _____

Some imperative do's and don'ts regarding safety talks: **DO** make sure everyone can hear the talk. **DO** give participants the opportunity to choose **NOT** to participate after the safety talk. **DO** make sure that everyone is paying attention and is not distracted. **DO** make sure that everyone is accounted for and present for the safety talk. **DON'T** do the safety talk on the bus unless the bus has an excellent PA system. **DON'T** do the safety talk after the trip has started.

Add humor, add jokes, make your talk funny and entertaining—as well as thorough and professional!!

☐ **Welcome**

☐ **Get Release Forms Signed**

☐ **Rafting Involves Inherent Risk**
*listen carefully-vital info in talk could improve your chances of survival

☐ **Questions Welcome**
*ask for clarification if you don't understand anything

☐ **Emphasize Teamwork**

☐ **Make Friends with Pandemonium**
*it's normal to feel overwhelmed in emergencies-you can still act effectively

☐ **Establish a Buddy System**
*immediately tell guide if someone is missing

☐ **How to Rescue a Swimmer**
*explain and demonstrate

☐ **What to do if You're the Swimmer**
*don't hang out on the downstream side of your boat; you can get crushed between boat and rock
*get out quickly from under raft-if you get separated from raft, 2 "swimming" techniques to choose from:
  –feet downstream, toes-at-surface sitting position for riding out big rapids
  –on-your-stomach crawl stroke for self-rescue
*listen to guides; look for hand signals from guides-guides always point where they want you to go
*always keep your feet at the surface to avoid foot entrapment
*never try to stop yourself or stand up in swift water deeper than your knees

☐ **Self Rescue**
*sometimes the fastest way out of water is to do it yourself
*avoid places where swift current sweeps through half submerged brush or trees

☐ **Flips**
*get out from under overturned raft as soon as you can
*put paddles on upside down bottom, grab floor lacing to pull yourself up onto overturned boat
*if you're separated from raft or can't climb onto slick bottom, may be best to swim toward shore

☐ **Collisions With Rocks**
*if raft slams broadside into a rock, guide yells, "HIGH SIDE!", move quickly to side of raft nearest rock to avoid wrapping or swimming

☐ **Low Branches**
*duck or get down low in boat if your boat sweeps under low branches

☐ **Vital Details**

*never jump headfirst into water
*most accidents happen on land
*be aware of slippery rocks along river's edge
*be careful with cigarettes
*drink lots of water, (not river water)
*secure hats and glasses with strap
*use plenty of sun screen, (not on forehead or backs of legs)
*inform us of any medical or special conditions we should know about
*no alcohol or drugs on the river
*follow guidelines for water fights

☐ **Ecological Awareness and Responsibility**

*please pick up any litter that you see on the ground, try to leave the river cleaner than we find it
*never pee in river, only pee at least 100 feet away (depends on river)
*all solid human waste is carried out (on wilderness trips)
*never use soap in river, even biodegradable
*be super careful with fire; no fire within 6 feet of anything flammable; no fire scars

☐ **Conclusion**

*are there any questions?
*if you don't want to go, you can still say no
*introduce guides and boats, talk about the river, what to expect during the day and the trip
*after talk, tell me of any medical conditions

Trip Leader's Safety Talk Checklist - Continued
INDIChapter Heading here — INDIVIDUAL MODULES FOR PUT-IN TALKS - *(Use Only When Appropriate)*

☐ **Toss Bag Module**
*grab line, not bag
*don't wrap or tie line around any part of your body
*roll over onto your back with line going over your shoulder so you can breathe

☐ **Hand Signal Module**
*1 whistle blast: urgent or emergency; pay attention to me for more signals
*point positive, where to go
*swimmer
*come to me
*I'm coming to you
*are you ok
*I'm ok
*we're ok
*I need First Aid
*don't know
*erase last signal
*I'm cold
*we barely made it
*I love you
*person or people missing
*we're searching for (#) of people
*everyone is accounted for, nobody missing

☐ **Strainer Module**
*very dangerous for swimmers; strong current can pin you to a strainer and you can easily drown
*if swimming, avoid strainers
*swim hard away from strainers at right angles to current, either toward shore or middle of river
*if you can't avoid strainer, swim headfirst toward it and pull yourself up and over it
*overriding concern is to keep your head above water
*never try to dive and swim under a strainer
*don't hit strainer feet first, you can slide under and either get stuck or pulled under water
*get rid of your paddle if it's in your way

☐ **Big Holes Module**
*treacherous reversals of current usually found just downstream of submerged rocks
*raft can get stuck in a hole, or even flip
*if boat is stuck in a hole, stay low in boat, jump to downstream side, draw stroke downstream
*if raft spins around in a hole, jump quickly to new high side *if you fall out of a boat in a hole usually you'll flush out immediately
*sometimes you can get caught in reversal and be tumbled around for a bit

☐ **Low Water Module**
*undercut rocks are dangerous; if swimming you can get stuck in them and held by strong current and drown
*if you're swimming, pay attention and look around for instructions
*extremely important to keep feet at surface to avoid foot entrapment

☐ **High Water Module**
*chances of long swims are greater; wraps, flips, and tube stands are far more common
*self-rescue is very important or you could be in for a long swim
*if swimming, immediately assess your situation; listen for directions, but don't wait to act; swim hard for nearest upright boat, or look for eddies and calm spots
*begin swimming early to catch an eddy and swim hard right angles to current
*stay away from strainers
*consider walking around a rapid you don't feel like running
*be absolutely sure to establish a buddy system to keep track of each other

PART 3: SAFETY TALKS

☐ **Class V Module**

*current is stronger, drops are bigger, holes are more violent, consequences of flipping or swimming are much more severe
*extremely important to pay attention to this talk
*team work is essential
*be absolutely sure to establish a buddy system to keep track of each other
*get swimmers back in raft immediately, listen to guides for directions
*self-rescue is very important or you could be in for a long swim
*if swimming, immediately assess your situation; listen for directions, but don't wait to act; look for eddies and calm
 spots
*begin swimming early to catch an eddy and swim hard right angles to current
*stay away from strainers

☐ **Hypothermia Module**

*potentially-fatal
*risk of hypothermia increases with cold water, cold air, windy conditions, wet clothes
*inform guide if you're feeling cold, continuously shivering, or feeling apathetic
*look out for each other
*wetsuits or drysuits are required
*wear warm and adequate insulating layer, no cotton
*eat plenty of food, drink lots of water; no alcohol or caffeine

I certify that each of the items I have checked above were covered in the trip safety talk I have just given on this day.

Date: _____

TL Signature: _____

Print Name: _____

MODULAR SAFETY TALK – WITNESS STATEMENT

By William McGinnis with Holly Cochran and Susan Maida

Dear Guest,

Please follow along with your trip leader and check off the points on this list as he/she covers them in the safety talk. Fill in the river, date and name of the person giving the safety talk below. At the bottom of page 2, please sign and print your name and date. Thank you very much for participating.

RIVER _____ DATE_____ TRIP LEADER_____

☐ **Welcome**

☐ **Get Release Forms Signed**

☐ **Rafting Involves Inherent Risk**
*listen carefully-vital info in talk could improve your chance of survival

☐ **Questions Welcome**
*ask for clarification if you don't understand anything

☐ **Emphasize Teamwork**

☐ **Make friends with Pandemonium**
*it's normal to feel overwhelmed in emergencies-you can still act effectively

☐ **Establish a Buddy System**
*immediately tell guide if someone is missing

☐ **How to Rescue a Swimmer**
*explain and demonstrate

☐ **What to do if you're the Swimmer**
*don't hang out on the downstream side of your boat; you can get crushed between boat and rock
*get out quickly from under raft-if you get separated from raft, 2 "swimming" techniques to choose from:
--feet downstream, toes-at-surface sitting position for riding out big rapids
--on-your-stomach crawl stroke for self-rescue
*listen to guides; look for hand signals from guides-guides always point where they want you to go
*always keep your feet at the surface to avoid foot entrapment
*never try to stop yourself or stand up in swift water deeper than your knees

☐ **Self Rescue**
*sometimes the fastest way out of water is to do it yourself
*avoid places where swift current sweeps through half submerged brush or trees

☐ **Flips**
*get out from under overturned raft as soon as you can
*put paddles on upside down bottom, grab floor lacing to pull yourself up onto overturned boat
*if you're separated from raft or can't climb onto slick bottom, may be best to swim toward shore

☐ **Collisions With Rocks**
*if raft slams broadside into a rock, guide yells, "HIGH SIDE!", move quickly to side of raft nearest rock to avoid wrapping or swimming

☐ **Low Branches**
*duck or get low in boat if your boat sweeps under low branches

☐ **Vital Details**
*never jump headfirst into water
*most accidents happen on land
*be aware of slippery rocks along river's edge

*be careful with cigarettes
*drink lots of water, (not river water)
*secure hats and glasses with strap
*use plenty of sun screen (not on forehead or backs of legs)
*inform us of any medical or special conditions we should know about
*no alcohol or drugs on the river
*follow guidelines for water fights

☐ Ecological Awareness and Responsibility

*please pick up any litter that you see on the ground, try to leave the river cleaner than we find it
*never pee in river, only pee at least 100 feet away (depends on river)
*all solid human waste is carried out (on wilderness trips)
*never use soap in river, even biodegradable
*be super careful with fire; no fire within 6 feet of anything flammable; no fire scars

☐ Conclusion

*are there any questions?
*if you don't want to go, you can still say no
*introduce guides and boats, talk about the river, what to expect during the day and the trip
*after talk, tell me of any medical conditions

Witness ~ Individual Modules *(Used only when appropriate)*

☐ **Toss Bag Module**
*grab line, not bag
*don't wrap or tie line around any part of your body
*roll over onto your back with line going over your shoulder so you can breathe

☐ **Hand Signal Module**
*1 whistle blast: urgent or emergency; pay attention to me for more signals
*point positive, where to go
*swimmer
*come to me
*I'm coming to you
*are you ok
*I'm ok
*we're ok
*I need first aid
*don't know
*erase last signal
*I'm cold
*we barely made it
*I love you
*person or people missing
*we're searching for (#) of people
*everyone is accounted for, nobody missing

☐ **Strainer Module**
*very dangerous for swimmers; strong current can pin you to a strainer and you can easily drown
*if swimming, avoid strainers
*swim hard away from strainers at right angles to current, either toward shore or middle of river
*if you can't avoid strainer, swim headfirst toward it and pull yourself up and over it
*overriding concern is to keep your head above water
*never try to dive and swim under a strainer
*don't hit strainer feet first, you can slide under and either get stuck or pulled under water
*get rid of your paddle if it's in your way

☐ **Big Holes Module**
*treacherous reversals of current usually found just downstream of submerged rocks
*raft can get stuck in a hole, or even flip
*if boat is stuck in a hole, stay low in boat, jump to downstream side, draw stroke downstream
*if raft spins around in a hole, jump quickly to new high side
*if you fall out of a boat in a hole usually you'll flush out immediately
*sometimes you can get caught in reversal and be tumbled around for a bit

☐ **Low Water Module**
*undercut rocks are dangerous; if swimming you can get stuck in them and held by strong current and drown
*if you're swimming, pay attention and look around for instructions
*extremely important to keep feet at surface to avoid foot entrapment

☐ **High Water Module**
*chances of long swims are greater; wraps, flips, and tube stands are far more common
*self-rescue is very important or you could be in for a long swim
*if swimming, immediately assess your situation; listen for directions, but don't wait to act; swim hard for nearest right-side-up boat, or look for eddies and calm spots
*begin swimming early to catch an eddy and swim hard right angles to current
*stay away from strainers
*consider walking around a rapid you don't feel like running
*be absolutely sure to establish a buddy system to keep track of each other

☐ **Class V Module**

*current is stronger, drops are bigger, holes are more violent, consequences of flipping or swimming are much more severe
*extremely important to pay attention to this talk
*team work is essential
*be absolutely sure to establish a buddy system to keep track of each other
*get swimmers back in raft immediately, listen to guides for directions
*self-rescue is very important or you could be in for a long swim
*if swimming, immediately assess your situation; listen for directions, but don't wait to act; look for eddies and calm spots
*begin swimming early to catch an eddy and swim hard right angles to current
*stay away from strainers

☐ **Hypothermia Module**

*potentially fatal
*risk of hypothermia increases with cold water, cold air, windy conditions, wet clothes
*inform guide if you're feeling cold, continuously shivering, or feeling apathetic
*look out for each other
*wetsuits or drysuits are required
*wear warm and adequate insulating layer, no cotton
*eat plenty of food, drink lots of water; no alcohol or caffeine

Witness:

I certify that the items I have checked above were covered in our trip safety talk.

Signature: _____

Print Name: _____

Date: _____

MODULAR SAFETY TALK OUTLINE
By: William McGinnis

Some imperative **do's** and **don'ts** regarding safety talks: **Do** make sure everyone can hear the talk. **Do** give participants the opportunity to choose not to participate after the safety talk. **Do** make sure that everyone is paying attention and is not distracted. **Do** make sure that everyone is accounted for and present for the safety talk. **Don't** do the safety talk on the bus unless the bus has an excellent PA system. **Don't** do the safety talk after the trip has started.

_____

Welcome

Get Release Forms Signed

Rafting Involves Inherent Risk
–Listen carefully, the vital information in this talk could directly improve your chances of survival, in other words, this talk could save your life.

Questions are Welcome
–ask for clarification if you don't understand anything

Emphasize Teamwork
–by working together as a team we are strongest
–every single one of us is a vital part of our team

Make Friends with Pandemonium
–in emergencies it's normal to feel scared and overwhelmed
–you can have these feelings and still act quickly, effectively

Establish a Buddy System
–immediately tell guide if someone is missing

How to Rescue a Swimmer
–don't jump in after them
–immediately pull them in, assuming it's safe to do so
–one person should pull in a swimmer; the rest of the crew should continue following commands
–extend your paddle handle so the swimmer can grab it and be pulled towards the boat
–have swimmer face raft, grab the shoulder of their life jacket, brace your knees against the tube, lean back, and pull them in-Questions?

What to do if You're the Swimmer
–hold on to your paddle-it can help you get in the boat
–at first, submerged, you'll probably be disoriented
–cold water may constrict your chest and throat, making breathing difficult
–no life jacket will float your head over the crest of the waves; breathe in the troughs between the waves
–panic often sets in as a normal and natural human response; try to relax and stay calm
–most of the time you'll pop up next to the raft and be rescued right away
–don't hang out on the downstream side of the boat; you can get crushed between the boat and a rock
–if you come up under the raft, face the bottom of the boat and quickly pull and kick your way out from under the raft
–if you get separated from the raft, there are basically two "swimming" techniques to choose from
    • the feet-downstream, toes-at-the-surface sitting position
    • the self-rescue, on-your-stomach crawl stroke

−every situation is different, so there's no single best strategy
−listen to your guide; look for hand signals from guides-guides always point where they want you to go
−look around, watch for toss bags or extended paddles; assess your situation and make the best decision you can
−unless there's a dangerous obstacle downstream, it's generally best to ride out big rapids in the feet-downstream sitting position; then in calmer water, self rescue by swimming in a crawl stroke toward either the boat or shore
−always keep your feet at the surface; dangling feet can become entrapped between rocks and you can drown
−never try to stop yourself or stand up in swift water deeper than your knees
−in the feet-downstream swimming position, you can:
  • see where you are going
  • maneuver by angling your body at about 45 degrees to the current and using a backstroke
  • use your legs, in a bent position, to bounce off rocks that you can't avoid
−questions?

Self Rescue
−sometimes the fastest way out of the water and back into the boat is to do it yourself
−the on-your-stomach crawl stroke is used to aggressively swim across white water and self rescue
−generally best to maneuver by swimming at right angles to the current
−to swim into an eddy, aim upstream of the eddy; start early and swim hard until your entire body is in the eddy
−avoid rocks by swimming around them, that is, into the water missing them
−avoid places where swift current sweeps through half submerged brush and trees; called strainers, these obstacles can be deadly traps because, while the current pours through them, bodies get caught.
−questions?

Flips
−sometimes boats flip over; if you bob up under the overturned raft, get yourself out from under the boat as soon as you can
−listen for your guide's instructions
−if upright boats are nearby, it is often best to swim for those.
−if there's not a serious hazard immediately downstream, a good choice can also be to stay with the overturned raft; grab floor lacing to pull yourself up and onto the bottom of upside down boat
−if you are separated from the raft or can't climb onto the slick bottom, it may be best to swim toward shore

Tube Stand
−sometimes boats ride up on one tube and people tumble out
−shifting your weight instantly and grabbing hold of something can help you stay in the boat

Collisions with Rocks
−if the raft slams broadside into a rock, move quickly to the side of the raft nearest the rock
−the command for this is "high side!"
−if the crew doesn't move quickly, the upstream tube can be sucked down, water can pour into the boat, and within seconds, the boat can be wrapped flat around the rock, pinned there by tons of force
−wrapped boats can take a long time to free; often the people who didn't high side quickly enough fall out
−shifting the crew's weight to the downstream tube usually lifts the upstream tube and allows current to flow under rather than into the boat; then, it's relatively easy to free the raft

Low Branches
−if your boat sweeps under low branches, you can get scratched and possibly even knocked out of the boat
−if your guide yells "duck" or "low branch", duck your head by leaning forward, not backward
−you may have to get down as low as possible into the center of the boat to avoid being taken by the branches
−once clear of the trees, get back to your position and be prepared to paddle

MODULAR SAFETY TALK OUTLINE

Vital Details

Loose Lines
–loose lines can tangle around your feet; stow all raft lines securely
–never tie yourself to the raft

Paddles
–when holding your paddle, always keep your hand over the T-grip to avoid injuring yourself or others

Thwarts
–it's okay to wedge your toes, but don't jam your entire foot under the thwarts, or you may find that your foot gets stuck and you can't get out

Footcups
–footcups assist participants from falling out of a boat, but they can also increase the risk of knee, ankle, and other injuries; the use of footcups is totally voluntary choice and like everything else, at your own risk

Jumping
–never, never jump headfirst or dive into the water; rocks can be invisible and you can hit your head
–jumping feet first can also be dangerous. Only jump into the water if you can see clearly that there are no obstacles
–after checking with your guide and making sure it is safe to do so, ease in feet first

Slippery Rocks
–most accidents happen on land; rocks at the water's edge are slippery; be extremely careful getting into and out of boats

Poison Oak (on Western North American Rivers)
–it has waxy green and red leaves in three-leaf clusters; if you don't know what it looks like, ask a guide to point out some
–can cause reactions from mild itching to severe pain and swelling to respiratory difficulties
–stinging nettles can cause painful, burning stings if you touch them

Snakes
–be alert for snakes around warm rocks, and keep your ears open for telltale rattling sounds

Cigarettes
–if you smoke, please be careful; don't leave burning embers on the ground; you might cause a fire
–don't throw your butts on the ground; put them in the trash bag or your pocket
–don't smoke within 6 feet of anything flammable

Water
–don't drink the river water; it may contain bacteria which can make you sick
–always drink from the water bottles or canteens in the boats
–make sure you drink lots of water to help prevent dehydration in hot water and hypothermia in cold weather
–it's safest to drink form your own personal water bottle which you can refill from the large water bottles in the boats

Glasses and Contact Lenses
–secure glasses to your head with a strap so you don't lose them
–if you wear contacts, close your eyes during water fights, when going through waves, and if you fall in the water

Hats
–secure hats to your head with a small piece of string, or wear a chin strap

Loose Gear
–Keep all loose items secured to the raft, otherwise they may be washed overboard and lost

Sunscreen
–below eye level only use sunscreen or sun block liberally to avoid sunburn
–sunscreen on your forehead is likely to get washed into your eyes, where it can burn painfully; wear a hat or visor to protect your forehead
–cover especially well those surfaces which are more horizontal; top of nose, back of neck, top of legs
–sunscreen on the back of your legs will make you slip around on the raft, increasing your chances of falling out

Special Medical Conditions
–please inform us of any medical conditions we should know about; we can carry your medications in our first aid kit

Alcohol
–no alcohol or drugs on the river. Drugs and alcohol use on the river increase the risk of injury and death

Water Fighting
–guidelines for water-fighting:
  • throw only river water
  • stay in your own boat; don't board other boats to continue the water-fight
  • don't pull or push someone else into the water
  • be considerate; don't bombard someone who is obviously not enjoying it
  • don't throw water at someone who has a camera out
  • hold on to your bucket; many people have been hurt by flying buckets
  • 1/4 full buckets are most effective in soaking the enemy; full buckets are heavy and harder to hold onto and control
  • no water-fighting if it's cold or if the risk of hypothermia is significant
  • never water-fight just above or immediately below a rapid
  • stop water-fighting ANY time your guide tells you to stop

Any questions?

Ecological Awareness and Responsibility

Basic Concept
–river is beautiful, special place and it's great that we can be here
–we owe it to the river and to ourselves to leave the river as we find it, or better, for those who follow
–we must be careful with four things: litter, human waster, soap, and fire

Litter
–pack out all unburnable garbage
–pick up any litter you see on the ground; let's all try to leave the river cleaner that we find it.

Human Waste
–all solid human waste is carried out; we'll explain about the porta-potty set-up in camp

Soap
–never use any soap, even biodegradable soap, directly in the river or in a side stream
–do your washing away from the river; after you're done, dump the water at least 100 feet away from the river

Fire
–forest fire is a very serious danger; we'll have only one group camp fire. So please do not make private fires on the side

–if you smoke, please do it in the cleared area around the main fire, not off in the bushes or in your sleeping bag
–put all butts and matches into the fire, not on the ground
–no smoking or open flame within 6 feet of anything flammable (a Forest Service regulation)

Conclusion
–if you don't fully understand anything, or if you have any questions, please ask a guide for clarification
–if you don't want to go, but choose instead to stay on the land and grow in other ways, it's not too late to say so
–introduce the guides and boats (point out the sweep with the emergency gear), and talk about the river and what to expect in the course of the day, the trip, including evening agenda and entertainment
–a reminder after talk, tell me of any special medical conditions, allergies, etc.

Swims & Pandemonium

One way to prepare people for swims and the accompanying pandemonium, is to say something like:

"When you go overboard or your entire boat flips: First, you get wet. Second, you panic. And third, you cope. You cope by getting your feet up and self rescuing at the earliest opportunity."

When integrated into this safety talk, this succinct phrasing makes these three key points easy to remember.

PART 3: SAFETY TALKS

INDIVIDUAL MODULES FOR SAFETY TALKS
(only use where appropriate)

Toss Bag Module
–if someone throws you a toss bag, grab the line, not the bag. If you grab the bag, you'll keep going until the line plays out.
–to avoid entanglement, don't wrap or tie the line around any part of your body—just hold it tightly with both hands
–roll over onto your back with the line going over the shoulder furthest from the bank—this gets your face downstream and lets you breathe. Putting line over shoulder furthest from bank swings you to shore faster

Hand Signal Module
–one whistle blast: urgent situation or emergency; pay attention
–point positive: go where indicated
–swimmer
–come to me
–are you OK
–we're OK
–I'm OK
–I need first aid
–don't know
–erase last signal
–I'm cold
–we barely made it
–I love you
–person or people missing
–we're searching for__(number) people
–everyone is accounted for, no one is missing in my boat/in boats indicated

Strainer Module
–strainers are obstructions in the river, such as a downed tree, logs, brush in the water, that allow water to flow under and through them, but trap solid objects, like humans, against them
–very dangerous for swimmers; strong current can pin you to a strainer, and you can easily drown
–if swimming, the best thing to do with a strainer is avoid it
–as soon as you notice a strainer, start swimming as hard as you can perpendicular to the current into water missing the strainer, either towards shore or the middle of the river, whichever way seems safer to you
–the key point here is to swim at right angles to the current to get into water that is missing the obstacle
–if you can't avoid the strainer, there are still some moves you can make to try to protect yourself
–overriding concern is to keep your body, particularly your head, on top of the strainer, above the water
–never, ever try to dive and swim under strainers; you could get permanently stuck in the tangled debris under the surface
–no two strainers are alike, so there's no single best strategy for dealing with them
–strainers come in three basic types: horizontal, vertical, and a confused tangle
–example of horizontal strainer: downed tree that is on or just below the river surface. If you can't avoid the log, swim aggressively toward it, headfirst; as you reach it, grab it with your arms, kick and pull yourself as high as possible up over the log or branches
–don't hit horizontal strainers feet first; your feet can slide under the strainer and you can either get stuck or pulled underwater
–example of vertical strainer: area where the trunks of several trees are partially submerged, with the water flowing through them but allowing debris to be caught between them; keep your body **on** the surface of the water, try to pass close to one side of a tree trunk, and swim or pull yourself into the downstream eddy formed by the obstruction
–in a confused tangle of branches, to protect your face and front, you can tuck into a tight ball just before you hit the strainer, and try to fight your way through the top part of it or over it
–if your paddle is in your way, get rid of it and put all your effort into swimming; do everything you can to avoid a strainer
–questions?

Big Hole Module
–treacherous reversals of current found just downstream of submerged ledges or rocks
–raft can get stuck in a hole, or even flip
–if your boat is stuck in a hole, stay low in the boat, move quickly to the downstream side
–if your raft spins around in a hole, keeping low, move quickly to the new downstream side to stabilize the boat
–use the downstream draw to help pull a raft out of a hole
–if you fall out of the boat in a hole, most of the time you will immediately be flushed out by the downstream current
–sometimes you can get caught in a reversal and be tumbled around for a bit
–in this situation, swim hard to the side to try to escape the hole
–also, as a last resort, try diving towards the bottom of the river to catch the downstream current, then swim hard
–questions?

Low Water Module
–smaller waves and more rocks
–more challenging because it requires precision timing and tight teamwork
–less margin for error in these technical moves, so teamwork is essential
–many more rocks are exposed; some rocks are undercut, which means there are places in which floating objects, including people, can get stuck and held by strong current
–often the only way out of undercuts is to be pulled back upstream against the force of the current; hard to do by yourself
 –if you're swimming, pay attention and look around for instructions. If a guide is pointing wildly, turn on your stomach and swim hard in that direction at a right angle to the current, to get into the water missing the obstacle
–when you're close to rocks that could catch and hold on to a dangling foot; it is extremely important to keep your feet at the surface in order to avoid foot entrapment
–questions?

High Water Module
–can dramatically change a run; chances of long swims are greater; wraps, flips, and tube stands are far more common
–nearly overwhelming feelings of fear and panic that can accompany these mishaps are perfectly human and normal–and each of you have the ability to both be scared and actively self-rescue at the same time
 –self-rescue is very important: unless you get yourself out of the water quickly, the swiftly moving current could carry you on into the next rapid in no time at all
–if swimming, immediately assess your situation and make decisions about self-rescue; listen for directions from your guide but don't wait to act; most generally the best option is to swim hard for the nearest right-side-up boat; if no boat is nearby look for eddies and calm spots
 –once you identify a safe place to swim to, begin early and swim hard, at right angles to the current. Continue swimming until your entire body is in calm water
 –if current is swift and strainers line the banks, it may be best to stay with the boat midstream–even if it's upside down—until it's time to start early for the next big eddy
–there can be great dignity in choosing to walk around a rapid that you don't feel good about running
–establish a buddy system within each boat whereby teams of two or three people keep track of one another at all times. Notify guide immediately if one of your buddies is missing
–questions?

Class V Module

–current is stronger, drops are bigger, holes are more violent, consequences of flipping or swimming are much more severe
–extremely important to pay attention to this talk—your chances of survival directly depend on how well you listen
–be especially alert, focused, and cautious
–take extra time to learn to hone your skills and work together as a team
–paddlers need to be able to respond instantly to whatever command a guide gives
–need to be able to paddle strongly and in unison, possibly for long periods of time
–distribution of weight and power in the boat is important, so guide may decide where each person will sit in the boat
–crews must learn to spot eddies, eddies are clam spots where water is actually flowing upstream; tend to form downstream of obstacles; eddies are our friends because they provide us with much-needed resting places
–holes tend to be big
–there is great dignity in choosing to walk around a rapid that you just don't feel good about running
–establish a buddy system within each boat whereby teams of two or three people keep track of one another at all times; notify guide immediately if one of your buddies is missing
–get swimmers back in raft immediately; listen to your guide for directions
–self-rescue is very important; if swimming, immediately assess your situation and make decisions about self-rescue; listen for directions from your guide but don't wait to act; look for eddies and calm spots
–once you identify a safe place to swim to, begin early and swim hard. At right angles to the current; continue swimming until your entire body is in calm water; current is extremely powerful; don't fight it but rather try to work with it
–questions?

Hypothermia Module

–potentially fatal condition in which the core body temperature drops dangerously low
–risk of hypothermia is greater when weather conditions are such that body heat is lost more rapidly than it can be replaced
–windy conditions increase the risk of hypothermia
–inform guide if: you're feeling cold and are not able to warm up; you're continuously shivering and are unable to stop; you're feeling lethargic and apathetic
–if you just took a swim and are wet, you're at greater risk of becoming hypothermic
–look out for each other; inform guides if someone looks like they are showing signs of hypothermia
–wetsuits or drysuits are required to reduce the risk of developing immersion hypothermia as a result of swimming
–wear adequate insulating layers and don't wear any cotton
–don't skip meals; eat plenty of food
–dehydration can actually increase your chances of developing hypothermia so drink lots of fluids, particularly warm ones but avoid alcohol and caffeine
–don't hesitate to ask for the trip to stop so that you can put on some additional clothes or get something high-energy to eat
–questions?

FULL MODULAR RAFTING SAFETY TALK
By William McGinnis

The Put-In Talk

Whenever a trip includes people new to rafting, it is vital to give a put-in talk. The talk can educate, inspire, and set the trip tone. Ideally, the put-in talk:

–warns people of the risks they accept when running a river
–shares information and skills to increase their chances of survival
–inspires respect and proper care for the river environment
–helps create a supportive atmosphere flowing with sincere positive strokes
–encourages teamwork
–lays a foundation of safety consciousness
–and does all this in a way that is personal, friendly, humorous, entertaining, and feels comfortable to you

In your own way strike a balance between humor and seriousness. Keep the talk warm and lively and funny, and at the same time set a serious tone that encourages caution and respect for the river. Where appropriate, illustrate key points with gestures.

Before You Begin:

Fit Lifejackets

Before you start the put-in talk, have everyone grab a lifejacket and show them how to fit it properly. Demonstrate with your own or a guest's, how to fasten all the buckles and cinch down the side straps so that the jacket is snug but not too tight. Explain that a loose jacket will ride up over your face while you sink low, maybe with your nose down in the foam. Remind folks to always wear their lifejackets when on or near the water. Show people how to check each others' jackets for proper fit and have the guides check also. Let them know that it should be loose enough so that they can breathe, but tight enough that when they raise their arms over head and exhale completely, a crew mate cannot slip it off their shoulders.

A Few Guidelines

Start off by asking the trip members to gather in a snug circle and make themselves comfortable. The essence of rafting, after all, is getting close and comfortable, and a compact audience allows you to speak at normal volume, which—since most talks last thirty minutes or so—saves your voice.

Clearly acknowledge that rafting involves inherent risks (i.e., risks that are impossible to eliminate due to the very nature of the activity itself) and other risks. Explain that your talk contains information vital to their survival, and request their undivided attention for the next 30 or so minutes.

If there are repeat clients or folks with prior rafting experience on the trip, make an effort to especially invite them to listen/ participate in the put-in talk. Acknowledge that they probably already know quite a bit since they've been rafting before and have heard put-in talks before, but that it's always good—even vital—to get a refresher and maybe they'll learn something new. This special invitation helps address the tendency that some repeat clients have to act bored and disinterested during the put-in talk.

Arrange things so the group is looking away from the sun. This generally means you must face the sun—so wear a hat or visor. We recommend that you not wear sunglasses when greeting people or giving the put-in talk. The eyes truly are windows to the soul—and sunglasses create an opaque barrier during this important time of initial contact. On hot days, if possible, give the talk in the shade.

When acknowledging the risks inherent in rafting, avoid making guarantees, especially about safety. Instead of saying, "If you do this, you'll be safe," it is better to say something like, "If you follow these suggestions, you'll increase your chances of survival". After all, no one can guarantee anyone's safety on the river. One can, however, share knowledge and skills which greatly increase people's safety margin.

Really give yourself to the talk, the trip, the moment. Strive to make each trip special; don't make it sound like "just another trip." Especially if you give a lot of put-in talks, you may have to make a point with yourself of breathing deeply and coming into the present moment. When you are fully present, the payoff in energy and aliveness is enormous for the group—and for you!

Find your own unique voice, humor and style. Speak in a way that is for you natural and comfortable—and clear and easy to understand. As you introduce words like eddy, haystack, hole and other examples of river jargon, explain each with clear, simple language and gestures. Remember that you don't have to live up to some perfect ideal—it's OK at times to fumble, search for words, and lose your train of thought (a checklist will get you back on track). These very fumbles are a part of your wonderful, unique humanness—and you, by accepting yourself, can help others accept themselves.

Create a Supportive Atmosphere: Appreciate People

Most people show up at river put ins not only eager and excited but also afraid—gripped by a number of conscious and unconscious fears. There is physical fear: "Will I survive? Will I be hurt?" Social fear: "Will I be accepted or rejected by this group?" And often biggest and deepest of all, fear related to self esteem: "Can I do this? Am I OK?"

A complete and nurturing put-in talk can greatly ease these fears and set the stage for transforming them in the course of the trip into confidence and joy. The talk's very thoroughness can both reassure people that they are in good hands and greatly increase their ability to raft safely—thus easing physical fear.

Your warmth, friendliness, and self-acceptance, and avoidance of machismo, competitiveness, elitism and judgement can create a supportive, caring atmosphere in which people become more accepting of themselves and others. Some keys to keep in mind: Cultivate a genuine interest in and caring for people. Listen with attention. And above all, express plenty of sincere positive strokes—whatever is true for you—including: "I'm really glad you're here." "Thanks for your attention." "I like the way you're holding that paddle." "Thanks for strong paddling." "Thanks for that question." Etc, etc.

Another key is to answer questions thoroughly and respectfully—the real question underlying most questions asked at put ins is, "Is this a safe place to be me?" Your thorough and respectful answers to any and all questions lets everyone know that it is indeed OK and normal to be a beginner and not know all the answers. OK and normal to be whoever you are and have whatever feelings you have—including fear. The idea is to accept and honor and celebrate *each* of the unique and valuable earth people—including yourself—-on your trip.

Rafting is a sport of cooperation and teamwork. By helping your companions feel accepted and a part of the team, you can not only ease their social fear and self-doubt, but also greatly enhance both their ability to just plain feel good and have fun—and their ability to work together to safely raft a wild river. As trip leader, you have a tremendous opportunity in your put-in talk to convey this spirit of cooperation, teamwork, and appreciation. I encourage you to foster this spirit within your boat, among all the boats in your group, and among all the people on and along the river.

Tailor the Talk to the River and the Group

The following basic put-in talk is for a typical class III raft trip with relatively inexperienced paddlers. Use your own judgement as to whether some of the more minor details are appropriate for your particular trip. At the end of this basic talk are a series of shorter talks on specific additional river hazards. These modules cover topics including ecology, strainers, low water, high water, big holes, hypothermia.

A BASIC PUT-IN TALK: LONG VERSION

Introduction

Welcome! Welcome to the _____ River. (Introduce yourself and the other guides and indicate which boat each will captain or row.)

Whitewater rafting involves inherent risk. You could get hurt, you could die. You can, however, improve your chances of survival by making yourself comfortable and giving me your undivided attention for the next 30 or so minutes.

I will talk about teamwork, pandemonium, swims, flips, collisions with rocks, low branches, mistakes to avoid, and how we can minimize our impact on this beautiful canyon.

Please feel free to ask questions at any time.

We Are A Team

It may come as a shock to hear this, but it's something we all need to know: There is no track which guides the boats safely down the middle of the river. It is only by working together as a team—paddling together, helping each other, pulling each other back in when we fall out—that we can hope to safely navigate this wild river.

We are a team. We are literally "all in the same boat." Each and every one of us is important. When everyone participates, everyone's chances of survival are improved. In fact, our entire group of boats is a team. All of us, in each and every boat, must look out for each other, and for the other boats.

Whether you are small or big, you are a vital member of the team. If you are small, you might think, "I'll just hold on—these big people can get us through." But each and every one of us is important. In fact, when the entire group paddles together in unison—when everyone's paddle blades move through the air at the same time, touch the water in sync, and power through the water in unison—the boat lunges forward with each stroke. It really moves. And this directly improves our chances of survival.

FULL MODULAR RAFTING SAFETY TALK

One of rafting's wonderful gifts is this whole experience of working together as a close team to create instant, beautiful results, such as making it through raging rapids right side up. By working together, helping each other, and, I might add, by really supporting and appreciating each other, we can raft more safely, have more fun, and connect more deeply with ourselves, one another, and our planet. I encourage you to foster a spirit of teamwork and appreciation within your boat, among all the boats in our group, and among all people on and along the river.

A suggestion: On this trip we make it OK to care about others and OK to show and say we care!

Making Friends with Pandemonium

Pandemonium is one name for the fear, panic, and sense of overwhelm that people often experience in a river emergency. When your boat flips or wraps, or someone goes overboard—whether you yourself are in the boat or in the water—it's likely your heart will pound wildly, your body will surge with adrenaline, and you'll feel an almost overwhelming—even immobilizing—sense of fear and urgency.

Two vital points: First, when this happens, don't take it personally. There is nothing wrong with you. You are not being singled out by the universe for this terrifying experience. You are simply becoming familiar with the very normal, very human fear, adrenaline, and panic of pandemonium.

Second, be aware that, on the river, pandemonium can suddenly rear its scary face at any moment. Just when you least expect it—Pow! You flip, wrap, swim or what have you and suddenly you're looking right down the terrifying, adrenaline-producing, panic-inducing throat of the beast pandemonium.

So, as well as you can, make friends with this beast. Be aware that pandemonium is simply what human beings experience in a river emergency, and that it can pop up anytime. This awareness, this friendship with pandemonium, will help you respond more calmly and effectively. The idea is: Notice that you're "gripped" and act fast to deal with the situation. Now let's talk about how to handle a number of emergency situations.

Emergencies

How to Rescue a Swimmer

What do you do when someone else goes overboard? First of all, don't jump in after them, because this more than doubles the problem. The best thing to do is to immediately pull them in, assuming it's safe to do so. Often for an instant or so after someone falls into the water, they'll be right next to the boat. But they won't stay there long, so they need to be pulled in quickly. One or two people should jump to grab the swimmer. It's important that everyone else continue paddling the raft—following the guide's commands.

If a swimmer gets separated from the raft, then continue following your guide's instructions, and as soon as it is safe to do so, the boat will maneuver toward the swimmer. As you approach, extend your paddle handle so the swimmer can grab it and be pulled toward the boat. If the swimmer is two paddle lengths away, you may be able to hook your paddle handle to the swimmer's paddle handle (demonstrate with t-grip paddles) and draw them to the raft.

To haul a swimmer up into the boat, turn them so they face the raft, grab them by the lifejacket at the shoulders, brace your knees against the tube, and, as you lean back, slide them belly-over-the-tube up and in. Swimmers can help by kicking their feet and pulling with their arms. Once the swimmer is in the boat, as quickly as you can, get back to your paddling position and resume following commands. In the sort of water where people get washed overboard, the boat needs all the power possible. By the way, if you see one of your boat mates teetering in their seats and starting to fall out of the boat, the best thing you can do is reach over and pull them back into the boat, before they even fall out!

What to Do if You're the Swimmer

Now, let's talk about what to do if you yourself go overboard. When you look up and see water (look and point up), and you look down and see sky (look and point down), chances are you're headed into the river—so take a big breath (take a big breath). Do your best to hold onto your paddle and, if you can, hold it out towards the boat (without clobbering anyone) as you're heading towards the water. This makes it easier for one of your boat mates to grab it and either keep you in or get you back quicker.

But let's say no one grabs your paddle and you go in. At first, submerged, you will probably be disoriented. This is almost like being suddenly thrust into some other dimension. You may wonder: Where am I? How did I get here? And if you're like me, there are bigger questions like: Who am I? Why am I alive? Within microseconds—which might seem like two or three lifetimes—it comes to you: Oh yeah, I just got washed overboard; I'm underwater; and, although I'm scared and have no air, soon my lifejacket will float me to the surface.

If you come up under the raft, face the bottom of the boat and, somewhat like you would crawl or scramble on all fours on land, as fast as you can, crawl, pull, scramble, kick, and stroke your way out from under the raft.

(Demonstrate this underwater crawl by leaning back and doing long, crawling, dog-paddle-like hand motions in the air as though on the underside of a raft.)

Once on the surface, you're likely to have a new sensation: Difficulty breathing. Cold water may constrict your chest and throat, making breathing difficult. Also, no lifejacket will float your head over the crests of the waves. Instead, your head will pass through the crests; so you must breathe in the troughs between the waves, and hold your breath in the crests. This comes naturally enough after a few waves.

The important thing is: Don't take it personally. First you're disoriented underwater with no air. Then you can't breathe on the surface. Panic can set in as a normal and natural human response. Remember though, that you are not being singled out by the universe. You're simply experiencing what human beings go through when swimming whitewater. And you do have a choice as to how you're going to react to this experience of being in the water. Some people give in to this feeling of panic, allowing it to overwhelm and paralyze them so that their overall experience in the water is miserable. Once they're rescued, they often insist upon getting back on the bus for the rest of the trip. Far preferable is the approach of recognizing that your fear and panic is normal and choosing instead to relax and stay calm and aware. Then, if you can, welcome the sensations you're having, and possibly even enjoy them, and recognize that you are in a far better position than anyone else to assist in your own rescue. Some folks become so adept at this that they actually ride out the rest of the rapid laughing, then swim to shore. So remember that although you may not have chosen to fall out of the boat, you can make choices while you are in the water that will greatly influence the nature of your experience. So, as well as you can, relax, welcome the sensations you're having—and hold onto your paddle.

OK, so you've just bobbed to the surface. Nine times out of ten you'll find yourself floating right next to the raft. Extend your paddle handle toward the raft (demonstrate by holding a paddle by the throat and extending the handle up and out as though toward a raft). Your paddle is your handle to safety. The people in the raft will grab it and pull you to the boat. To help your rescuers get you back in the boat, face the raft, kick with your feet and pull with your arms—while the people in the boat pull you in by the lifejacket at the shoulders. So, lickety split, nine times out of ten, you'll be pulled right back into the boat.

Occasionally, however, you will be separated from the raft or see that for some reason you will not be pulled in right away. In this case, there are basically two techniques to choose from: The feet-downstream, toes-at-the-surface sitting position (demonstrate), and the self-rescue, on-your-stomach crawl stroke (demonstrate).

Every situation is different so there is no single best strategy. Listen to your guide. Look around. Look downstream. Assess your situation. And make the best decision you can. It's generally best to ride out big rapids in the feet-downstream sitting position, and then, in calmer water, self rescue by swimming in an all-out crawl stroke for either the boat or shore. (Repeat this sentence for emphasis.) The big exception to this is if there is an especially dangerous obstacle just downstream—in this case it may be best to crawl stroke as fast as possible either to shore or' into water missing the obstacle.

Whichever position you choose, it's extremely important when swimming whitewater that you keep your feet at the surface. A foot thrust downward can become entrapped between rocks. The rest of your body then submarines under water to join your feet: you become entrapped with your head under water and are not able to breath. So never try to stop yourself or stand up in swift water deeper than your knees.

In the feet-downstream, toes-at-the-surface sitting position you can maneuver by angling your body to the current and using a backstroke. Angle your back, say, 45 degrees toward the right bank to move toward river left (demonstrate), and 45 degrees toward the left bank to move toward river left (demonstrate). By the way, river right refers to the right side of the river as seen when looking downstream (demonstrate with points and gestures), and river left refers to the left bank as seen when looking downstream (point). In shallows, you can keep from hitting rocks with your fanny by flattening out your body like a board (demonstrate) and keep those feet up!

In the feet-downstream swimming position, you can see where you are going. When you see rocks ahead of you, if possible avoid them by swimming perpendicular to the current to get into the water missing them. If you can't avoid a rock, use your legs, with knees slightly bent, to bounce off of the rocks. Most rocks have a cushion of water piled up against their upstream face so if you do run into them the impact is usually not that hard. However, whenever possible avoid rocks.

Don't cling to or climb onto midstream rocks—unless there is a terrible hazard directly downstream, or the water is excruciatingly cold, or there is some other reason you must get out of the water immediately. It might be hard for us to get you off the midstream rock, so we only want you there if it's more dangerous for you to stay in the water. A possible exception: If you move like a fish in whitewater—that is, if you are a truly adept whitewater swimmer—an occasional rock may make a good temporary resting or scouting spot—but not a place to stay for long.

Avoid at all costs places where swift current sweeps through half submerged brush and trees. Called strainers, these obstacles can be deadly traps because, while the current pours through them, bodies get caught—like spaghetti in a colander.

FULL MODULAR RAFTING SAFETY TALK

Self Rescue

The key point to remember is that you are not helpless just because you fell out of the boat. There is a lot you can do to affect your own rescue. Of course, the guides will be doing everything possible to get you back into the boat as soon as possible. Sometimes, however, the fastest way out of the water and back into the boat is to do it yourself, especially if there are several swimmers in the water and you are the farthest one from help.

The on-your-stomach crawl is used to aggressively swim whitewater. In this position your feet should naturally be at the surface. When doing the crawl stroke, it is best to maneuver by swimming at right angles to the current (illustrate with gestures). This is often the most efficient way to both get to shore and get into the water missing obstacles (demonstrate with gestures).

There are many ways in which you can self-rescue. Some examples include: swimming toward a boat so that the crew can pull you in, climbing on top of an overturned raft, swimming toward shore, swimming into an eddy or other calm spot.

To swim into an eddy you begin by aiming upstream of where you want to end up. If you aim directly at where you want to go, then the current will sweep you right past it. So aim upstream and start early. Swim hard and continue swimming until your entire body is in the eddy.

The key points again when swimming whitewater: You're likely to be disoriented and have difficulty breathing, but don't take it personally. Keep your feet up. Hang onto your paddle. Listen to your guide. Assess your situation. Look downstream for hazards. Watch for toss bags and extended paddles. Look for hand signals from guides. Even if you can't hear or understand what your guide is saying, know that he or she will always point positive—guides always point where they want you to go. Try to avoid rocks, big holes, and strainers. Generally, ride out fast, turbulent water in the feet-downstream toes-at-the-surface, sitting position. And as soon as you get to a calm or you see a good opportunity to swim either to the boat or shore, go into active self-rescue mode: Roll onto your stomach and crawl stroke hard and fast. Don't forget to breath: inhale in the troughs between the waves. And through all this as much as you can, be calm, and savor the experience.

Flips

Sometimes boats flip over. (As you say this do the flip signal for emphasis—that is, starting with both arms out horizontal pointing to one side, swing 'em both up and over until both point horizontally the other way). If you look down and see the raft and sky (look and point down), and look up and see the river coming at you (look and point up), the chances are your boat is flipping. Take a big breath, hold onto your paddle, relax, enjoy the experience.

If you bob up under the overturned raft, there is an air space in which you can take that long-awaited first breath, but this is not a safe place to stay for very long. As soon as you can, get yourself out from under the boat. After a flip, the first thing we guides do is count heads—and if we don't see enough heads, we start checking under the boat. So come out as quickly as you can.

If you bob up near the flipped raft, toss your paddle and any other loose items up onto the bottom of the boat. Listen for your guide's instructions. He or she may tell you to swim toward a nearby rescue boat, swim to shore, or climb up on top the overturned raft. Provided there is not a big rapid or some serious hazard immediately downstream, the safest place is often aboard the overturned raft. If the raft is a self-bailer, reach up over the tube and grab the floor lacing or put your fingers through the drain holes, found where the floor meets the tube on either side of the boat, then pull and kick your way up onto the upside-down raft. (As you speak, act these motions out in pantomime). With non-self-bailers, two people can boost and pull one another up. Or one person can board by taking a bow or stern line, running it through a side D-ring, throwing it over the raft to the other side, and going around to that other side and pulling her or himself hand over hand up this line onto the raft.

Once aboard, you can paddle the flipped boat to shore—or, in some cases, right it in midriver in the next calm by standing and leaning back on lines run through the side D-rings.

If you are separated from the raft or can't climb onto the slick bottom, it may be best to swim toward shore. Use the same swimming techniques described earlier: Generally, while in rapids, float in a sitting position with your feet downstream and toes on the surface. Then, in a calm or at the first good opportunity, roll onto your stomach and swim hard toward shore.

Tube Stands

Sometimes boats can ride up on one tube, completely abandoning the horizontal world for a moment and becoming mostly vertical. Gravity then takes over and people tumble out. When the boat comes back down, it is right-side up and very often the guide is the only one left in it. This is because the guide reacted instantly. You can do this too. Shifting your weight instantly and grabbing hold of something can help you stay in the boat.

PART 3: SAFETY TALKS

Collisions with Rocks

If the raft slams broadside into a rock, move quickly to the side of the raft nearest the rock. The command for this is "High side!" If the crew doesn't move quickly, or, worse, if the crew doesn't move at all, the upstream tube can be sucked down, water can pour into the boat and within seconds, the boat can be wrapped flat around the rock, pinned there by tons of force. (Illustrate this by wrapping one hand, representing the raft, around your other hand closed in a fist, representing the rock. You can also represent the raft with a hat and the rock with a child's head.) Once a boat is wrapped it can take quite awhile to get it off the rock—sometimes hours—and all those folks who didn't make it to the high side fast enough usually end up swimming. So, to avoid all that, when your guide's eyes get as big a saucers and she or he yells, "High side," jump toward the side of the raft that's against the rock. As you jump, be careful not to bop yourself or anyone else with your paddle.

Shifting the crew's weight to the downstream tube usually—but not always—lifts the upstream tube, and allows the current to flow under rather than into the boat. (Demonstrate with gestures.) And often the crew winds up sitting in a little row with their backs against the rock. If this happens to you, lean back and relax. Savor the sudden contrast between the tumult of the rapid and the serenity of the rock. By the way, virtually anything you say on a midstream rock—including, "I appreciate you," "This is life," and even, "The sky is blue"—takes on extra meaning—so if you're like me you'll take advantage of this rare opportunity to sound profound.

The next step will be to free the raft. This is often done by shifting everyone's weight to one end of the raft and jumping up and down so that the current twirls us off and away back into the downstream current.

Low Branches

Another river hazard is low branches. If your boat sweeps under low branches, you can get scratched by them and possibly even knocked out of the boat. If your guide yells "duck" or "low branch," duck by leaning forward, not backward, to protect your face and throat. At times you may have to get down as low as possible on the floor of the boat to avoid being raked by the branches. (Conventional boat: When rafting in boats with thin, non-self-bailing floors it is generally best not to put knees or tailbone down on the raft floor, where they could be injured by rocks passing under the raft. However, ducking under low branches—provided there are no rocks near the surface below the branches—can be one of the few situations in which going knee down to the floor may be the best/ least dangerous choice.)

Mistakes to Avoid In the Boat

Loose Lines

Loose lines can tangle around your feet. Stow all raft lines securely, either in pockets on the raft or coiled and hung over the bow and stern. Tie all gear in tight, and secure loose ends of gear lines. Never tie yourself to the raft. If the boat flips, you want to be free to float to the surface, not tied under the boat.

Shoes

Always wear them. Bare feet can get cut, bruised, and crushed. Sandals provide protection only for the soles of the feet; for more complete protection, wear sneakers or booties.

Lifejacket

Keep it snug. Always wear it when you're on or near the water. Have a crew mate check it for tightness. It should be loose enough for you to breathe, but tight enough that when you raise your arms over your head and exhale completely, a crew mate cannot slip it off over your shoulders.

Thwarts and Footcups

Don't jam your feet under thwarts, or you may get stuck when you don't want to be, or you can break an ankle. It's OK to wedge your toes under a thwart, but never a whole foot. If there are footcups in your boat, make sure your foot can't fit all the way through the strap or cup and get caught. Footcups can help keep you in the boat, but they have, in some rare cases, actually caused ankle and knee injuries. Like everything else, use them at your own risk.

Sharp Edges

Some equipment has sharp edges that can cut or bruise you. This can include ice chests, first aid kits, and the raft frame in an oar boat. Look for sharp edges and stay away from them. Tell your guide if any protective padding seems to be coming loose.

FULL MODULAR RAFTING SAFETY TALK

Paddles

Try to avoid hitting the person behind or in front of you while you're paddling. You think rafters wear helmets to protect themselves from rocks in the river; we really wear them to protect ourselves from paddles! If you're not paddling, keep your paddle in your outside hand, away from your crew mates. Keeping control of your paddle can prevent chipped teeth, cut chins, etc.

Jumping

Never, never jump headfirst or dive into the river. Rocks can be hidden just below the surface and you can hit your head. Jumping feet first can also be dangerous, as you can cut, break, or bruise your feet or legs. Only jump feet first into the water if you are very close to the water and you can see clearly that there are no obstacles in it.

Bailing

In a self-bailing raft, this is not a problem, but in a non-self-bailing raft, it is important that the crew members keep the raft bailed free of water. A raft full of water is heavy, hard to control, and vulnerable to puncture.

Mistakes to Avoid on Land

Snakes

Be alert for them around warm rocks, and keep your ears open for that telltale rattling sound in rattlesnake country. You don't want to step on a poisonous snake and make it mad.

Ticks

Ticks are common. Check yourself thoroughly after side hikes or after any time you've been tromping through the brush.

Slippery Rocks

Most accidents happen on land. Be extremely careful getting into and out of boats because rocks at the water's edge tend to be slippery. Always wear shoes and don't jump onto wet or slick looking rocks.

Poison Oak (on Western North American rivers)

Avoid it. It has waxy green and red leaves in three-leaf clusters, and can cause reactions from mild itching to severe pain and swelling to respiratory difficulties. If you don't know what it looks like, ask a guide to point some out. If you do touch any, wash it off immediately with cold, soapy water if it's available, or just with cold river water. If you do have a reaction to poison oak, it will likely start several days after you touch it. Also stay away from stinging nettles, which, if touched, can cause painful, burning stings.

Drugs and Alcohol

Whitewater and drugs or alcohol don't mix. You need all you wits about you. Drug and alcohol use increase the risk of injury and death. In other words, your life could literally be in peril if you raft when intoxicated or drugged.

Cigarettes

If you smoke, please be careful. Don't leave burning embers on the ground; you might cause a fire. Don't throw your butts on the ground; put them in the trash bag or in your pocket. Cigarette butts are litter and should be packed out. Please be considerate of non-smoking crew mates when you're smoking.

Fire

All fires must be completely smothered and out cold before leaving shore.

Vital Details

A few details that can make your trip more comfortable, safe, and enjoyable. (The trip leader may want to leave these items for the individual guides.)

Water: Don't drink the river water. It may contain bacteria which can make you sick. Always drink from the water bottles or canteens in the boats. Make sure you drink lots of water—drink some every hour. Drinking plenty of water helps prevent dehydration in hot weather and hypothermia in cold weather.

Glasses: If you're wearing glasses or sunglasses, secure them to your head with a strap. If you don't, you may lose your glasses to a rogue wave or a fall in the water. If you don't have a headstrap, ask your guide to cut you a piece of string from our generous supply.

PART 3: SAFETY TALKS

Contacts: If you wear contact lenses, close your eyes during water-fights, when we're going through waves, and if you fall in the water.

Hat: If you wear a hat, tie it on with a small piece of string, or wear a chin strap. Keep straps small and light so you can break them if you fall in the water and they become entangled in branches or something else underwater, or use some quick-release device on the strap, like a clothespin, paper clip, or binder clip.

Loose gear: Keep all loose items secured to the raft. Tie loose clothing and small items to the boat. Otherwise, they may be washed overboard and lost. Boats should always be rigged as if expecting to flip.

Clean feet: Rinse your feet before you get into the raft. If you bring sand or mud into the boat with you, it can get into the seams of the raft and abrade them, plus you'll have to sit in a muddy boat.

When you get into or out of the raft, try not to step on sloped or slippery rocks at the water's edge. Be careful.

Sun screen: Use sunscreen or sunblock liberally to avoid sunburn. The water reflects the sun back at you, so you're getting more sun than you may think. Protect any exposed areas such as your nose, ears, tops of legs, and the back of your neck. But don't put sunblock above your eyes. Sunblock above eye level is likely to be washed into your eyes, where it will burn painfully. Wear a hat or visor to protect your forehead instead. Also, avoid putting sunscreen on the back of your legs, as it will make you slip around on the tubes of the raft.

If you have any medical conditions we should know about, please tell me and your guide immediately after this talk. We can carry your medication in our first aid kit. If you have any allergies, such as to bee stings, or you use prescription drugs, or if you have asthma, which can be activated by a plunge into cold water, please tell me or your guide.

There will be no alcohol or drugs on the river. Having a drink or two in camp at night is fine, but we all need clear minds and strong, steady hands to get down the river safely. Drugs and alcohol greatly increase the risk of rafting and can quite literally result in serious injury or death.

Water-fighting

Water-fighting is a popular river pastime. A few words about it:
–Throw only river water; don't throw dirty bilge water from the bottom of your boat. Nobody likes to get sand in their eyes.
–Stay in your own boat; don't board other boats to continue the water fight or to throw someone in the water. Don't pull or push someone else into the water.
–Throw water "with love"; that is, be considerate. Don't bombard someone who is obviously not enjoying it. Don't throw water at someone who has a camera out.
–Hold on to your bucket! Many people have been hurt by flying buckets, and it's easy to let it slip out of your hands when you fling the water. Throw only partly-full buckets. Full buckets are heavy and harder to hold onto, and you'll be able to throw a small amount of water further. Quarter full buckets have the best range and are most effective in soaking the enemy.
–We won't be water-fighting if it's cold. Hypothermia is a serious danger on any river trip, and we won't water-fight in conditions that promote hypothermia.
–Never water-fight in or just above a rapid. Chaos above a rapid almost guarantees chaos in a rapid. In fact, stop water-fighting ANY time your guide tells you to stop.
–Follow your guide's instructions at all times. Your guides are concerned for your safety and know whereof they speak.

Ecology

Introduction

We are earth people. This is our planet and our river. We belong here, and being on this river is a clean, fun, healthy, and natural way to celebrate being alive on this beautiful planet, right here, right now! But along with the gift of this voyage comes a very serious responsibility to take care of the river and its environment. We owe it to the river and to ourselves to leave the river as we find it, or better, for those who follow.

Now, a raft, by its very nature, leaves no footprints, no treadmarks, no trace of its passage down the river. But in our temporary toeholds, put ins, lunch spots, and camp sites, it is important that we leave no permanent trace of our presence. To do this, every one of us must be careful with four things: litter, human waste, soap, and fire.

Litter

We will pack out all unburnable garbage. On this trip, and on any other nature trip, devote a pocket to litter. The following things are all litter: pull tabs from cans, cigarette butts, matches, orange peels, watermelon seeds, bits of lettuce, paper, and foil. You may not think of food scraps as litter, but they are, for several reasons. One, food scraps are unnatural and don't belong there. Two, they can attract rodents, which in turn attract rattlesnakes to the camp areas and lunch sites. Three, the local wildlife can become dependent on your food scraps, which disappear at the end of rafting season, leaving the little critters to starve.

When you see any litter on the ground, pick it up and put it in your litter pocket. If you don't have a pocket, give it to someone who does. Later, burn everything flammable—except plastic—in the campfire and put everything else in the garbage bags which the guides will set up. Let's all try to leave the river cleaner than we find it.

Human Waste

Bring your toilet paper back and burn it in the campfire or put it in the garbage. Remember, toilet paper is litter too, even if you bury it, so pack it out or burn it instead. (Mention the location of any toilets or outhouses at the put-in, take-out, and at any stops along the way.)

(Give one of the following three talks depending on which technique is being used for human waste disposal on this trip. Some rivers have regulations regarding the disposal of human waste: make sure you understand and abide by the regulations, and use the disposal method approved for the river you're running.)

A. Lime Can

We will carry out all solid human waste in a big, tight-sealing, metal can about so big (gesture to indicate size of can). In a secluded spot near each camp, the can will be set up with a toilet seat and a bag of lime or powdered chlorine bleach close by. The can is for solid human waste only, popularly known as "Number 2." After you've made your contribution, use the scoop provided to sprinkle a small amount of powdered lime or bleach into the can. Then take the toilet seat off and carefully replace the lid on the can, making sure it fits tightly. This is vital to prevent flies from carrying germs from your waste to your food, which could result in serious disease. So remember keep the lid on the can between uses.

Optional: By the way, along the approach to the lime can, there will be a paddle. When the paddle is up or across the path, the can is occupied. When the paddle is down or alongside the path, the can is free. Just holler when you get close if you're not sure.

During the day, the lime can is available on request. If you have to go Number 2, please use the lime can, not the bushes.

B. Porta-Potty

We will carry out all solid human waste in a porta-potty. A porta-potty will be set up in a tent or secluded spot near each camp. Be sure to read the instructions posted next to the porta-potty. The crucial thing is that the potty is for solid human waste only. Please try not to pee in the potty. Also, don't put toilet paper in the potty. Instead, burn it in the campfire or put it in the garbage.

Because waste tends to pile up in the center of the holding tank, the potty may appear to be full before it actually is. Close the trap door and rock the potty from side to side to even things out. If the potty is actually full, please tell one of the guides *before* it overflows. We'd appreciate your help on this point more than we can say.

During the day, the porta-potty is available on request. If you have to go Number 2, please use the porta-potty, not the bushes.

C. Buried Waste

We will bury all solid human waste. When you feel the urge, take one of our shovels which you'll find in camp, and head out into the woods. Pick a good spot well above and away from the river. Try to get a spot with a good view. Dig a hole about six inches deep. The elements which cause the most rapid decomposition of human waste are in the top six inches of soil, so don't bother to go deeper. Then get comfortable, take your time, and savor the experience. Afterwards, fill in the hole with dirt. But, because paper decomposes slowly, don't bury your toilet paper. Instead, wrap it up in a bit of extra paper, bring it back to camp, and burn it or put it in the garbage. Don't be shy and sneak back into camp—hold your T.P. bundle high, like a badge of achievement, and walk proudly! Also, when you return the toilet paper roll, remember to tuck the end into the tube so it won't unravel all over camp, or if it's in a plastic bag, return it to the bag and close the flap so it won't get wet from overnight condensation or rain.

Soap

You may be interested to learn that most of the soap we use today is biodegradable. But even biodegradable soap takes time to decompose, and a small amount can create a lot of ugly suds, which are a form of litter on the river. So, never use soap directly in the river or in a side stream. Instead when you want to wash or brush your teeth or do your dishes or whatever, take one of the bailing buckets, scoop up some water, and carry it away from the river. After you're done washing, dump the water at least 100 feet away and as far above the river as you can get. That way, the soil will purify the water as it seeps down to the river.

PART 3: SAFETY TALKS

Fire

Forest fire is a very serious danger. At camp, we will have only one group fire. Please do not make private fires on the side. If you smoke, please do it only in the cleared area around the main fire, not off in the bushes or in your sleeping bag. Also, please put all butts and matches into the fire, not on the ground.

(Say one of the following depending on the technique being used.)

A. Established Campfire Sites

We will build our campfires in approved, established campfire sites. Before leaving each camp, we will thoroughly douse and stir the coals until they are cold to the touch.

B. Fire Pans

In order to avoid leaving ash and fire scars in our camps, we will build our fires in a fire pan and we'll carry the ash out with us.

Conclusion

That concludes this safety talk. Please remember to tell us now about any medical condition you may have that may require our attention. Does anyone have any questions?

Just out of curiosity, how many of you can swim? Please raise your hands. (Note the people who can't swim; you may need to keep an eye on them in an emergency.)

(At this point, the guide should describe the flow of the river, anticipated weather, and what lies downstream, river-wise. Describe any unusual features of the river, such as quiet zones or portages. Estimate the number of miles and hours before the lunch stop. Describe the rapids before and after lunch. Explain when and where the day will end and, or multi-day trips, outline the evening agenda, including happy hour, dinner and evening entertainment.)

Thank you very much for your patient attention. If you do not fully understand anything I have said, please ask me or the guide in your boat for clarification. Please remember to be alert and cautious. Use your good judgement. Follow your guide's instructions at all times. Leave no trace that you were here. Do you still want to go? Are you sure? It is not too late to choose to stay on the land and grow in other ways. You want to go? Great! Then let's pull together to make this the best possible river trip. Let's all support each other and work together as a team, because each of us will be an integral part of this voyage. Please choose a boat and a paddle, and have a fun and safe trip down the river!

After the Put-In Talk

After the put-in talk is over and people have chosen their boats and paddles, each guide should have the crew members in his or her boat introduce themselves to each other. The guide should explain how to check for lifejacket fit (arms held above head, fully exhale— your crew mate should not be able to pull your jacket up over your shoulders) and the guide should check the fit of everyone's lifejacket. The guide then proceeds to the in-boat training talk.

In-Boat Training Talk for Paddle Boats

First, the guide clearly and carefully explains and demonstrates all of the paddle strokes and commands. He or she demonstrates the correct and incorrect way to do the forward and backpaddle strokes. When demonstrating the backpaddle, the guide emphasizes the need to fulcrum off the hip, use the entire torso, and shows the crew how to really lean back into each backstroke. The crew is told to sit aggressively forward on the tube, using their legs with knees bent to maintain their balance, and to lean out over the tube to get a good strong pull on each stroke and to avoid scraping their fingers. The turn commands are reviewed, and the crew practices the turns repeatedly, right there at the put-in. Seasoned guides spend plenty of time on this, especially when launching just above rapids, where turns will quickly be needed.

Explaining the turn commands can be tricky. Everyone understands "forward paddle" and "backpaddle" well enough, but turning is much harder to grasp. Most guides use the commands "right turn" and "left turn." One method of explaining these commands is to say, "When I say 'right turn,' the right side backpaddles and the left side paddles forward. When I say 'left turn,' the left side backpaddles and the right side paddles forward. Whichever turn I call, if you're on that side, you backpaddle. If you're not on that side, you paddle forward. Tell yourself right now which side you're on—right or left? Then be prepared to backpaddle when I call out your side, and forward paddle when I call out the other side. I know you can do it! Now let's try it. Right turn!"

If the guide plans to use the downstream draw stroke, which is useful for getting the boat out of holes and tight spots, he or she explains it something like this: "When I say 'downstream draw,' everybody on the downstream side should drop a knee to the floor to get their weight low in the boat, lean your body way out over the tube to get good leverage, dig your paddle deep into the water, and pull hard straight in toward the boat. This draws the boat straight downstream." The crew practices this stroke at put-in and also periodically downriver (when relaunching after the lunch stop is also a good time to practice this), so they really learn how to do it. The variations of "draw left" and "draw right" should also be practiced if the guide expects the crew to use them later. The guide may also wish to teach the pry stroke, and how the bow strokers can help dig through holes. The pry stroke can be very effective if there is something to pry off of (i.e., push against) and digging from the bow can pull the boat out of some amazingly large holes.

Throughout the practice session, the guide gives a great deal of support and encouragement to the crew, saying things like "Good," "That's it," "That's better," and "You're doing great." When a crew member does something incorrectly, the guide gently and firmly explains the correct way to perform the maneuver and makes sure that he or she gets it right before they continue. The guide must communicate very clearly what is needed and why it is needed, so that each crew member sees the importance of doing it right. The beginning of the trip is the best (and perhaps only) time to teach the crew how to control the boat. Showing the crew how the boat responds to their efforts makes them feel like they have some control over the situation and gives them confidence both in themselves and in the guide who has taught them the technique.

One of the guide's primary responsibilities is to keep people in the boat. When the boat goes through rough water, the team will keep better control of the boat if they all continue paddling. But if they feel the need to hold on, they should do so rather than be washed out of the boat. Emphasizing the need to stay in the boat (especially in difficult or high water), the guide teaches the crew to respond to the command "Hold on and lean in." At the sound of this command, crew members hold on, preferably to handholds tied to the top middle of the thwarts and lean far into the center of the boat. To avoid cracking heads, they should point their shoulders, not their heads, at the person across from them. Also, teach crew members to be careful not to bop, pop or poke themselves or others with their paddle handles.

When holding on to a safety line around the perimeter of the raft, crew members should use their outboard hand, so they can lean their body in toward the center of the raft and avoid being flushed overboard. When holding on to safety lines tied around the thwarts, they should use their inboard hands. There is a delicate balance to be struck between holding on and paddling. A crew with some experience may not need to hold on at all, and may be able to keep paddling through all the rapids, maintaining their balance by wedging a toe under the thwart or by putting a foot in a footcup on the floor.

In especially tough water, the guide may call "Hold on, lean in, get down." In this case, the crew members, in addition to holding on and leaning in, should slide their weight down off the tube so as to stay low in the boat. "Get down" in this case doesn't mean "get down and boogie!" Finally, crew members are taught to grab anybody who seems to be washing overboard and pull them back in. All of these maneuvers should be practiced, with the guide calling the commands in an appropriately strong urgent voice.

The guide reviews the main points of the trip leader's put-in talk. Crew members are reminded how to swim rapids, how to highside, how to pull a swimmer into the boat, what to do in case of a flip. If there is a strong possibility of colliding with a rock or hitting low branches, the guide has the crew practice highsiding and ducking in response to the guide's commands. Optionally, the guide may have the crew practice swimming and pulling swimmers in; practicing these techniques depends on the water temperature and the river conditions. If the water is cold, the crew can practice pulling a swimmer in on dry land. Practice is invaluable, as it trains both the crew's minds and muscles to respond to the guide's commands.

The guide designates the two people in the bow as the "strokes" and emphasizes the need for everyone to take their queue from the "strokes" and paddle in unison. The guide can say something like, "When everyone's paddle blades flash up into the air at the same time, hit the water in unison, and pull the boat forward with a single powerful sweep, we do not bang our paddles together, our strokes are more effective, the boat lunges ahead with each stroke, a powerful harmony develops, and most important, we look good."

The guide reinforces the importance of the "strokes" by sometimes speaking to them when giving a command. For example, if the boat is about to cross a long calm stretch, the guide might say, "OK, Bob and Betty, set an easy, slow, but powerful stroke that we can all follow to move across this pool." To balance the importance of the "strokes," the guide also periodically reminds the crew that everyone matters, no matter what their size or fitness level, and that it is important, when they're feeling overwhelmed, to keep trying to follow the guide's commands. The guide makes it clear that he or she depends on each crew member, and that they are a team, working together.

The guide selects one of the strokes, preferrably a strong, agile person, to be the "line person." or "agile bow person." This person is in charge of keeping the bow line coiled and up off the floor, but ready for quick use. In some boats, the bow line is stuffed in a pocket on the bow; on most boats, it is coiled and hung through the outboard D-ring (the guide demonstrates how the line is handled in each boat). The guide teaches the bow person how to jump ashore: First, stow your paddle, second, grab the line, third, jump out. With one foot on the tube, the line person launches the other foot forward through the air, landing on the bank just as the boat sweeps into the bank and before it bounces away. The line person also needs to understand that, once on the bank, he or she, especially when stopping in strong current, must brace him or herself strongly or wrap or tie the line to something solid, like a tree or a rock, to avoid being pulled into the river.

The guide reviews the main points of river ecology: pick up all litter, smoke only near the campfire and don't use soap in the river. The guide describes again any local hazards such as poison oak or ivy, snakes, or stinging nettles. Basic safety guidelines are reiterated: keep your feet inside the boat, don't wedge your feet under a thwart so far that you can't get them out, keep your shoes on, and keep your lifejacket on. Keep bailing buckets and lines properly stowed away, keep the raft bailed if it's not a self-bailer, and lean into the center of the boat when hitting big waves, but keep paddling if the guide says to paddle. The guide also adds any details that the trip leader forgot to include in the main put-in talk. Finally, the crew members are taught to leave their paddles in their places in the boat if they change places or leave the boat. After a few more practice turns, they're off and running!

In-Boat Talk for Oar Boats

(This talk contains much of the same material found in the in-boat paddle boat talk, without the paddle commands and with a few topics specific to oar-boats.)

Emphasizing the need to stay in the boat (especially in difficult or high water), the guide teaches the crew to respond to the command "Hold on and lean in." At the sound of this command, crew members hold on and lean far into the center of the boat. To avoid cracking heads, they should point their shoulders, not their heads, at each other.

When holding on to a safety line around the perimeter of the raft, crew members should use their outboard hand, so they can lean their body in toward the center of the raft and avoid being flushed overboard. When holding on to safety lines tied around the thwarts, they should use their inboard hands.

In especially tough water, the guide may call "Hold on, lean in, get down." In this case, the crew members, in addition to holding on and leaning in, should slide their weight down off the tube so as to stay low in the boat. Finally, crew members are taught to grab anybody who seems to be washing overboard and pull them back in. All of these maneuvers should be practiced, with the guide calling the commands in an appropriately urgent voice.

The guide reviews the main points of the trip leader's put-in talk. Crew members are reminded of how to swim rapids, how to highside, how to pull a swimmer into the boat, what to do in case of a flip. If there is a strong possibility of colliding with a rock or encountering low branches, the guide has the crew practice highsiding and ducking in response to the guide's commands. Practice is invaluable, as it trains both the crew's minds and muscles to respond to the guide's commands.

The guide places a strong, agile person in the left bow to be the "line person." or "agile bow person." This person is in charge of keeping the bow line coiled and up off the floor and ready for landing. In some boats, the bow line is stuffed in a pocket on the bow; on most boats, it is coiled and hung through the outboard D-ring (the guide demonstrates how the line is handled in each boat). The guide teaches the bow person how to jump ashore: With one foot on the tube, the line person launches the other foot forward through the air, landing on the bank just as the boat sweeps into the bank and before it bounces away.

The guide reviews the main points of river ecology: pick up all litter, smoke only near the campfire and don't use soap in the river. The guide describes again any local hazards such as poison oak, snakes, or stinging nettles. Basic safety guidelines are reiterated: keep your feet inside the boat, keep your shoes on; keep your lifejacket on, keep bailing buckets and lines properly stowed away, keep the raft bailed if it's not a self-bailer, and lean into the center of the boat when hitting big waves. Everyone is cautioned not to sit where they could get struck by an oar, and to be careful of the oars at all times.

Modules

Toss Bag Module

Include on rivers where toss bags are likely to be used—such as rivers with rapids where people with toss bags are posted in key rescue positions.

(Have someone throw you a toss/ rescue bag. Hold a paddle by the throat out to one side with its t-grip handle extending your reach for the catch. Demo what happens when you grab only the bag—then grab the line.) If someone in the boat or on shore throws you a rescue bag, grab the line, not the bag. If you grab the bag, the line will keep paying out and you'll continue to float downstream. To avoid entanglement, don't wrap the line around your wrist or tie it to you—just hold it tightly with both hands. As you swing to shore—especially if you are in swift water—you will probably want to roll over onto your back with the toss/ rescue line going over the shoulder furthest from the bank (demonstrate). This gets your nose around to the downstream side of your head—which enables you to breathe when the current piles up in a water pillow on the upstream side of your head. And passing the line over the shoulder furthest from the bank causes you to pendulum to shore much more quickly.

FULL MODULAR RAFTING SAFETY TALK

Hand Signal Module

–one whistle blast: Urgent or emergency; pay attention to me
–point positive: go where indicated
–swimmer
–come to me
–are you OK
–we're OK
–I'm OK
–I need first aid
–don't know
–erase last signal
–I'm cold
–we barely made it
–I love you
–person or people missing
–we're searching for (number) people
–everyone is accounted for, no one is missing
–in my boat/ in boats indicated

Strainer Module

For people overboard: Look for downstream rocks and strainers (trees, bushes and logs in the water). If you see any, swim as hard as you can perpendicular to the current to get into the water missing them! The force of the current can pin you against a rock or a log and you can drown. If you can't avoid the strainer, swim headfirst at it and thrust yourself up and over it, to avoid entrapment. Don't hurt yourself on a protruding branch, and above all, don't go underwater.

(This module should be inserted under *Emergencies* when you're running a river that is known for having strainers.)

This river has an unusually large number of strainers. Strainers are obstructions in the water, such as trees, bushes and logs, that allow water to flow under and through them, out trap solid objects. Strainers are very dangerous for swimmers. Think of draining noodles in a colander; the water flows through, but the spaghetti—that's you—stays behind. The force of the current pins you to the strainer, and you can easily drown.

The best thing to do with a strainer is avoid it. If you're swimming, swim as hard as you can at a right angle to the current into water missing the strainer. Swim hard and fast toward shore or toward the middle of the river, whichever way seems safer to you. However; if you can see that you cannot avoid the strainer, there are still some moves you can make to try to protect yourself.

No two strainers are alike, so there is no single best strategy for dealing with them. However, strainers come in three basic types: horizontal, vertical, and the confused tangle. I'm going to tell you how to recognize each type and some possible ways to survive them. In each case, the overriding concern is to keep your body on top of the strainer, above the water. Never, ever try to dive and swim under a strainer. There is likely to be debris tangled beneath the surface, and you could get stuck with your oxygen supply cut off!

A typical example of a horizontal strainer is a downed tree that is on or just below the river surface. Float toward the strainer with your entire body on the surface of the water, positioned sideways to the strainer. When you reach the strainer, throw your downstream arm and leg over the top of the strainer, and pull yourself up onto it. Another method is to float toward the strainer headfirst, and when you reach it, grab it with your arms, kick with your feet and press with your arms to pull yourself as high as possible up over the log or branches. Don't hit the strainer feet first, in the normal rapid-swimming position, because your feet are likely to slide under the strainer and you can either get stuck or pulled underwater.

Vertical strainers often include an area where the trunks of several trees are partially submerged, causing the water to flow through them but allowing debris to be caught between them. Try to pass close to one side of the tree trunks and swim or pull yourself into the downstream eddy formed by the obstruction. From the eddy, try to climb up onto the strainer so you can look for further opportunities for rescue.

Sometimes a strainer is a confused tangle with no obvious horizontal or vertical main branches, and many of the branches may be protruding toward you. To protect your face and front, you can tuck yourself into a tight ball just before you hit the strainer, and then try to fight your way through the top part of it or over it.

I trust you can see that the best method of survival is to avoid strainers altogether. If you're swimming and you see brush or a log downstream, swim as hard as you can immediately toward shore or toward the middle of the river, whichever you judge to be safer and more reachable at the time. Do everything you can to avoid strainers.

Big Holes Module

Holes, or reversals, are often found just downstream from where the river pours over a submerged rock and at the bases of waterfalls. As the water pours down a waterfall or over the downstream face of a rock, it generally plunges to the river bottom and flows downstream on the bottom for a distance. This leaves a gap or low pressure zone on the surface of the water at the base of the falls or rock. This gap is filled by white, aerated foam rising and flowing upstream, forming a treacherous circular motion of water where the two currents meet. (Demonstrate with hands.)

A raft can get stuck, swamped, or flipped in a hole because the downstream water is pushing the raft back upstream, and the water flowing down from upstream is trying to push the boat down and fill it. If your guide yells "highside," stay low in the boat and move quickly to the downstream side. This shifts the weight away from the tube which is being pushed under by the falling water.

A hole can be a very turbulent, confusing, and violent environment. A raft can spin wildly in a hole, so that the downstream side quickly becomes the upstream side. Some call this a "switcheroo," and you need to jump quickly to the new high side to stabilize the boat.

One technique that helps get rafts out of holes is the downstream draw. To "draw downstream," everyone gets knee down on the floor on the down stream side of the boat, puts their armpits over the downstream tube, and does deep draw strokes straight downstream. (Demonstrate.)

If you fall out of the boat in a hole, most of the time you will be flushed out of the hole immediately by the downstream current. Sometimes, however, you can get caught in the reversal and be tumbled round and round. It's like being in washing machine. If you find yourself in this situation swim hard sideways to escape the hole. Sometime just getting an arm out into the main current is enough to pull the rest of your body out of the hole. If that doesn't work, you can try diving and swimming hard downstream to catch the downstream current.

Celebrate the fact that the river of each human soul tends to be deep and wide and multi-layered and ever flowing. It is normal for us to have multiple and even contradictory feelings about issues, ourselves and one another all at the same time. As guides we can model and inspire in others an acceptance and celebration of this ever unfolding, multifaceted, mysterious richness! It is totally OK that at times parts of us don't like certain things about others. As human souls, even with all of our differences, we have an infinite number of things in common. When you have people on a trip who outwardly are very different from one another, you as the guide can in fact use this to enhance the group's experience. First, set an example of finding and focusing on things everyone has in common (as humans in any setting but especially when working together to run a river, we have just about everything in common, fundamentally). Later, as the group's bonds and sense of unity strengthen, appreciate and celebrate the differences—which turn out not to be so different after all. When a group of us humans has a really good time together, our very differences, seen from the perspective of all we have in common, can greatly add to the fun we find in being together!

Be humble, that is, include everyone in your coolness: Perhaps the single most influential thing a guide can do to inspire openness, trust and true camaraderie—and, hence, deep fun—is to simply be humble and appreciate others.

4: RIVER SIGNALS

Introduction

On an early high-water trip on California's class V Forks of the Kern just before the advent of self-bailing rafts, our Avon Pros were brimming half way through the longer rapids. Our runs were completely wild and we were squeaking through, truly, by the skin of our teeth. Now, 25 years later, I still cherish the moment when my life-long river buddy Dan Grant caught my eye from across the river—both of our paddle crews were looking the other way—and we both slid a finger across our bared teeth signaling, "We're making it by the skin of our teeth." Having that communication, and knowing I wasn't alone in my fear and stress, made all the difference!

On the river, where distance and the roar of the rapids can make it impossible for speech to be heard, hand and whistle signals can be useful in all sorts of situations, including coordinating groups of boats, enabling fast, effective responses to life threatening emergencies and making those all important emotional connections.

In the course of my 42 years of river running, I—and many of my boating companions over the years—have adopted the "language" of hand and whistle signals shown on these pages. Some of these signals were already universal; many are based on signing, the language of the deaf; and we've tried to make as many as possible intuitive, that is, understandable at first glance. Like any language, this one is ever evolving; and I welcome suggestions for improvements and additions, which I hope to incorporate into a future editions of this book and perhaps a set of laminated cards.

By facilitating clear communication in situations where it would otherwise be impossible, a widely used language of hand and whistle signals can enhance cooperation and good will within and between boating groups, and help make all of our river journeys safer, smoother and more fun.

Two key points:

–Signals should be used only in earnest and never in jest. For example, never use signals to lure people into water fights. If we have to first determine whether or not a signal is meant seriously or as a joke, precious time could be lost in situations in which every second counts.

–Always acknowledge receiving signals with a wave or an OK signal, and pass signals on to more distant boats or people whenever appropriate.

UNIVERSAL SIGNALS

Single medium to long blast: Pay attention to me for more signals, possible emergency.

Three blasts repeated or three short bursts and three long blasts followed by three short bursts: SOS, Mayday, universal distress signal.

Also see whistle signals for blind swimmers.

WHISTLE SIGNALS

A paddle held with blade up or an arm held straight up means go down the center. If the paddle or arm is angled 45° one way or the other, go down the side indicated.

POINT POSITIVE

Note: Always point in the direction you do want someone to go, never in the direction you don't want them to go. Turn paddle blade flat to receiver for maximum visibility.

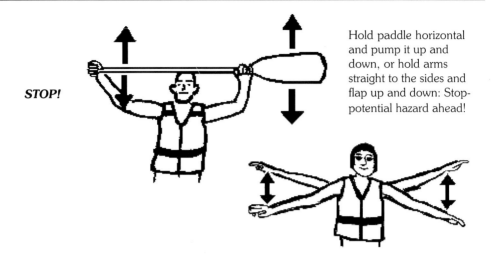

STOP!

Hold paddle horizontal and pump it up and down, or hold arms straight to the sides and flap up and down: Stop-potential hazard ahead!

HELP/ EMERGENCY

While giving three long blasts on your whistle, wave a paddle, life jacket, helmet or hand over your head in a big arc from side to side: If you don't have a whistle, use the visual signal alone: Help-emergency-assist the signaler as quickly as possible.

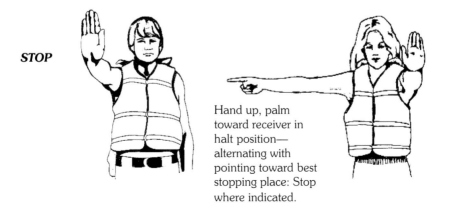

STOP

Hand up, palm toward receiver in halt position—alternating with pointing toward best stopping place: Stop where indicated.

With arm forming an O, repeatedly lift and tap finger tips on top to head or helmet: are you OK?

ARE YOU OK?

Form an O with one arm with fingers touching top of head or helmet.

I'M OK

Form O with thumb and forefinger: OK. Also, you're looking good. (If last signal was come closer or move back, this means position is now good— you've moved far enough.)

OK

Form an O over head with both arms: OK. Same as smaller OK, but easier to see at a distance.

LONG DISTANCE OK

YES

Nod your head up & down.

LONG DISTANCE YES

With profile toward receiver, swing both arms, preferably with a bandana or other cloth in hand, up and down together in front of you: Yes.

NO

Shake head from side to side.

LONG DISTANCE NO

Facing receiver, swing both arms, with a cloth in hand, from side to side in unison: No.

GROUP MODES OF OPERATION

Hold paddle vertical with blade up. At a put-in eddy, for example, after each crew completes their in-boat training and their boat is fully prepared to go (all lines are coiled and up off the floor, everyone's life jacket is fastened and snug, etc.) the captain sits with her or his paddle vertical with blade up. Oar boat guides hold up an arm. When all of the boats in the group are making this signal, the trip leader knows everyone is ready to pull out into the current together. A very useful signal!

OUR BOAT IS READY

With a questioning look, sender holds thumb up and points at receiver with index finger.

ARE YOU READY?

With fingers folded, hold thumb straight up: We're in good shape. Also, we're ready and raring to go.

WE'RE READY

ONE MINUTE

Single, vertical forefinger: Wait one minute; or get ready to go very soon.

CAN PROCEED SHORTLY

Arm extended horizontally to side: Can proceed shortly.

WAIT FIVE MINUTES

Make "stop" signal with one arm while indicating number of minutes to wait by holding up fingers and thumb of other hand. Three digits means wait three minutes, etc.

WE'RE GOING TO TAKE PICTURES

Hold hands as though holding camera— with one index finger moving: We're going to go downstream and get into picture-taking position.

Moving fist in circular motion like locomotive wheel: Speed up. It's important that we make time.

SPEED UP

"Wiping brow" motion with back of forearm: Slow down, we're getting tired.

SLOW DOWN

Point at your own chest; then, in a down-sweeping motion, point toward receiver: I'm coming to you.

I'M COMING TO YOU

Point at receiver; then, in a down sweeping motion, point to yourself: Come to me.

YOU COME TO ME

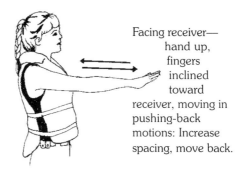

INCREASE SPACING

Facing receiver—
hand up,
fingers
inclined
toward
receiver, moving in
pushing-back
motions: Increase
spacing, move back.

COME CLOSER

Fingers together,
palm toward
sender, hand and
forearm moving in
"come here"
motions: Decrease
spacing, move
closer.

COME HERE ALONG ROUTE INDICATED

Same as above, but at end, point along a particular route (for instance, along the beach or along the river): Come here in manner indicated. If a land route is indicated, walk. If a river route, bring a boat (or swim).

GO WHERE INDICATED

Point first at receiver, then toward some other location, such as someone or something needing rescue: Go provide assistance or rescue as indicated.

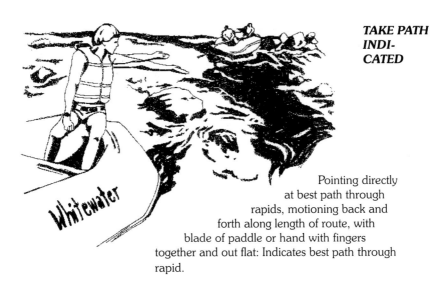

TAKE PATH INDICATED

Pointing directly at best path through rapids, motioning back and forth along length of route, with blade of paddle or hand with fingers together and out flat: Indicates best path through rapid.

COPING WITH DROPS

EDDY OUT

With upraised finger make circles in a level plane: Eddy out.

SCOUT

Flat, horizontal hand at brow, sometimes with slight forward and back motion: Scout. Usually combined with a stop or eddy out signal and an indication of which bank on which to stop.

LOOK

With index and middle fingers forming a V, point to eyes then twist and point out: Look

Open, flat hand, palm up, moving in up and down, carrying motion above shoulder: Portage

PORTAGE

With lifted foot, make a vigorous mid air kick toward the river, as though kicking a raft out into the current: Ghost boat, which means, we're going to push our boats out into the current and let them float empty through the rapid.

Note: Obviously, only ghost boat appropriate rapids with no places likely to hang up boats and with a good place below to recover your boat.

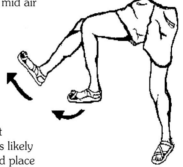

GHOST BOAT

With left hand open palm down & fingertips to right, wiggle fingers of right hand over and down little finger side of left hand: Waterfall.

WATERFALL

RIVER EMERGENCIES

ENTRAPMENT!

One hand pinches throat while the other hand points to victim: Oxygen supply endangered—begin entrapment rescue! One of the most time urgent of all emergencies.

PERSON OVERBOARD

With profile to receiver, make swimming motions in the air: Person overboard. Between every two or three air strokes, with whole arm point toward swimmer.

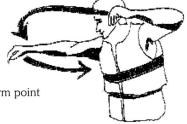

PERSON OVERBOARD

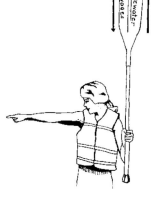

Single vertical paddle with blade up (or a single arm with hand flat and fingers pointed up) moving up and down: An alternate way to say person overboard.

Form a circle with both thumbs and forefingers, hold hands in front of chest: Our boat is damaged.

BOAT DAMAGED

Both palms clasped to forehead: A boat is wrapped.

WRAP

FLIP

Starting with forearms horizontal and pointing to one side with fingers flat and extended, swing forearms up and over 180°: A boat flipped.

SOMEONE MISSING

ARE YOU...MISSING...HOW MANY?

ARE YOU...?

Starting with extended index finger beside head, swing finger down to point toward receiver: Are you...?

MISSING

Start with fingers of right hand slightly spread above encircling left hand. Then drop right hand down from left hand while pressing right fingers together.

(Memory aid: Fingers "disappear" or become missing.)

HOW MANY?

Start with fingers of both hands together, tips up. Keeping palms up, spread fingers with a snap.

YOUR...MISSING...(ONE, TWO) PEOPLE...ARE THERE

YOUR

Point to your
receiver.

Start with fingers of right hand slightly
spread above encircling left hand.
Then drop right hand down from left
hand while pressing right fingers
together.

MISSING

(Memory aid: Fingers "disappear" or
become missing.)

**ONE,
TWO...
PEOPLE**

With one swing of whole arm
up and out representing each
person, count off number of
people. At the same time,
count off number with fingers.

Point to once-missing,
now-found people.

**ARE
THERE**

WE HAVE EVERYONE, OUR GROUP IS COMPLETE

Start with two fists thumbs together knuckles forward. Move fists outward in a circle until the little fingers touch.

WE ARE SEARCHING FOR

With closed hand make big circle two or three times in front of face.

NUMBER OF PEOPLE

With one swing of whole arm up and out representing each person, count off number of people. At the same time, count off number with fingers.

MISSING PERSON WAS LAST SEEN WHERE INDICATED

One hand waves bye-bye over shoulder, while other arm points to location where missing person was last seen.

With arm upraised, the number of fingers held up indicates the number of swimmers.

I HAVE YOUR SWIMMERS

WE NEED...

**FIRST
AID
KIT**

Cross forearms with one forearm vertical, the other horizontal: We need the first aid kit.

AMBULANCE

Make a cross on upper left arm with bunched fingertips of right hand.

PUMP

Keeping hands a few inches apart, move 'em up and down as though operating a pump: We need a pump.

With hands open, flat and level, press palms together repeated: We need repair kit.

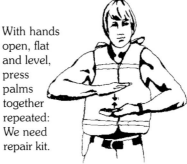

RE-PAIR KIT

LINE

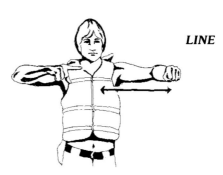

Repeatedly grab and pull on single, outjutting forefinger as though pulling rope out of hand: We need line.

RIVER ETIQUETTE

MAY WE PASS

With both palms toward receiver, move one upwards past the other, as in one boat passing another.

Note: Before asking to pass, have your entire group together and be ready to pass quickly.

PLEASE

Rub palm in clockwise circle against upper chest. (This is a nice signal to add when asking permission to pass.)

YOU'RE WELCOME TO PASS

Beginning with open hand in front of chest, swing your whole arm in broad welcoming gesture in the direction group will pass.

Note: A thumb to your chest followed by an eddy out signal indicates: We'll eddy out soon to let you pass.

Both hands flat with palms toward receiver, fingers up, one hand directly above the other.

Memory aid: If the hands represent boats, one boat is blocking the other.

WE'RE WAITING ON/BEING SLOWED DOWN BY THE GROUP AHEAD OF US

Circle closed hand on chest.

SORRY

Touch the lips with the fingertips of one or both flat hands, then move the hands forward until the palms are facing up. It's natural and OK to smile and nod while making this sign.

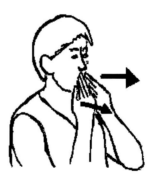

THANKS, THANK YOU, YOU'RE WELCOME

CAMARADERIE & OTHER STUFF

HI

GOOD RUN

With fingers up, knife flat hand straight out from chest, something like a smooth, slow karate chop: My compliments to you on a fine run.

EXCELLENT

With both hands making the OK sign, jerk both hands forward slightly.

Note: Another way to signal "excellent!" is to make exuberant hand-to-head OK signals while dancing around in a circle!

Place the fingers of the right open hand on the upturned left palm. Close the right fingers as they are lifted and touched to the forehead.

LEARN-ING OPPOR-TUNITY

Memory Aid: If the left hand represents a book, the right hand is taking information from the book and placing it into the mind.

Note: A positive aspect of mishaps and mistakes is that they can be valuable learning opportunities.

With hands open, palms in, alternately brush finger tips of both hands upward on chest.

I'M EXCITED

With both palms facing forward and fingers spread to sides, shake in nervous fashion: Nervous.

NERVOUS

For emphasis, open eyes wide.

Hold both hands open, fingers curved and apart, with palms in, one a little below the other, both hands in front of face and drop slowly.

I'M SAD

I'M HAPPY

Brush open hand
up chest twice with
quick, short
motion.

**WE BARELY
MADE IT**

Flat hand or single
forefinger passed
level in front of
bared teeth: We
made it by the skin
of our teeth.

**BE CARE-
FUL**

With both hands flat,
fingers forward,
thumbs up, place right
above left then slowly
circle both hands
forward and
backward: Be careful.

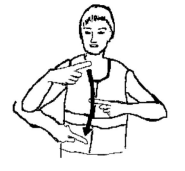

CAN'T

With both index
fingers pointing
toward each other,
strike tip of left index
with tip of right
passing on down:
Can't.

Jerk thumb back over shoulder: Won't.

WON'T

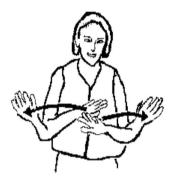

Starting with both hands open, palms down, one on top the other, draw hands forward and apart forcefully: Don't.

DON'T

Straight forefinger pointing into open mouth: We're hungry. We want to stop for lunch, or dinner.

HUNGRY

Head tilted over onto hands, palms together, in sleeping gesture: We want to stop and make camp, or rest.

SLEEPY

WE'RE COLD

Wrap your arms around yourself, making shivering motions, rubbing yourself as though to generate heat: We're cold.

YOU

Point index finger at receiver: You.

CARRY, TRANSPORT

With both slightly curved hands held side by side palms up, move both simultaneously in an arc from right to left, or vice versa: Carry, transport.

DON'T KNOW

Shrug shoulders with palms up: I don't understand or I don't know.

CONFERENCE

One or both arms, beginning wide apart, moving horizontally in broad "come here" motions, with hand(s) almost touching chest at end of each gesture: Conference! Come here fast, grab hold of my boat, and stand by for a conference. The boats furthest away should make all possible speed, so as not to hold up the proceedings.

ERASE

Hand, with palm toward receiver, waved from side to side in easy motion, like eraser on blackboard: Forget last signal.

SOMETHING OF INTEREST

Sight along arm with forefinger pointing (or paddle with handle pointing) at something of interest, such as wildlife, etc.: Indicates something of interest.

OAR OR PADDLE OVERBOARD

Move hands together and apart horizontally, over and over, as though sliding hands along shaft of paddle or oar. Alternately point toward lost item.

CONFIDENCE

With shoulders back and chest out, tap shoulders.

Memory Aid: Strong shoulders suggest the sender assumes responsibility and can be relied on.

PRIDE

Move thumb from belly button straight up center of chest.

Memory Aid: This signal represents the less-than-ideal attitude of, "It's all about me."

FOCUS

Like blinders, vertical flat hands move straight out from both sides of head.

EXPERIENCE

Touching cheek as though stroking beard.

Interlock the right and left index fingers and repeat in reverse: Friend.

FRIEND

Memory Aid: Suggests the link of friendship.

I LOVE YOU

WHISTLE SIGNALS TO ASSIST BLIND SWIMMERS

The blind signals below I created with Phil Wojdak (pronounced wo-jack), a blind Los Angeles district attorney whose hobbies include double-diamond skiing, roller blading and whitewater rafting. Blind swimmers can sense the direction of the current, but need signals telling them whether to swim toward river right or left, ride out the rapid in feet downstream position, or swim for the boat — in the latter case, they need a constant series of signals coming from the boat to guide them all the way back into physical contact with the boat.

Note: • = Short, momentary burst or chirp

     — – Longer (1 - 2 second) blast

Swim toward river left: • • (2 sec. pause) • • (2 sec. pause) • • etc.
  (Memory aid: little = left)

Swim toward river right: — (2 sec. pause) — (2 sec. pause) — etc.

Float downstream feet first: • — (2 sec. pause) • — (2 sec. pause) • — etc.

Swim to me: • (2 sec. pause) • (2 sec. pause) • (2 sec. pause) • etc.

Repeat blind signals at frequent (2 to 3 second) intervals as long as that message stands.

**MORSE
CODE**

To communicate longer messages, such as to a blind person on a mid-rapid rock or in a sheer-walled, inaccessible eddy, use Morse Code:

a • –	s • • •
b – • • •	t –
c – • – •	u • • –
d – • •	v • • • –
e •	w • – –
f • • – •	x – • • –
g – – •	y – • – –
h • • • •	z – – • •
i • •	1 • – – – –
j • – – –	2 • • – – –
k – • –	3 • • • – –
l • – • •	4 • • • • –
m – –	5 • • • • •
n – •	6 – • • • •
o – – –	7 – – • • •
p • – – •	8 – – – • •
q – – • –	9 – – – – •
r • – •	0 – – – – –

SIGN LANGUAGE ALPHABET

When most people contemplate outdoor adventure activities like whitewater rafting, it is entirely normal to experience fear, consciously or unconsciously, on a number of levels. There is physical fear: Am I going to get hurt? Am I going to die? There is social fear: Am I going to be accepted or rejected by this group? And biggest of all, for most of us, are fears around issues of self esteem: Can I do this? Am I OK? Skilled river guides can implicitly assuage all of these fears in the very way they prepare people and guide them down the river. Every trip begins with a thorough safety talk and in-boat training which teach everything trip members need to know to make it safely down the river— thereby addressing physical fear. And by doing this with warmth, caring, good humor and respect, professional guides create an atmosphere of acceptance and support and good fun in which social fears and fears around issues of self esteem melt away.

Seize the moment: Be present in the moment—don't wait for take-out, tomorrow, etc. Whenever you notice yourself thinking about or yearning for take-out or anywhere else, ask, "What can I do right now to make this trip, this moment in this boat, in this camp, more enjoyable, fun, and supportive for all of us?" This is it! There is only now. In a very important sense there is nothing else. Our best option is to be here now!

5: RESCUE

EMERGENCIES

In any emergency, guides take care of the boaters first. For example, when it starts to rain unexpectedly in the middle of the night, guides do *not* simply grab a tarp, cover up, and let everyone else fend for themselves. Rather, they display concerned leadership. Donning rain coats and taking up flashlights, they seek the boaters out, help those that need it put up their tents, give tarps to those without tents—and, if necessary, put up a tarp shelter or raft lean-to.

CARE FOR BOATERS FIRST

In the split second before a flip, nimble guides grab a D-ring or safety line. This keeps them with the raft. Immediately after the flip, while counting heads and tossing loose paddles and other items up onto the bottom of the overturned boat, the guide gives directions and reassurance to the crew, saying things like, "Relax, everything's alright. This is how I always run this rapid." "OK. Move over here away from the downstream side of the raft." "Swim with your feet out in front of you. Use your feet to bounce off the rocks." "Hi. You look so calm and beautiful." If someone is missing, the guide, generally using his or her legs, checks to see if they are caught under the raft. Unless there is an urgent reason for not doing so, the guide rights the boat midriver—or stays with the raft until another boat comes to the rescue or until she or he can beach the flipped boat—either by swimming a line to shore or by crawling up and paddling it ashore.

FLIPS

COUNT HEADS

SAVE PADDLES

GIVE REASSURANCE

RIGHT BOAT OR STAY WITH IT, GET IT ASHORE

After racing to the rescue of a flipped raft, pulling in swimmers and paddles, and taking the cumbersome, upside-down raft in tow, rescue rafts tend to be extremely heavy and hard to stop. If a long calm or large eddy handily presents itself, great. Or, if the river is not too turbulent, the flipped boat can sometimes be righted in midriver by pulling on a line attached to the flipped boat's far side. Often, however, flips occur—and rescues must be performed—when the river is high, fast and rough, when good eddies are scarce, and, perhaps, when the current sweeps through the trees on either bank. In this situation level-headed guides, unless there is a compelling reason to stop immediately at all costs, do *not* power headlong for the bank, where a heavy boat

AFTER QUICKLY PICKING UP SWIMMERS AND TAKING FLIPPED RAFT IN TOW, RESCUE BOAT WAITS FOR LARGE EDDY TO STOP

would be driven into the trees, forced along through the brush and raked by low branches while its crew grabs futilely at passing tree trunks and clamors in pandemonium. Instead, rescue guides stay out in midcurrent, bide their time, speak calming words to their crews, and wait for a large, approachable eddy to come along. Using a downstream ferry, the rescue guide starts very, very early for the eddy, steadily develops more and more momentum, and pops into the eddy at its uppermost end, punching neatly across the eddy line.

TRY TO COPE WITH SITUATION

The vital thing in any emergency is that the guide hang in there, remain outwardly calm (regardless of his or her true feelings), and try—make some kind of effort—to cope with the situation. This *attempt* to handle the emergency is the thing—this is what being a river guide is all about.

Example: A paddle raft flips in a big hole. The crew, after finally swimming ashore, is spread out for half a mile along both banks, while the boat, which was caught in the hole long enough for another boat to approach, has been pulled into a large eddy just below the rapid. The guide (who was unable to stay with the boat in the violent turbulence of the hole) rounds up what paddles and crew members he or she can find, hikes back up to the raft, rights it, and zig zags down the river picking up the rest of the crew and stray paddles.

Another example: A heavily loaded oar boat in sweep position, after having fallen a bit behind and just out of sight of the other rafts, ruptures two air chambers on a sharp rock. The guide rows the listing, water-filled boat to shore as fast as possible, jumps out, tells the two crew members to hold the boat, and runs quickly downstream to get help from the other rafts.

KEEP TRIP MOVING

Whenever possible, Whitewater Voyages guides handle emergencies in such a way that the trip keeps moving with minimum delay. Delays of over two hours are to be avoided.

PROVIDE DIVERSION DURING DELAYS

When a delay is unavoidable, it is combined with something to fill the time and entertain the guests, such as an early lunch, games, or a nature walk. A diversion of some sort during delays longer than a half hour is strongly recommended because it takes everyone's mind off the mishap, prevents a tense, worried mood from taking over, and reassures our guests that we are professionals still very much in control regardless of some temporary problem.

HEAD TRAUMA

When a person receives a blow to the head, check immediately— and repeatedly during the following 24 hours—for signs of head trauma (concussion). These signs include: pupils that do not react or are of unequal size, vomiting, and inability to respond and move appropriately. If these signs appear, get the victim to a doctor as soon as possible.

In the event of injury or loss, experienced guides do everything possible to cope with the situation and ease suffering. They also show all the concern they feel, but they never admit negligence, or say anything that implies that they are to blame. Instead, experienced guides say something like, "We all know whitewater rafting is dangerous, and sometimes these things happen."

NEVER ADMIT NEGLIGENCE

If at all possible, apply no temporary patches. Instead, redistribute people and run the damaged boat as half a raft, a "stub." Or put an inflatable thwart inside the damaged chamber. Or take a half hour to apply a permanent patch.

PATCHING

Except in dire emergencies, do not use duct tape on rafts. The glue left by this tape is extremely difficult to remove—and the tape is seldom effective anyway.

NO DUCT TAPE ON RAFTS

Save *all* of the pieces of broken oars. We can glue or fiberglass them back together.

SAVE BROKEN OARS

EMERGENCY BACKBOARD MADE FROM LUNCH BOARDS

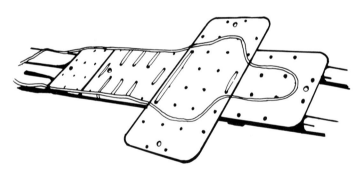

Tightly weave flat nylon line through holes to form backboard shape as shown.

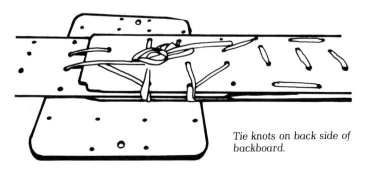

Tie knots on back side of backboard.

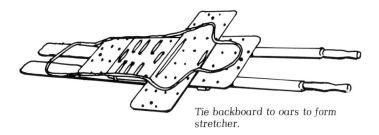

Tie backboard to oars to form stretcher.

Place victim on backboard as shown. Use towel for cervical collar and rolled tarp or sleeping bag around head to prevent all motion of head in relation to body. Secure to backboard in manner illustrated in Red Cross manual.

METHOD FOR WADING ACROSS SWIFT CURRENT

By tightly gripping one anothers' life jackets at the shoulders and keeping the row of people in line with the current, two or more people can wade through very swift water without being swept off their feet.

146   **Whitewater Voyages.com**   The Guide's Guide *Augmented*

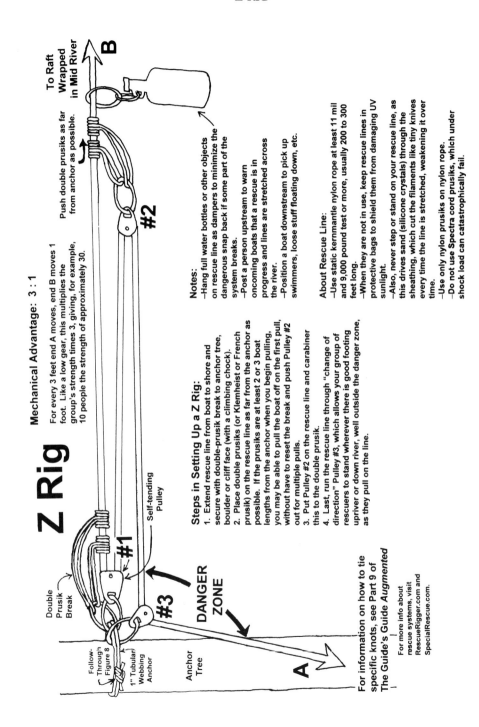

Z Rig

Mechanical Advantage: 3 : 1

For every 3 feet end A moves, end B moves 1 foot. Like a low gear, this multiplies the group's strength times 3, giving, for example, 10 people the strength of approximately 30.

To Raft Wrapped in Mid River — B

Push double prusiks as far from anchor as possible.

#2

Self-tending Pulley

#1

Double Prusik Break

Follow-Through Figure 8

1" Tubular Webbing Anchor

Anchor Tree

#3

DANGER ZONE

A

For information on how to tie specific knots, see Part 9 of *The Guide's Guide Augmented*

For more info about rescue systems, visit RescueRigger.com and SpecialRescue.com.

Steps in Setting Up a Z Rig:

1. Extend rescue line from boat to shore and secure with double-prusik break to anchor tree, boulder or cliff face (with a climbing chock).

2. Place double prusiks (or Klemheist or French prusik) on the rescue line as far from the anchor as possible. If the prusiks are at least 2 or 3 boat lengths from the anchor when you begin pulling, you may be able to pull the boat off on the first pull, without having to reset the break and push Pulley #2 out for multiple pulls.

3. Put Pulley #2 on the rescue line and carabiner this to the double prusik.

4. Last, run the rescue line through "change of direction" Pulley #3, which allows your group of rescuers to stand wherever there is good footing upriver or down river, well outside the danger zone, as they pull on the line.

Notes:

–Hang full water bottles or other objects on rescue line as dampers to minimize the dangerous snap back if some part of the system breaks.

–Post a person upstream to warn oncoming boats that a rescue is in progress and lines are stretched across the river.

–Position a boat downstream to pick up swimmers, loose stuff floating down, etc.

About Rescue Line:

–Use static kernmantle nylon rope at least 11 mil and 9,000 pound test or more, usually 200 to 300 feet long.

–When they are not in use, keep rescue lines in protective bags to shield them from damaging UV sunlight.

–Also, never step or stand on your rescue line, as this drives sand (silicone crystals) through the sheathing, which cut the filaments like tiny knives every time the line is stretched, weakening it over time.

–Use only nylon prusiks on nylon rope.

–Do not use Spectra cord prusiks, which under shock load can catastrophically fail.

Piggyback Rig

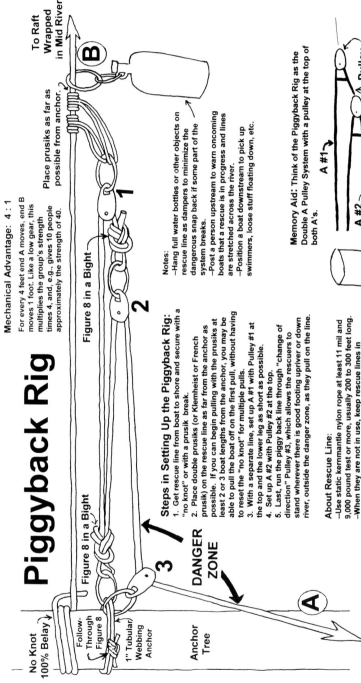

To Raft Wrapped in Mid River

B

Place prusiks as far as possible from anchor.

Mechanical Advantage: 4 : 1

For every 4 feet end A moves, end B moves 1 foot. Like a low gear, this multiplies the group's strength times 4, and, e.g., gives 10 people approximately the strength of 40.

Figure 8 in a Bight

1

Figure 8 in a Bight

2

3

DANGER ZONE

Figure 8 in a Bight

No Knot 100% Belay

Follow-Through Figure 8

1" Tubular Webbing Anchor

Anchor Tree

A

Notes:
—Hang full water bottles or other objects on rescue line as dampers to minimize the dangerous snap back if some part of the system breaks.
—Post a person upstream to warn oncoming boats that a rescue is in progress and lines are stretched across the river.
—Position a boat downstream to pick up swimmers, loose stuff floating down, etc.

Steps in Setting Up the Piggyback Rig:

1. Get rescue line from boat to shore and secure with a "no knot" or with a prusik break.

2. Place double prusiks (or Klemheist or French prusik) on the rescue line as far from the anchor as possible. If you can begin pulling with the prusiks at least 2 or 3 boat lengths from the anchor, you may be able to pull the boat off on the first pull, without having to reset the "no knot" for multiple pulls.

3. With a separate line, set up A #1 with Pulley #1 at the top and the lower leg as short as possible.

4. Set up A #2 with Pulley #2 at the top.

5. Last, run the piggy back line through "change of direction" Pulley #3, which allows the rescuers to stand wherever there is good footing upriver or down river, outside the danger zone, as they pull on the line.

About Rescue Line:
—Use static kernmantle nylon rope at least 11 mil and 9,000 pound test or more, usually 200 to 300 feet long.
—When they are not in use, keep rescue lines in protective bags to shield them from damaging UV sunlight.
—Also, never step or stand on your rescue line, as this drives sand (silicone crystals) through the sheathing, which cut the filaments like tiny knives every time the line is stretched, weakening it over time.
—Use only nylon prusiks on nylon rope.
—Do not use Spectra cord prusiks, which under shock load can catastrophically fail.

Pulley

Pulley

A #1

A #2

Remember: Make the lower leg of A #1 as short as possible.

Memory Aid: Think of the Piggyback Rig as the Double A Pulley System with a pulley at the top of both A's.

For more info about rescue systems, visit RescueRigger.com and SpecialRescue.com.

For information on how to tie specific knots, see Part 9 of The Guide's Guide *Augmented*

Continuous-Loop Load Distribution System
Used to attach a rescue line to a wrapped raft.

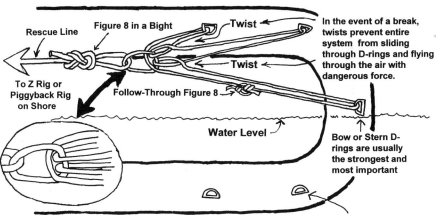

Rescue Line

Figure 8 in a Bight

Twist ←

In the event of a break, twists prevent entire system from sliding through D-rings and flying through the air with dangerous force.

Twist ←

To Z Rig or Piggyback Rig on Shore

Follow-Through Figure 8

Water Level

Bow or Stern D-rings are usually the strongest and most important

Run loop through lower D-rings if possible, but in most wraps they are out of reach underwater.

Steps to Set Up a Continuous-Loop Load Distribution System
1) Run a sturdy line through as many D-rings on the far end of the boat as you can reach.
2) Tie the two ends together with a figure-8-follow-through knot to create one continuous loop.
3) As shown in the diagram above, gather the strands between D-rings together, give one or two a twist as shown, and carabiner them together.
4) Clip this carabiner onto the rescue line.

Notes:
–Sturdy lines 40 feet or so in length work best–this is a good reason to outfit all boats with bow and stern lines suitable for this use.
–Why pull on the far end? D-rings are strongest when the pull is on the sheer of the D-ring patch, and weakest when the pull is straight out perpendicular from the patch. Hence, attaching to the D-rings on the far end of the raft, which pulls on the sheer of the D-ring patches, is best. Also, inflatable boats can handle compression better than stretching, and pulling on the far end tends to compress rather than stretch the boat.
--Hang full water bottles or other objects on rescue line as dampers to minimize the dangerous snap back if some part of the system breaks.

If you are the guide on the wrap rock, your three immediate tasks are:
1) Get your people to safety: Depending on the situation, you may be able to get your crew out of the danger zone by having them hunker down on the far side of the wrap rock, having a second boat catch the eddy below the wrap rock and take them to shore, having them swim, etc. It is often helpful to keep one able-bodied volunteer with you on the rock.
2) Decide on the direction of pull and signal this early on to the rest of your group, so they can begin as early as possible getting into position to free your boat. The key thing here is to go in the direction favored by the current, but also consider distance, accessibility, availability of suitable anchors, intervening obstacles, and what will happen after the boat comes off.
3) Attach a continuous-loop load distribution system to all the D-rings on the far end of your boat that you can reach. Because wrapped and wedged boats can be drawn down below the surface, it is a good idea to do this right away!

It is only normal and human for guides who have just wrapped their boat to feel rattled and self critical. One way to help guides in this situation who might be beating themselves up inside, is to send them the "learning opportunity" and "I love you" signals. Instead of harshly judging one's self, it is better to focus on learning from what happened. And it helps us all, of course, to get the message that we are loved and appreciated, especially when we are down.

Entrapment Rescue Options

by William McGinnis, Whitewater Voyages Guide School

One of the most time critical of all river emergencies! As fast as possible, first, stabilize the victim's head above water, and then free the entrapped limb!

Overall Summary

1. Send entrapment signal and indicate victim's location. This signal, like all emergency signals, is immediately passed on to all boats.

2. Choose the rescue option(s) best suited to the situation, and communicate/coordinate a plan with other rescuers (usually via signals).

3. Jump into the most urgently needed rescue role you can.

4. Secure victim's air supply.

5. Free entrapped limb.

6. Get victim and all rescuers to safety.

7. Be careful! Do not create more victims!

Signal:

One hand pinches throat while the other hand points to victim.

Oxygen Supply Endangered Person Trapped Underwater Begin Entrapment Rescue!

Rescue Team Organization

In entrapment rescues, often there is not time to methodically plan out who will do what. Instead, guides need to quickly assess the situation, enroll and coach able volunteer clients on the fly, and jump in where needed. For example, if a guide already has a team on river left, the next guide to arrive might spontaneously head for river right. And the third guide to arrive, seeing teams on both banks, and realizing, for example, that the river is wider than a single toss bag throw, might quickly prepare and, as he/she floats past (being careful to avoid the victim), simultaneously throw connected toss bags to teams on both banks–and then eddy out downstream ready to pick up the victim, etc. Above all, be careful! It is vital that rescuers no only act quickly but also take care to avoid creating more victims. Some typical rescue team roles:

– **Leader**: Coordinates overall rescue mainly with hand signals. Gets in a high, prominent spot where leader can see and be seen by the victim and all rescuers.

– **Strong Swimmer Rescuer**: Should have quick-release rescue harness life jacket.

– **Line/Belaying Teams**: Depending on power of current, these teams may need from 2 to 10 or more people each. Multiple line/belaying teams may work simultaneously. For example, two teams (one on either bank) can put in place and monitor a Carlson Cinch/stabilization line holding the victim's head above water, while other teams work on a snag/drag line to free the entrapped limb.

– **Person Upstream**: Warns approaching boats that a rescue is in progress.

– **Guide with Boat Downstream**: Waits ready to pick up freed victim, etc.

– **Gofer**: General helper, runs errands, delivers messages, goes and gets things, helps wherever necessary.

– **Client Counselor**: If all other roles are covered, a guide stays with the victim's family and the rest of the group to explain the proceedings; provide reassurance that everything possible is being done; prevent loved ones from taking crazy risks/injuring themselves/interfering with the rescue/adding to the problem/etc.

Keep in mind the old adage: If someone is in the way, give them a job.

The Carlson Cinch

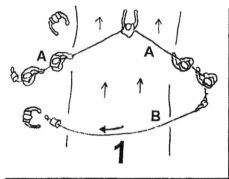

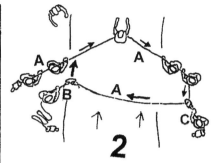

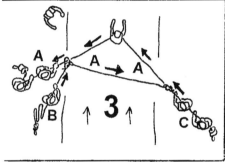

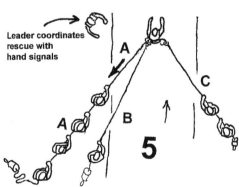

Leader coordinates
rescue with
hand signals

The Carlson Cinch: 1. Toss

Bag B is hooked into the river right end of
Line A, and thrown to river left. 2. Line C is
hooked into Line A while the river right end
of Line A is pulled to river left by Toss Bag
B. Line A is then clipped to itself on river
left. 3. & 4. Lines B & C are slowly let out
while Line A is pulled in, cinching Line A
tightly around victim. 5. Once Line A is
cinched tightly around victim, the primary,
strongest pull must be continuously applied
to Line A. Pulling too hard on lines B or C
could loosen the cinch and cause it to slip
off the victim. All of these steps must be
done with great care, all the while making
sure the victim's head is stabilized out of
the water and making sure the line does not
slip off the victim.

In some cases one Carlson Cinch will enable rescuers to pull a victim
upstream enough to free the entrapped limb. In other situations, a closely
monitored Carlson Cinch–or simple stabilization line–is used only to stabilize
the victim's head above water, while a snag/drag line–or second Carlson
Cinch–is used to free the entrapped limb.

Line Crossing Options:
Mid River Double Toss-Bag Throw

As the boat passes down the middle of the river (being careful to avoid the entrapment victim), two connected toss bags are thrown simultaneously to people on each bank. To prevent the lines from raking the raft, they should be thrown from the boat's upstream end. Angle throws slightly downstream to provide more time for the grabbers to grab before the ends are pulled off and away downstream by the current. Also, the grabbers can greatly increase their chances of a successful catch by extending their reach with an outstretched paddle handle with t-grip end pointed up as a hook.

Another option: Paddle the end of a long line from bank to bank across the calm above the rescue rapid. Two teams, one on each bank, then walk the line down into position, maintaining tension to keep the line up out of the river. Inevitably, at times the line will sag into the river which will exert a tremendous pull–and both teams will have to pull very hard to lift the line free.

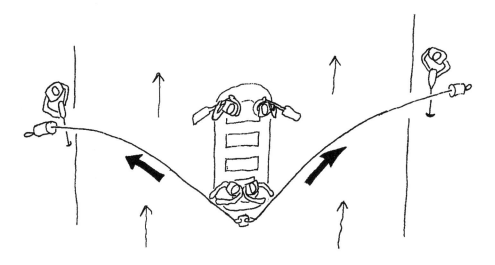

Strong Swimmer Rescue

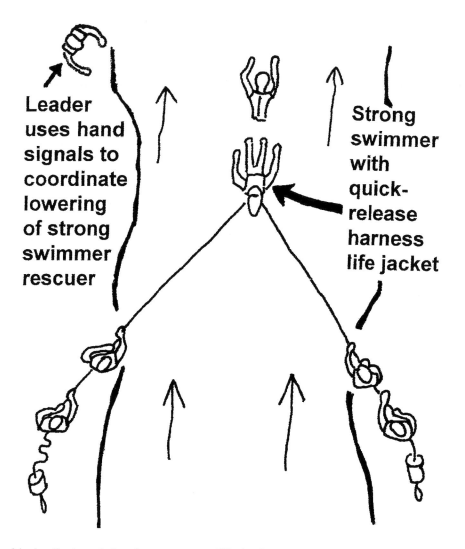

Leader uses hand signals to coordinate lowering of strong swimmer rescuer

Strong swimmer with quick-release harness life jacket

Clipped in by their quick release rescue life jacket, a strong swimmer rescuer is carefully lowered down current to the victim. A cinch is passed around the victim's torso and hooked into the rescuer's quick release harness. Next, the rescuer and victim are pulled back upriver far enough to free the entrapped limb. And lastly, the rescuer and victim are swung in to shore. Even the strongest strong swimmer rescuers become rapidly exhausted and must be ready to pull their quick release if necessary.

Stabilization & Snag/Drag Lines

First, secure the victim's head above water with a stabilization line–carefully monitor and adjust this line as necessary to make sure the victim does not slip off and go back underwater. Then, use a snag/drag line to free the entrapped limb. Often, an excellent option is to incorporate these lines into a Carlson Cinch.

Drag lines are weighted with rocks to get them to drop to the river bottom where they can engage an entrapped limb. Unfortunately, drag lines tend to get hung up, so unweighted snag lines are often used. To get snag lines (and also drag lines) to drop to the river bottom, hold the ends below the river's surface just off each bank.

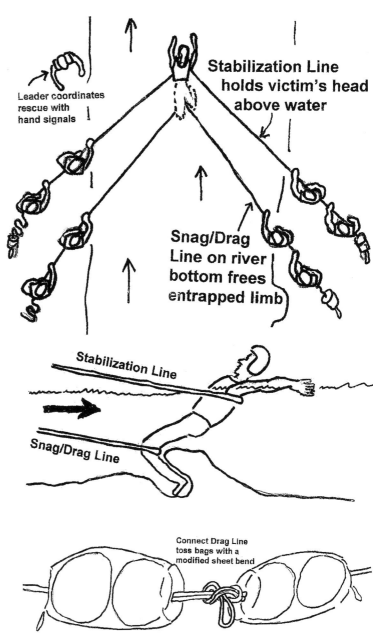

Leader coordinates rescue with hand signals

Stabilization Line holds victim's head above water

Snag/Drag Line on river bottom frees entrapped limb

Stabilization Line

Snag/Drag Line

Connect Drag Line toss bags with a modified sheet bend

To make a drag line, fill two toss bags with big grapefruit-sized rocks and tie the bags together with a sheet bend.

Telpher Lower

1. Extend strong rescue line across river in calm above rescue rapid, and securely belay both ends.
2. Position rescue raft directly up current from victim. Lower boat on pulley held in place either by a prussik or positioning lines from shore.
3. Lower boat down current being careful to reach but not run over victim.
4, Pass harness/loop/cinch around victim's torso.
5. Pull boat back upstream to free entrapment limb & pull victim into boat.
6. Depending on situation, get boat to shore in quickest, safest manner. Run rapid and eddy out or pull boat back upstream and then to shore. Pulling boat upriver is likely to require many, many people plus one or two mechanical advantage pulley systems. One of these pulley systems can be mounted between the cross river line and the boat, the other can be a z-rig or piggy-back rig set up on shore.

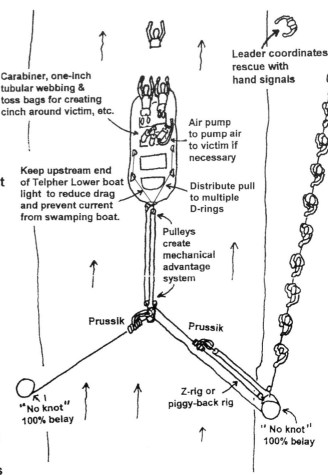

Leader coordinates rescue with hand signals

Carabiner, one-inch tubular webbing & toss bags for creating cinch around victim, etc.

Air pump to pump air to victim if necessary

Keep upstream end of Telpher Lower boat light to reduce drag and prevent current from swamping boat.

Distribute pull to multiple D-rings

Pulleys create mechanical advantage system

Prussik

Prussik

Z-rig or piggy-back rig

"No knot" 100% belay

"No knot" 100% belay

Pump Air to Underwater Victims

In some situations, rescuers can get close to a victim but can not immediately bring them to the surface. In this case, be prepared to pump air to the victim with a raft pump.

Boat Plug: In some situations, lowering a boat and sinking/floor wrapping it above a narrow chute may divert enough water to enable rescuers to free an entrapment victim.

Swiftwater Crossing: The Wedge

Form the wedge on the bank and side step out into the river. The point person calls each step with loud calls such as, "One step to the right." The point person, who faces upstream and leans into the current bracing against the shaft of a paddle in a tripod stance, is supported, held down and kept from being "blown out" by two lines of team members, each of whom stays in the point person's eddy and tightly grips and holds down the person just ahead and the person to the side. Pointed upstream and staying in line with the current, the wedge side steps to a point directly up current from the entrapment victim, and then carefully backs down with one line of team members on each side of the victim. Also, as the wedge backs down around the victim, team members can use their inside hands to free the victim and help them to shore.

Wedge formations, when executed with strength and determination, can cross amazingly deep, fast current and have saved lives. Still, for the wedge team there is inherent risk of foot entrapment and of being "blown out" and washed down river. Always exercise caution and only use a wedge where it is reasonably safe to swim out downstream.

The wedge forms on the bank and side steps into the river.

The point person calls each step.

Important: Keep the two lines tight together and in line with the current!

The wedge sidesteps to a point directly up current from the victim, then backs down with one line on each side of the victim.

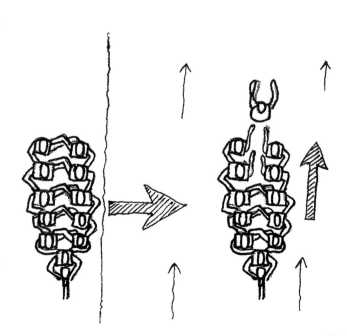

Emergency Evacuation Procedures
Emergency Evacuation Action Plan

The priority is to give the highest level of care and concern for the safety and well being of victims(s), guests, and guides.

1. Stabilize victim(s)   ABC-C (Use protocols below, and reference book in first aid kit as needed). <u>One staff member should stay with victim through entire evacuation process, if at all possible. Use Patient Assessment Form on Sheet 1 to gather important information to send out with the runner.</u>

2. Regroup   If possible and safe, get everyone in one place, in order to communicate the plan, and designate assignments.

3. Gather guides/staff   For brief assessment of situation.

4. Determine action plan   The initial key decisions that need to be made are:

Evacuation Plan A, B, and C. Using the map and information on Sheet 1, the circumstances of the emergency situation, and your best judgement—determine the best evacuation strategy-Plan A. Consider evacuation by road, by trail, by helicopter, or by combination of any or all of these. Critical consideration must be given to the condition of the victim. Can they be moved? If not, helicopter evacuation should be a strong consideration. Evacuate by river only if the injury is minor, if the downstream white water is mild or, if the risk of delay is greater than the major risks of taking an injured person through Class V rapids. Create contingencies based on changes in weather, condition of victim, speed of evacuation, night fall, etc. Outline at least a Plan B, and consider a Plan C. **Make sure runner(s) (and team) are clear on the plan, and that they write it down on the Evacuation Plan A, B, C.**

Send runner(s)/team. See runner packing list below. It is vital that runner(s) have a clear understanding of Evacuation Plan A, contingencies, and as much information on the victims(s) as possible (e.g., Patient Assessment).

Other key staff assignments
-Victims care (should be one person from site to hospital)
-Care of relatives/friends of victim
-Communication with guests, and look after their needs (trip leader if possible)
-Big picture (food/warmth/shelter/safety of group)
-Consider guest assignments. An old bit of wisdom: If someone is in the way, give them a job.

5. Communicate the plan to the guests and ask for their patience, understanding and assistance.

6. Implement the plan

Runner Packing List
*Patient Assessment Form, Evacuation Plan, and Evacuation Information (and Map)
*Coins/phone card for pay phone
*Lifejacket (for flagging down help)
*Hiking first aid kit
If overnight is possible or likely:
*Matches
*Water, food
*Flashlight and flare
*Emergency blanket, sleeping bag, dry clothes

ABC-C Protocols
A - Establish/maintain airway
B - Breathing
C - Circulation/stop bleeding
C - Cervical immobilization if suspected neck injury. Emergency back board.

Evacuation Plan A (write it down!!!):_____

_____
_____
_____
_____
_____
_____
_____
_____
_____
_____
_____
_____
_____
_____
_____
_____
_____
_____
_____
_____

Plan B...if, _____

_____
_____
_____
_____
_____
_____
_____
_____
_____
_____
_____

Plan C...if,_____

_____
_____
_____
_____
_____
_____
_____

Patient Assessment Form

After conducting a primary survey (ABC-C) and the patient has been stabilized, use this form to gather further information, and to assist you in performing a secondary survey. Use this form to inform the hospital, ambulance, sheriff or search and rescue emergency medical personnel of the situation.

Name of Patient _____

Age_____ Sex _____ Weight_____

Chief complaint _____
_____

Level of Distress (Circle one):   Mild~Moderate~Severe~Unconscious

What happened? (Medical or Trauma) Describe briefly the events leading up to the accident.
_____
_____
_____

Is the patient taking any medications? (Check for medic alert tags)
_____

Does the patient have any known allergies? If so list here:
_____

Initial vital signs (monitor regularly, and note changes):

Pulse_____ Respirations_____ BP (If possible)_____

Temp_____ Pupils_____ Skin Color _____

Level of Consciousness (monitor and note changes very closely in case of head injury)
_____
_____
_____

Describe any other problems here, such as deformities, areas of pain or tenderness. Check distal pulse to any suspected fractures of extremities, and make note of it here.
_____
_____
_____
_____
_____

This is a sample of what you might prepare for each river or run:

Whitewater Voyages
Emergency Evacuation Information
Tuolumne River

Priority Phone Calls

Tuolumne County Sheriff **911** or	(209) 533-5911
Groveland Forest Service	(209) 962-7825
Stanislaus NF Dispatch	(209) 533-1130
High Sierra Office/House	(209) 555-0851
Satellite Phone	(254) 555-5555
Manager's Cell	(415) 555-5555
Main Office **(800) 400-7238** or	(510) 222-5994
Mid Sierra Office	(530) 555-7215
Bill McGinnis (Home)	(510) 555-5555
Alternates:	
Sonora Ambulance	(209) 532-8101

Nearest Phones

1. Residence on Ferretti Road
2. Residence at the top of Tuolumne Power House Rd.
3. Residence at the top of Indian Creek Confluence
4. Wards Ferry Bridge. If no vehicle transportation is available, hike road north (river right) to ridge-top residence.

Casa Loma Store	(209) 555-5555
Casa Loma Payphone	(209) 555-5555
Tuolumne River Shuttles	(209) 555-5555

Trail Escape Routes

1. From Lumsden put-in to the confluence of the Clavey River: The best route out is going upstream along the south (left) bank of the river, until you can get up tp Lumsden Rd. Follow Lumsden Rd. west to County Rd.
2. Directly at the Clavey confluence, you can take the Hamby Trail on the south bank up to the ridge-top fire road. Turn left and follow the fire road to a trailer residence on Ferretti Rd. Estimated hike-out time to contact is 1.5 hours.
3. Clavey River Confluence to Indian Creek Confluence. Unmaintained fishermens' trail runs parallel to the river on the south (left) bank. An abandoned road reaches the river on the south side of the river at Indian Creek. (Tuolumne Powerhouse Rd). Follow road to ridge top or barn. Turn right into residence. Estimated hike out time to contact is 1.5 hours.
4. Indian Creek Confluence to Mohegan Mine (old foot bridge). Float to foot bridge, take trail up south (left) side to unmaintained jeep trail. Follow jeep trail to ridge top and continue in a southerly direction to residence on right. Estimated hike-out time to contact is 2.0 hours.
5. Mohegan Mine to Wards Ferry Bridge. Raft to bridge. If no available transportation, hike road on north (right) side to ridge top residence. Estimated walk-out time is 1.5 hours.

Nearest Medical Facilities

Sonora Community Hospital
One North Forest Rd.
Sonora (209) 532-3161

Directions:
* Take Wards Ferry Rd. north and follow signs to Sonora
* At Highway 108, go west into Sonora
* Take a right onto old Highway 108 (DO NOT continue WEST on the new 108 bypass past Sonora!)
*Go right on Stockton St. in downtown Sonora (at signal near Sonora Inn)
* Go right on Forest Rd. and follow signs to hospital.

> Important note: The information contained in this Emergency Evacuation Kit is accurate to the best of our knowledge at the time of printing. However, this information may be neither completely accurate nor current. The best preparation for emergency evacuation is firsthand knowledge. Hike the trails, find the phones, know the helicopter landing zones, check priority phone numbers for changes—before an emergency. Use all of the information contained in this Emergency Evacuation Kit at your own risk.

Helicopter Evacuation

Tuolumne County Sheriff (911) will contact the closest airborne transport. Be as specific as possible with the Sheriff dispatch. Use the Patient Assessment form and the Emergency Evacuation Plan you have outlined. Dispatcher will determine the need for a helicopter.

Vital Information to Communicate:

• **Your name, phone number and location you are calling from**
• **Emergency situation: medical or trauma**
• **Patient assessment (see Patient Assessment Form)**
• **Exact location of victim/ accident (use geographic clues)**
• **Time accident took place**
• **Evacuation plan of action**
• **Specific request for assistance (helicopter, etc.)**
• **Stay on the phone line, until they hang up!**

© Copyright Whitewater Voyages, 2005

Trip Leader's Emergency Evacuation Sheet
Big Picture Considerations

Remember the most important priority is for you and your staff to demonstrate the highest level of care and concern for the safety and well being of the victim(s) and guests, and to transport the victim(s) with all due speed to professional medical care.

When dealing with a serious injury or a fatality, it is important to communicate courteously, honestly and professionally to the group. Here are some guidelines to assist you and your staff in communication.

Do:

—Whatever you can to have the most (medically) qualified staff member stay with the victim all the way into the emergency room. This is probably the most important factor in avoiding a law suit
—Tell the group the general plan for evacuation
—Tell the group you are doing the best you can to get help for the victim
—Tell the group you are in a remote situation, and it could take some time to get out
—Show empathy and sympathy for what victim(s) and their family and friends are experiencing
—Gather as much information about the facts of the accident as you can. Use the Trip Leader Journal, and all of the appropriate forms included in this packet
—Take written witness statements
—Encourage each guide to write down their own written account of what happened. Again, stick to the facts
—Use the following basic guidelines in your written reports:

> What happened? Where did it happen?
> When did it happen? Who did it happen to?

—If written statements are not possible or appropriate, take verbal statements, and make notes on your TL journal
—Avoid any statements that may be damaging later on
—Take pictures of the accident site and victim if possible
—Maintain a high level of care and concern for the well being for the rest of the group
—If questions about how the accident could have been prevented arises—talk only about what the guest(s) could have done differently (e.g. swim harder for the eddy, grab the toss bag line, etc.)
—If the question arises about refunds/ trip credits—tell guests that our office staff is very fair, and will gladly answer any questions they may have

Do not:

—Make guarantees of a speedy evacuation—even a helicopter evacuation can take far longer than one might think
—Say or write anything that may be damaging later
—Put in writing any analysis of why an accident happened
—Make admission of guilt, wrong doing, or negligence
—Make value judgements or statements about what happened
—Write anything but the facts on any of the reports (no feelings or judgements)
—If questions about how the accident could have been prevented arise, do not talk about what the guides might have done differently. Such speculation could be damaging later on
—Forget about the highest care and well being of the rest of the group
—Promise refunds or trip credits

Dealing with the Media

—It is important and appropriate to withhold the name of victim(s), pending notification of next-of-kin
—Do not deny the accident occurred
—Do not speculate. When the answer to a question is not known, state that it is not known
—NO ONE, including a company spokesperson, should release information that identifies responsibility for the accident without first consulting legal council
—**See "Notes on Handling the Media" on next page.**

Dealing with a Fatality

—Names of deceased persons, must first be released by a Coroner's Office, after notifying next-of-kin
—Do your best to console the friends and family of the deceased, expressing your sorrow and sympathy for their grief
—It is important to recover the body, and get it out of the water if at all possible

Insurance and Helicopter Evacuation costs

Helicopter evacuation is expensive. Here are a few things to remember if the question arises of who will bear the cost of the helicopter evacuation:
—Most importantly, this question of cost should not slow down the evacuation process in any way.
—This is a good time to get information about the victim(s) personal insurance carrier, which often times will cover the costs of evacuation.
—Often times, the county of a victim's residence will have emergency evacuation coverage.

The Aftermath: Notes on a thorough and professional follow-up

Once the evacuation is complete, and the trip is over, it is important to make sure that thorough follow-up of the accident is carried out. As trip leader, you should take responsibility for seeing this process through. Here is a guideline and some notes to assist in a complete follow-up.

—Schedule a debriefing meeting as soon as possible after the trip

If possible, have someone from the main office attend and facilitate this meeting. Ideally, this person will be the owner, general manager, or the person who will be working closest with the insurance agencies and other authorities in the follow-up. All staff who were involved in the accident should attend this meeting. One of the primary purposes of this meeting is to begin an important foundation of mutual support for yourself and your staff. Everyone should have the chance to talk about the facts, as each person saw them unfolding. The first person to speak should be the person most directly involved.

—Compile your written report

Immediately! Your written report will include:

-Trip Report (**with release form of injured party)**
-Trip Leaders Emergency Evacuation Journal
-Witness Statements
-Any other forms required for the specific river

—Fax your report to the main office

Within 24 hours, for immediate distribution to:

-Local Sheriff/Authorities
-Managing Agencies of the river (BLM, USFS, etc.)
-Worker's Comp/Insurance Agents*
-Other required agencies for the specific river

Note that someone in the office, either the owner, general manger, or office manager will take responsibility for handling the report to workers' compensation and the insurance carrier. The trip leader should clarify who in the office is doing this, and make sure that whoever it is, has everything they need and has a clear understanding that it must be done immediately.

—Contact the victim(s) family

At least one guide from the trip, preferably the guide most directly involved with the accident or victim, should personally contact the victim(s), and/or their family to check on their progress, and express our continued concern and sympathy. This may include a visit to the hospital, and should happen as soon and as often as appropriate and possible.

—Notes on handling the media

One person, usually the owner or manager, should be designated to handle all inquiries from the media. Others should resist the temptation to be an "expert" and should instead simply refer all media calls to this designated contact person. If asked about the accident, persons other than the media contact person can say something like "**yes, we did have an accident and there was an injury/death on the "X" river. That's all I really know. The person who has all of the facts is the Owner/ Manager, and I am sure he/ she will answer your questions as best as he/ she can. His/ her phone number is "X"."**

The overall goal vis a vis the media is to honestly share all the facts in a non-sensational, non-dramatic manner. In other words, we want to stick to the facts—and remove the story, the sensation, the drama. Instead of going into detail about how, after a boat hit a rock and flipped, the powerful current sucked a person down, and they struggled and tumbled in the current... and we tried valiantly to rescue them for hours, etc. etc. It would be better to simply say **"Yes, we had an accident on the "X" river. A boat turned over and a person was drowned."** End of story. No story. OUR message needs to be: There is no front page (or even back or inner page) story here.

Names of deceased persons must first be released by the coroner's office. It could even be grounds for a lawsuit if one were to release the name before the coroner. The goal is to make sure the next-of-kin are notified in person before the news goes out through the media.

—Emotional turmoil, self-forgiveness & the healing process

In the terrible emotional turmoil following serious injury or death, there is a natural tendency for guides and trip leaders to blame themselves, to feel responsible, to replay the event over and over in their minds wishing they had done things differently. Here are some crucial steps in the healing process: Realize that these thoughts and feelings are completely normal and are in no way, in and of themselves, an indication of wrong doing or negligence. Realize that part of the inherent risk in rafting is the fact that the guides, being human, occasionally misjudge rapids, blow maneuvers, and make other mistakes. Be aware that hindsight is 20/20, and no one could have known ahead of time the exact events preceding the accident would turn out as they did. **Everyone involved in the accident is highly encouraged to consider Post Traumatic Stress Counseling.**

Trip Leader's Emergency Evacuation Journal

_____

_____

_____

_____

_____

_____

_____

_____

_____

_____

_____

_____

_____

_____

_____

_____

_____

_____

_____

_____

_____

_____

_____

_____

_____

_____

_____

_____

_____

_____

_____

_____

_____

Report of Injury to Client or Guest

This form must be completed and faxed to the main office within 24 hours of your return from the river, along with the Release Form of the injured party, witness forms, and any other pertinent information. In the case of emergency evacuation a Patient Assessment Form must also be included. All injuries must be reported- No matter how small!!

Date and time of injury: _____/_____/_____@_____am/pm   **River:** _____

Trip Leader: _____ Guide: _____

Exact location on river injury occurred: _____

Full name of injured person: _____

Date of Birth: _____/_____/_____

Home address: _____

City, State, Zip: _____

Home Phone: _____ Cell Phone:_____

Email Address: _____

Weather conditions: _____

Nature of injury: _____

Describe how injury occurred: _____
_____
_____

Describe action taken and first aid rendered: _____
_____
_____

Where was the injured party taken? _____

Did the injured party contribute to the accident?   ☐ Yes   ☐ No

Were there other contributing factors? Explain.
_____
_____
_____

Signed:

Trip Leader _____ Date: _____/_____/_____

Guide: _____ Date: _____/_____/_____

Area Manager: _____ Date: _____/_____/_____

General Manager: _____ Date: _____/_____/_____

Note key witnesses on the back of this form, and if possible have them complete witness forms.

Witness of accident or injury

Name: _____ Phone: _____

Address: _____ Cell:_____

_____ Email:_____

Name: _____ Phone: _____

Address: _____ Cell:_____

_____ Email: _____

Information on any government agency employee(s), law enforcement person(s), or other accident response person called to the scene of the accident, or that may file a report.

Name: _____ Phone:_____

Address: _____ Cell: _____

_____ Email:_____

Information on other employees directly involved with the accident and/or treatment, transportation, etc. of injured party.

Name: _____ Phone: _____

Address: _____ Cell:_____

_____ Email: _____

Name: _____ Phone: _____

Address: _____ Cell:_____

_____ Email: _____

Name: _____ Phone: _____

Address: _____ Cell:_____

_____ Email: _____

Report of Injury to an Employee

This form is due within 24 hours of your return from the river. If this is incomplete, benefits will be withheld until it is completed correctly. It is the injured parties responsibility to make sure this form is received in the main office. If this injury is serious and needs further medical attention it is imperative that you inform your area manager. All injuries must be reported—no matter how small!! Note key witnesses on the back of this form, and if possible have them complete witness forms.

Date of injury:_____   **Time injury occurred:** _____

Trip leader: _____   **River:**_____

Injured Employee Full Name:_____

Date of Birth:_____ / _____ / _____   SS#:_____ - _____ - _____

Home Address:_____   Phone Number:_____

_____   Cell Phone: _____

_____   Email: _____

Information about injury. Please be brief and accurate.

City and County of occurrence:_____

Was guide on the river when the injury occurred?   ☐ Yes   ☐ No

Did injury occur on Whitewater Voyages' property?   ☐ Yes   ☐ No

Describe injury and explain how injury occurred:_____
_____
_____

Location of injury on the body: _____

Object or substance that directly injured guide: _____

Information about treatment

Was guide seen by physician?   ☐ Yes   ☐ No

Physician's Name: _____   Physician's Phone: _____

Address: _____

Will guide lose any days of work due to this injury?   ☐ Yes   ☐ No   How many? _____
Did guide receive full pay for the injury occurred?   ☐ Yes   ☐ No
Was another person responsible for this injury?   ☐ Yes   ☐ No   Who?_____

Signed:

Area Manager:_____   Date:_____ / _____ / _____

Injured Employee:_____   Date:_____ / _____ / _____

Witness of accident or injury

Name:_____   Phone:_____

Address:_____   Cell:_____

_____   Email: _____

Information on any government agency employee(s), law enforcement person(s), or other accident response person called to the scene of the accident, or that may file a report.

Name:_____   Phone:_____

Address:_____   Cell:_____

_____   Email: _____

Information on other employees directly involved with the accident and/or treatment, transportation, etc. of injured party.

Name:_____   Phone:_____

Address:_____   Cell:_____

_____   Email: _____

Name:_____   Phone:_____

Address:_____   Cell:_____

_____   Email: _____

EMERGENCY EVACUATION KIT

WITNESS STATEMENT

Our professional trade association requires us to collect witness statements as part of the procedure for properly documenting any emergency situation. Thank you for your assistance.

DATE OF ACCIDENT:_____   DATE OF STATEMENT: _____

INJURED'S NAME:_____

WITNESS NAME:_____
PERMANENT ADDRESS:_____
HOME PHONE: _____ BUSINESS PHONE:_____
EMAIL: _____ CELL:_____
AGE:_____   OCCUPATION: _____

TEMPORARY ADDRESS:_____
UNTIL:_____ PHONE:_____
RELATIONSHIP TO INJURED PARTY:_____
SPECIFIC LOCATION OF INJURY:_____

WITNESS STATEMENT: DESCRIBE ACCIDENT CONDITIONS:
_____
_____
_____
_____

WITNESS DESCRIPTION OF INCIDENT:
_____
_____
_____
_____
_____
_____
_____
_____
_____
_____
_____
_____
_____
_____
_____
_____

I HAVE READ THE ABOVE STATEMENT AND I AGREE THAT IT IS A TRUE, ACCURATE, AND COMPLETE FACTUAL REPRESENTATION OF MY OBSERVATIONS OF THE DESCRIBED INCIDENT. SIGNED UNDER THE PAINS AND PENALTIES OF PERJURY, THIS _____ DAY OF_____ _____ 20____.

WITNESS SIGNATURE:_____

STATEMENT TAKEN BY:_____

WHEN TRAGEDY STRIKES: DEALING WITH SERIOUS ACCIDENTS, POST-TRIP DEBRIEFING, REPORTING AND CARE

The following is an outline of a talk given by Bill McGinnis at the America Outdoors' Confluence in Fort Myers, Florida.

Introduction
- So, the accident happened, first aid was given, the evacuation was done. It's at this point that the company owner/manager gets that dreadful phone call.

Feelings
- Potential liability aside, the feelings are unbelievably awful—and the liability worries make these feelings even worse.

- Just as doing CPR on a dummy cannot adequately prepare a person for the real thing, nothing can adequately prepare a person for these feelings. However, if you have some understanding of how awful it is, you'll be better able to:
  1) <u>respond effectively.</u>
  2) <u>get support for your staff and yourself</u>; also, having a glimpse of what others have gone through in similar situations may help.

- So you get the dreadful phone call and you're overwhelmed by awful feelings, what do you do? More immediately to:
  1) Learn and record all the facts.
  2) Support your staff and yourself.
  3) Contact and file accident reports with a number of entities:
     - your insurance company
     - the permitting agency(ies)
     - the local sheriff
     - in California, the State Department of Boating and Waterways
  4) Of course, you will also want to give support to the victim and the victim's family, and you'll be dealing with the press. These will be covered later.

Debriefing Meeting
- You can begin to learn the facts and begin the process of supporting your guides by getting everyone who was involved in the accident together as soon as possible for a debriefing meeting. I'd like to offer some thoughts about debriefing meetings.
  - I recommend that you yourself, as company owner/manager, meet with your guides.
  - One way to begin is to focus on the facts: ask each guide to tell what actually happened, beginning with the person most directly involved.
  - They need to hear from you that self-blaming thoughts and feelings of guilt are completely normal and do not at all mean they were negligent or did anything wrong.
  - One basic reassuring message you can offer: hindsight is 20/20. But no one could have known <u>ahead of time</u> that the particular events preceding the accident would turn out as they did. Really letting this sink in is a key to self-forgiveness.
  - It is important that you set a tone that is <u>supportive</u> and <u>free of blame, judgement, or accusation.</u>

- Eventually in the course of the meeting you will want to cover the specifics of the guide's written statements:
  - Encourage each guide involved in the incident to write an account of what happened, sticking to the facts:
    what happened?
    where did it happen?
    when did it happen?
    to whom did it happen?
  - But let the guides know that they should never deal with the "why" of what happened in writing. They need to be forewarned about the importance of avoiding written statements which could be damaging later on.
  - Many accident forms include some form of the question: "How could this accident have been prevented?" or "How could you have prevented this accident?"
  - In response, the guides should write about what the client could have done to prevent the accident. For example, "the client could have swam more aggressively to the eddy," or "the client could have walked around the rapid."
  - Do not write about what the guide could have done to prevent it. One way to say this to the guides is to advise them to: Truthfully say what happened and stick to the facts—but avoid comments which could be damaging later on. Do not, in the emotional turmoil, admit guilt, cast blame, judge, or accuse.
  - This brings up the whole issue of Discovery, which I'll address in just a bit.

- Another specific issue to cover during the debriefing meeting deals with CPR.
  - If the rescuers did CPR, there is no need to write about the specific details, such as whether or not the ratio of breaths to compressions was exactly by the book.
    All they have to say is: "We did CPR."

- You'll also want to talk about how to deal with the media.
  - Ask all guides to avoid the temptation to be "an expert" in the eyes of the media, and to refer all inquiries about the accident to you (owner/manager) —by saying something like, "Yes, we did have an accident, and someone drowned. I don't really know all the facts. John or Janice, the company owner/manager, will do his or her best to answer all your questions."
  - And brief them on media strategy in a nutshell, which is: reveal all the facts, but take the sensation, the story, out of them.

- There are a few other points to present in the meeting.
  - Stay in touch. Because lawsuits can be filed years later, it's important that guides keep you informed of their current address for years to come.
  - While you have everyone together, plan a date(s), the sooner the better, for meeting with a therapist or psychologist skilled in counseling victims of posttraumatic stress. More about this later.
  - A subject to be thinking about, but maybe to pursue in detail in a later meeting after emotions have had time to heal, is:
  - What can we learn from this experience?
  - How can we improve our operation to reduce the chance of this happening again?
  - I understand that, at least in California, there is a law which prevents changes in one's operation made following an accident from being used in court as an indication of or admission of negligence.

The Issue of Discovery
- What is Discovery?
  - If there is a lawsuit, the plaintiff's attorney, through a process called discovery, can ask for access to any written records that you have pertaining to the accident, such as, trip rosters, signed release forms, brochures, and written statements by guides involved in the accident. The court is likely to grant such access.
  - The only way I know of to prevent these records from being discoverable is to invoke what is called "attorney-client privilege" by having an attorney ask you beforehand to have the guides write the statements. This can be done with a phone call, but a letter is better because it creates a paper trail that can be produced as evidence later.
  - So, to invoke or not to invoke attorney-client privilege, that is the question.
  - I'd say: If all the facts in the case are clearly in your favor, you probably don't need to—and not invoking the attorney-client privilege can show openness and confidence in a strong case—which could discourage the enemy attorney from pursuing the case.
  - However, if some of the facts weaken your case, or could be so construed, it would probably be best to invoke attorney-client privilege. Because most cases have their strong and weak points, I suspect attorney-client privilege is invoked more often than not.
  - A word of caution: Some lawyers will ask you to send them copies of the statement for review—which starts their hourly fee clock ticking big time. I'm not saying don't send it. I'm just saying be careful—and know that you very possibly do not have to start this expensive clock ticking right away.

Contacting and Filing Accident Reports with the Agencies
- As soon as possible after initiating the evacuation, your guides should make the initial calls to the sheriff, the managing agency, and to you.
- You will also want to call your insurance agency as soon as possible.
- Within 24 hours, written reports must be sent to all of these agencies (the agency managing the river, the sheriff, and the insurance company), plus in California, the State Department of Boating and Waterways.
  - The agencies in California ask us to use the Department of Boating and Waterways "Boating Accident Report Form," which is basically a Coast Guard accident form designed for marine accidents between ships. It doesn't exactly fit the circumstances but seems to serve the purpose well enough.
  - The only thing to watch out for on this form is the tricky question: "What could have prevented this accident?" Be careful here not to say anything which could be damaging later on. Focus on what the client could have done differently and not on what your guides could have done differently. No matter how awful you feel in the turmoil following the accident, keep this in mind.

Dealing with the Sheriff or Other Law Enforcement Agencies
- The ideal situation is to have built a relationship of mutual respect and communication with the local sheriff beforehand.
  - We've been working on this in California.
  - For example, my guides and I did a river rescue workshop for the Trinity County Sheriff Department.

- And the outfitters on the Kern River have worked to build closer ties with the sheriff there.
- During an evacuation, of course, the crucial thing is to cooperate fully with any sheriff or deputy on the scene.
- Following an accident, the crucial thing regarding the local sheriff is that the sheriff's report says it was an accident, rather that something else, like negligence.
- The level of interest in a river accident on the part of local law enforcement agencies can vary greatly—some may not show much concern.
- Soon after a serious accident, I recommend calling the main local sheriff.
  - Tell him or her that you're the owner/manager of the company which had the accident.
  - Ask if he or she has any questions that they'd like to ask you, and offer to help in any way they need.
  - This call can be a gesture that is deeply appreciated—and it can give the sheriff an opportunity to resolve any questions or doubts which might otherwise show up in the report.
  - Bear in mind that the sheriff may not know anything about rafting and may be wondering if rafting outfitters are a bunch of lunatics who have no idea what they are doing.
  - Tell the sheriff about your company, about your many years of experience outfitting river trips, about the thousands of people you have successfully taken down rivers, about how your company has run that particular river at much higher water levels, etc.
  - Your goal is to assure the sheriff that you and your guides are responsible professionals who have experienced an unfortunate accident, rather than a bunch of lunatics negligently risking people's lives.

Post-Traumatic Stress
- It seems to me that each of us has within us an unconscious judge which can, if left to its own devices, mete out terrible judgement and punishment.
- A number of years ago, a fourth year guide with another outfitter flipped his oar boat on the class III South Fork American River. In the flip, one of the passengers was struck by an oar and later died. To all appearances, the guide was handling this tragedy extremely well—but within six months he became involved in a terrible car accident which left this formerly handsome young man disfigured. There may have been no connection between the two events, but who can say for sure?
- Had this young man received post-traumatic stress counseling, had he been given more of an opportunity to consciously work through what might have been survivor guilt, or guide guilt, or other harsh inner judgements, perhaps he would not be disfigured today.
- When this accident happened—I think it was in the mid '80's—none of us in California knew about post-traumatic stress counseling.
- Today, in California, and probably in other states as well, most counties now have county-funded Critical Incident Stress Debriefing Teams.
- The sooner guides are brought into this counseling, the better. Go yourself, and participate; talk about your experience. Also, seriously consider getting additional counseling for yourself separately.

If you can say how you feel to at least one other person, it can free you to feel something new.

The goal is to include, accept and appreciate—and to send the message that everyone is truly OK, great and wonderful— just as they are right now! This is one of the most healing of all messages—and puts the group on the path to deep fun!

6: SPECIFICS

COMPANY POLICIES

It is vital that guides protect themselves from the sun's potentially harmful UV rays, which can cause skin cancer and other problems. Whitewater Voyages policy specifies that guides wear adequate sun protection at all times when on the river and out of doors, including sun block, broad brimmed hats and full length clothing to cover arms and legs as necessary.

SUN PROTECTION

Whitewater Voyages staff are hired "at will."

AT WILL

In order to minimize potential injuries, think about the following:

HAZARD AWARENESS

— Move carefully on land, and rocks—don't panic or run in an emergency. Injury to yourself would seriously complicate any rescue efforts already in progress.
— Always wear a life jacket, and helmet when appropriate, on the water and on shore when scouting, portaging, and assisting in safety or rescues.
— High-top shoes with ankle support will help avoid foot injury. Bare feet, and even strap-on sandles, are not recommended. Many guides have received foot injuries while wearing open-toed strap-on sandles.
— Get others to help you lift heavy boxes, coolers and rafts.
— When entering steep drops or big holes, slide off the back tube into the rear compartment to keep from being launched—grabbing a hand hold helps, but getting your weight down into the boat is key. Also, be careful with the grip of your paddle to keep it from smacking you or your neighbor. You can also look down, in case your neighbor's paddle (or elbow, knee, helmet, etc.) comes flying your way.
— In some rapids, guiding from the bow might be safer (practice beforehand a lot).
— Placement of people for safety (for example, neighbors in a crowded stern compartment might fall on your knee and blow it out).

Whenever working with raft glue, glue solvents, and any and all other toxic chemicals and substances, all Whitewater Voyages staff members are required to use our fresh air power respirators.

FRESH AIR POWER RESPIRATORS

GUESTS OF GUIDES & BORROWING BOATS

The family and close friends of our full-time guides may raft midweek only with Whitewater Voyages for half the regular price with firm reservations in advance. On weekends, however, we can not accommodate discounted guide guests, we are just too full. With the prior approval of the area manager, guides may—strictly on rare occasions on weekdays only—borrow our unmarked boats for private trips with family and close friends.

TELL 'EM NOT TO TELL

It is important that all friends, family and lovers paying less than full fare be asked not to tell the other boaters of their discount. Otherwise the boaters could feel excluded from the ''in group'' getting the discount. This could harm the quality of the trip.

GROUP LIMITS

Whitewater Voyages is careful never to exceed government group limits. Exceeding those limits jeopardizes our permits and, hence, the existence of our company. Government regulations state that *all* of our permits can be cancelled if there are violations on any one river. An example of those regulations is the rule on the Merced which limits us to 25 boaters and six guides (one guide for each boat).

BLM TRIP TICKETS

When filling out Bureau of Land Management trip tickets only paying boaters are listed. Trainees, photographers, news people, and others going free are mentioned in a note in the margin, saying something like, "plus one guest."

BOOKING COMMISSIONS

Whitewater Voyages guides may earn travel agent commissions when they book groups or individuals for our trips. But to qualify the clients must be new to Whitewater Voyages and the guide must handle all of the booking arrangements.

CREDIT CARDS

Company credit cards are to be used only for company business. Unless a person is specifically authorized to keep a card for a longer period, all cards are returned to the office as soon as possible after being used for the specific purpose for which it was issued. By the way, when returning from trips do not leave credit cards, checks, cash, etc. in the trip file. Instead, turn them in with the trip report. Report lost cards *immediately* to the office.

RECEIPTS

Without exception, a receipt is obtained whenever company money is spent. Five things should be written on the back of the receipt:
1) name or type of item purchased
2) name of purchaser
3) date
4) whether cash, credit card or check was used. Note: If a check was used, write the check number on the receipt.
5) area of operation

THEFTS

Guard against thievery at all times. On trips, two or more guides sleep on or right next to the rafts. Report all thefts including *full* descriptions, details, etc., to the office with all due speed.

COMPANY POLICIES

At the beginning of the season, all guides must sign a W-4 form and provide the office with three copies of their up-to-date first aid, CPR and, if they have them, WFR and/or EMT cards. Bus drivers must sign a W-4 form and supply copies of their driver's license and health certificate.

W-4 FORM, FIRST AID, DRIVER'S LICENSE

Guides: Throughout the year, please keep the office informed of your current address, email address and phone number. Besides needing to be able to contact you, we want to be able to forward your fan mail.

CURRENT ADDRESS

Nobody—neither guests, guides nor friends of guides—is allowed to bring his own boat on our trips. This also means that no privately-owned boat—rafts or kayaks—are allowed to tag along. Not only do private boats create an extra burden of responsibility and liability insurance problems, they degrade the experience of our clients. Our guests have paid a lot for a professional trip. For someone who has not paid to tag along, often in a smaller boat that might seem more daring and more fun, and to benefit from the security umbrella of our presence and to receive the attention of our guides, makes our guests feel like outsiders. They might also feel a little dumb to have paid dearly for what someone else is getting free. (Of course, we rescue anyone in distress. But we don't escort them down the river unless they are already part way down and unable to proceed safely on their own.) There is an exception to the rule about not allowing kayaks to tag along: If there are boaters at the put-in who don't know the river or if it is a lone boater at the put-in who doesn't want to travel downriver by himself, common river etiquette suggests that we consent to allow them to follow us. But use good judgement and don't encourage tagalongs.

NO PRIVATE BOATS

Another exception to the above rule: On some class IV and V rivers one expert kayaker, at the discretion of the head boatman, may occasionally be allowed to tag along to provide rescue support below difficult rapids and waterfalls.

SAFETY KAYAKS ON CLASS IV & V

Whitewater Voyages doesn't loan or rent equipment. Our equipment is the means of our livelihood. Any use which doesn't produce income for the company isn't a good idea. Exception: We readily assist other rafting companies in any way we can whenever possible. Cover the company name on loaned boats.

NO LOANS OR RENTALS

Guides who wish to take their watertight bags home after trips are encouraged to purchase their own. Under certain special circumstances guides may be assigned items of company equipment on a long-term basis, but this use must be cleared—and signed for—in the office. All such equipment must be returned at the end of the season or whenever the guide will be away for an extended period of time.

COMPANY EQUIPMENT

GOOD DEAL ON WET SUITS

Whitewater Voyages will buy wet suits and booties at wholesale prices for our guides. The cost will be deducted from future pay. Delivery time from the manufacturer is usually six to eight weeks, sometimes more.

GUIDES DON'T USE COMPANY WET SUITS

The company's rental wet suits and booties are to be used by guides only in an emergency, and even then only after checking the wet suit reservation book and obtaining the manager's approval. These wet suits were purchased at great expense to provide a service for our guests. They have a limited life span—especially on rivers. If they are to serve their intended purpose—and if the company is to recoup its investment—they must be used only by the guests.

BE AVAILABLE

We ask guides planning private trips not to lure away other guides during peak periods. Guides who disappear for private trips during peak periods without first getting the approval of their area manager will not be given priority in scheduling.

NO PRIVATE DEALS

Without Bill's specific approval, Whitewater Voyages employees and associates do not strike private deals, run side businesses or rent their own gear out of any location connected with Whitewater Voyages. Such deals can create a conflict of interest. Further more, in El Dorado county, it is illegal to rent out rafting equipment.

NO PRIVATE TRIPS FOR HIRE

Our guides don't conduct trips for hire with contacts made through working for Whitewater Voyages. Also, needless to say, it is not OK for Whitewater Voyages guides to conduct or part-icipate in illegal pirate or bootleg trips, that is, any trip without a commercial permit that is not a truly shared-expense trip. To be legal, all expenses on a private trip must be shared equally by all trip participants. If any participant pays less than his or her fair share or receives pay or equipment in return for "guiding" or "trip leading," the trip is illegal. It is very important that Whitewater Voyages guides not take part in such trips, because, among other things, to do so seriously jeopardizes our reputation with the Forest Service, BLM, and other managing agencies.

STAY OFF RIVER IF SICK

To avoid the spread of communicable disease, guides with diarrhea or any intestinal ailment should stay off the river—and not return until two days after the symptoms have disappeared.

AGE OF GUIDES

At least two-thirds of the guides on each trip must be 20 or older.

AS ALWAYS, ABSOLUTELY NO DRUGS

In our present legal system, we are completely liable if our guides take part in or condone illegal drug use. We can practice every safety precaution and be totally professional in every other way, and still be deemed completely negligent and liable in the event of injury or death if any guide or driver so much as takes a single puff of marijuana or uses any other illegal drug. As a result, our policy is simple and strict: **No drug use**

whatsoever. Of course, we cannot police what our clients do in camp in the privacy of their own sleeping bags. But we must actively discourage any and all illegal drug use whenever we learn of it. We can and should refuse the right to participate in our trips to anyone who will not follow this policy. Explain it in the same way we explain our policy against drinking alcohol during the day—as their choice: They can use drugs and <u>not</u> go rafting, or they can <u>not</u> use drugs and go rafting. Everyone associated with Whitewater Voyages should be very clear on this policy: **Any guide or driver who uses illegal drugs on our trips will be fired with no opportunity for a second chance**.

As of January 1, 1996, both the Federal and California governments enacted a drug and alcohol testing program for commercial drivers. At Whitewater Voyages' expense, drivers must submit to drug and/or alcohol screening tests. All class B drivers will be tested.

ALCOHOL AND DRUG TESTING FOR CLASS B DRIVERS

Drivers who arrive to work under the influence of alcohol, or drink while working will be immediately removed from service and will not be asked to drive again.

DON'T MIX DRINKING AND DRIVING

Guides should limit their intake of alcohol carefully in camp on overnight trips. It is important that guides and especially trip leaders be able to deal with any in-camp emergencies with clear heads. Furthermore, it is important that our guests feel that their guides are clear-headed enough to be able to deal with any emergencies. It's a good thing for guides to be able to relax with our guests and join them in having a beer or wine cooler during happy hour. Please be careful, though, that your alcohol consumption, both during happy hour and at some later time, does not approach the point that either you are becoming intoxicated or that our guests might think you are becoming intoxicated.

GUIDES AND ALCOHOL

HOUSE CODE

Those living on company land are asked to follow this house code. It is hoped that we will create for one another an atmosphere of friendship, sensitivity, and mutual support. We are not rivals or competitors. If we succeed it will be because we cooperate and help one another. Our goal: To learn, grow, feel good, and work hard to provide the finest river trips possible.

WELCOME

Please keep our living areas, bathrooms, parking areas, etc. neat and presentable. Pick up after yourself. Wash your dishes and cooking utensils—plus a few extras—right after eating. In the long run, it takes less energy—and is so much more uplifting—to keep things clean as we go.

KEEP OUR HOME NEAT & CLEAN

A basic guideline: Do your best not to make a mess, and if you do, clean it up ASAP! Do not do mechanical work on personal vehicles or leave old parts, oil, junk or dead vehicles on company property!

DON'T MAKE A MESS

**LAST ONE OUT
LOCKS UP**

The last person leaving the office, warehouse or staff house makes absolutely sure the heater, stoves, air conditioner, lights and other appliances are all turned off, and carefully locks all windows, doors, and gates. In El Sobrante, even if someone is elsewhere on the property, when the office and warehouse are empty lock 'em up tight.

**LOCK UP
AT NIGHT**

At night, both in winter and summer, keep the warehouse and office doors closed and locked. At El Sobrante, at the Kern House, at all company facilities and on all rivers, be vigilant and guard against thievery. Thieves are just waiting for us to relax.

KEYS

With the manager's approval, people living on company land may carry a set of company keys. However, if you are going to be gone for more than a few weeks, return all keys.

PREVENT FIRE

Be especially careful in regard to fire and avoid above all else doing anything that could burn the place down. Never place wood or combustibles on, under or near a wood-burning stove. Please be alert to fire hazards, and correct them or call them to the manager's attention.

**TAKE PRIDE IN
OUR PLACES**

Keep the place neat and clean and well swept. Wash your own dishes immediately after use—don't let them pile up. Regularly clean the facilities you use: Scrub the shower, sinks, and toilet. Pick up any and all litter you see on the grounds or in the warehouse. Be particularly careful to notice and pick up any nails on the ground where vehicles drive. If they seem to need it, water the plants and trees. Generally, take pride in and help keep up the fine places we are so fortunate to have.

**USE THINGS AS
INTENDED,
WHERE
INTENDED**

Use things in an appropriate manner, in their appropriate place. Do not take indoor furniture outside. Do not take bunkhouse mattresses outside or elsewhere.

**PUT TOOLS
AWAY PRONTO**

Return each tool, appliance, utensil, etc. to its proper place immediately after use. If, after finishing with something, you set it down for a few minutes, the chances are increased you will forget to put it away. So put it in its proper spot the instant you finish the task.

**BORROW ONLY
WITH
PERMISSION**

Borrow tools, etc., *only* with the manager's express permission and then return them as soon as humanly possible. If the manager can not be found, permission to borrow anything is denied.

PLEASE

Use company vehicles *only* for company business. After parking our vehicles, unless it is quite hot, keep windows closed.

**CONSERVE
ENERGY &
WATER**

Conserve electricity, gas, and water. Keep the office doors closed to conserve warmth—or, when the air conditioner is on, coolness. Turn out lights when they are not needed—exception: Fluorescent lights require an energy surge to turn on; it is cheaper to leave them on if they will be needed again within the next few hours.

Those living on company land are expected to contribute four full hours per week—in exchange for rent—to warehouse projects such as raft patching, cleaning and maintaining vehicles, and cleaning, painting, and maintaining buildings and grounds. First check with the warehouse manager. Record work in warehouse log. This warehouse work is not to be confused with the everyday housework described above in "Take Pride. . ."

WAREHOUSE & MAINTENANCE WORK IN LIEU OF RENT

Fully record in the phone log—and later pay for—all personal telephone calls made on company phones. Do not tie up company phone lines during office hours.

RECORD & PAY FOR PHONE CALLS IN EL SOBRANTE

In the evenings, the main office is a quiet space for reading, writing, and thinking.

TRANQUILITY

Consider our neighbors: Keep noise and music down low. Don't yell. This is particularly vital from 10 p.m. to 9 a.m.

QUIET

THE WAREHOUSE

Our guides do a thoroughly good job on all tasks. That includes everything from applying a patch to keeping tools and spare parts organized to building a shelf. If a job is worth doing, it's worth doing well.

DO A GOOD JOB

Warehouse work is first cleared with the warehouse manager. Later, after completion, each job is recorded in the warehouse log.

WAREHOUSE LOG

Keep the warehouse and toolroom clean and organized. Return tools to their proper place as soon as you are finished with them. Take a little time whenever you are in the toolroom or warehouse to straighten up things that need it.

KEEP PLACE ORGANIZED

Keep only company gear in the warehouse. Keep the decks clear for action.

NO PERSONAL GEAR

Only if each of us takes a little extra care putting things away and maintaining order can we keep creeping chaos and impending collapse at bay. Like a teeming jungle, disorder surrounds us and is always closing in. Folks, only perpetual vigilance, effort and cooperation on the part of all will keep us from being shut in by ever encroaching clutter.

TAKE A LITTLE EXTRA CARE

Occasionally, the warehouse floor is occupied with raft patching and other projects. This is okay, so long as it doesn't interfere with packing and unpacking for trips. If it does interfere, try to

KEEP WAREHOUSE CLEAR WHEN BUSY

do it somewhere else or wait for a more convenient time.

LOCK UP AT NIGHT Whenever possible, bring all rafts and other equipment inside and lock up the warehouse for the night.

STENCIL ALL GEAR All new boats and other equipment must be stencilled with our company name before taking them on the river. Stencil new wooden equipment between the first and second coats of spar varnish. Using an electric pencil, engrave the company name on all new small equipment. Also, attach our decals.

OBLITERATE CO. NAME WHEN GEAR SOLD Whenever a raft or other piece of gear is sold, paint over the company name. Otherwise the company may be inadvertently charged for user days if the gear is used on rivers we run.

FOUR COATS Give oars and decks three or four coats of spar varnish. Don't put any spar varnish on the oar handles.

WHEN PAINTING Don't use river tarps as drop cloths, and be careful not to splatter paint on river gear.

KEEP LINE When shipping rafts back to the manufacturer, first remove our bow, stern and perimeter safety lines.

ONGOING WAREHOUSE JOBS

—Repair damaged gear.
—Organize and restock first aid kit supplies. Double check kits.
—Organize and restock repair kit supplies. Double check kits.
—Organize and restock peddlers' suitcases with decals, visors, emblem patches, bandanas and a full selection of t-shirts.
—Empty and clean potty cans.
—Replenish supply of brochures on dash boards of all vehicles.
—Wash vehicles inside and out. Check water, tires, batteries, oil. Top off all gas tanks.
—Keep a supply of duffle bags filled with firewood. To this end, cut up scrap wood on hand and make wood runs.
—Organize and restock Friends of the River boxes. Mail letters.
—Organize and restock kitchen box supplies. On a regular basis, thoroughly clean kitchen boxes.
—Once a year refinish all oars, lunch boards, decks and other wooden gear.
—Mend, scrub and organize rental wet suits and booties.
—Refill propane bottles for dishwashing unit and stoves.
—Put away all dry coolers.
—Fill ice trays in freezers.

—Every two months, defrost freezers.

—Restock items such as charcoal, ligher fluid, etc.

—Restencil "Whitewater Voyages" on equipment when the old stencil starts to wear off.

STOVES: KEEP 'EM CLEAN!

We have several 4-burner Cook Partner Stoves. Each stove has its own rocket box, so please keep them together. Also, each stove has it's own propane hoses. It is essential to keep the hoses inside the stove when not in use. This will keep them from getting lost. The stoves will last indefinitely if cared for properly. Never set pots on the sand or dirt and then onto the stove, the sand falls into the stove and clogs it up. Either rinse off the bottoms if you have no alternative, or set the pot on a cutting board or something else that is clean. We all need to do this for it to be effective. It also looks bad to clients to see their food being cooked on unclean surfaces.

JON-NY PARTNER PORTA-POTTIES

We use Jon-ny Partner porta-potties on the Tuolumne, Merced, and Middle Fork American. The Jon-ny pot is a 20-pound aluminum box, measuring about 18 inches tall. It comes with a toilet seat and an aluminum cover that snaps into place using clamps. When properly closed, the rubber gasket eliminates any leakage, even when turned upside down. There is a 5-pound pressure relief valve for the release of any excess gas pressure. The Jon-ny pot has a capacity of 50 to 60 days for 1 person so that means about 25 to 30 people for 2 days and 16 to 20 people for 3 days.

The Jon-ny pot must be emptied at either an approved RV dump station or at an authorized disposal site. It is illegal to dump human waste in a landfill! Trip leaders need to be aware of where the approved dump sites are for the river they are working. In the High Sierra, there is an RV dump facility on Garotti Grade (old Hwy. 120 just east of Groveland) and another one in Big Oak Flat.

To empty the Jon-ny pot, use the giant funnel and hose set-up so that the waste empties out through the set-up and you don't have to do anything but hold the sealed Jon-ny pot inverted. Disposal works best if the consistency of the waste is that of a slurry. To achieve this it's probably best to suggest that the women on the trip can pee directly into the pot but the men should pee off to the side. If you're on a trip that's really small and the women can't create enough of a slurry on their own, perhaps everyone should pee in the pot. It might be a good idea to check the consistency of the waste at the end of the trip, after the guests have left. That way, if you need to add some water, you can and there will still be time during the ride home for the mixture to arrive at a perfect slurry consistency.

When connecting the aluminum funnel to the Jon-ny pot for disposal, a little bit of Vaseline can be used to lubricate the connection, if needed. **However, never put any Vaseline on the**

rubber gasket or it can begin to dissolve and it will no longer be leak proof—YUCK! It's probably a good idea before each trip to check the rubber gasket to make sure it is actually there and that it is in good shape. <u>Also, before each trip, spray the inside of the Jon-ny pot with PAM (the non-stick cooking spray) so that the slurry won't stick.</u>

Due to the bulky size of the Jon-ny pot, it's unfortunately not suitable for Forks trips because of the pack-in. Forks trips will continue using the rocket box set-up while making sure that the waste is disposed of properly.

HOW TO APPLY LARGE DECALS TO BUSES OR TRAILERS

Visually select a good place for the decal. Then thoroughly clean the area. With a spray bottle of Windex or similar glass cleaner (something that contains lots of alcohol), thoroughly wet down the entire area to be covered by the decal. Peel the back of the decal and place in position. The coating of Windex allows the decal to be slid around in order to achieve a perfectly level position. Finally, when the decal is positioned perfectly, squeegee the Windex out from behind the decal and when it dries, it's exactly where you want it.

OFFICIAL HOOPI LENGTHS

Red:	40"
Yellow/White/Green:	6'
Purple:	12'
Black:	Boat floor lacing

Due to years of extensive use and consumption, we have depleted the world of yellow hoopi. Then we moved onto white hoopi but that has turned out to be a limited commodity. Therefore, green hoopi has joined the ranks as an officially sanctioned color for 6-foot lengths.

Hoopi is one of those mysterious items that always seems to be disappearing. Please go through you closets, cars, river gear, etc., and round up those missing pieces of hoopi and send or bring them back to us!!

SADDLE BAGS

The idea behind our thwart saddle bags is to carry rescue/sweep boat gear, (including first aid kit, repair kit, and long line) in two snug, padded bags with quick tie-in and minimum entanglement risk.

If you find that the bags take too long to tie in, maybe leave them tied on to certain boats which would always be rescue/sweep boats. (Check with your area manager beforehand to make sure this meets with his/her plan for your area.)

STERN FRAMES

Our beautiful, rugged, breakdown, stern frames are made by the same manufacturer who did our bomber Tuolumne frames. There are some special notes to be aware of with regards to these frames:
— The components of the frames are not necessarily interchangeable from one frame to another. Consequently, the

parts of each frame are numbered (#1, #2, . . .#8) and each joint (4 joints per frame) is coded with a certain number of dots to help identify which part goes where. Generally, try to keep these frames assembled to avoid mixing parts. Only take them apart when packing into the Forks, etc. When a frame is apart, be careful to keep the parts together so that they don't wander off and get confused with the parts of another frame. When reassembling a frame, check that all the components have the same number and thus all are part of the frame you are trying to reconstruct. Also, use the dots to match joints.

— The oarlock towers are held in place by cadmium set screws. Each area will have extra screws. Also, keep a few extra screws in a ziplock in each repair kit!

— The plastic slant boards are a bit slippery. Each guide can figure out his or her own solution to this—perhaps tie on a small pad.

TRAINING

To benefit most from a whitewater school or training program, prepare thoroughly and pitch in wholeheartedly. Make a point of being there when things are done, for example, when the boats are inflated, when the D.O. is used, etc. As with most things, you get out of a school what you put into it. Your learning and growth will be greatest if you embrace the experience with all your energy and ability. By the way, if during a whitewater school a beginner has dreams about the river—and, at times, these dreams are frightening—he or she should be reassured. Such dreams are quite common.

TO BENEFIT MOST

Beginning raft guides learn faster if they first concentrate on either paddle captaining or rowing. Later, after one technique is mastered, the other is learned with relative ease. Trying to learn both at the same time is often too confusing and tends to extend the time needed to master either.

CONCENTRATE ON ONE TECHNIQUE

The steps in learning to guide a raft:

STEPS

First, the beginner reads everything available about rafting. Also, learn first aid and CPR techniques.

STUDY BOOKS

Second, the trainee observes an experienced guide. Riding in the boat while the expert rows or captains, the student listens to the expert's explanation of each action as it is performed.

OBSERVE EXPERTS

Third, the trainee takes over with the instructor staying close enough to step back in whenever necessary. The instructor talks the beginner through each rapid and each maneuver, always

DO IT WITH EXPERT GIVING DIRECTIONS

with an understanding that the veteran guide will take over a bit before the raft gets into any serious difficulty. Gradually, the student does better and better and the instructor says less and less, until finally the expert rides mute, awestruck at the extent of the newcomer's learning.

PRACTICE WITH-OUT INSTRUCTOR Fourth, the novice practices with other trainees or with daring volunteers.

POUR ON THE ADVICE For a veteran guide to withhold advice or instruction out of a reluctance to seem bossy or too exacting does the trainee no favors. The average trainee will spend only one week in a boat with an expert. After that, except for a week or two practicing with peers, he'll be on his own with crews who know little or nothing about rafting. So these training trips are very important. The more information and counsel the expert offers, the better a guide the trainee will become. So, even if the novice can't absorb and put into practice each bit of advice, the words will lodge somewhere in his mind and probably be useful later.

GIVE ENCOURAGE-MENT BUT STEP IN WHEN NEEDED Instructors give trainees as much encouragement and positive reinforcement as possible. But they don't hesitate to step in whenever necessary for the safety of the boat or crew.

LEARN GOOD TECHNIQUES The point is not merely for the trainee to get the boat down the river, it is to maneuver down the river using the best techniques. The goal is to teach sound techniques including proper boat angles, strokes, commands, etc., that, once they become second nature, will enable the novice to run more difficult rivers. Veterans don't let trainees slide by with poor techniques that will have to be unlearned before she or he can progress to more challenging rivers.

CAPTAINS SAY STOP After giving commands, beginning paddle captains learn to say "stop" as soon as the crew's response is sufficient. If a command is ever left standing so long that the paddlers stop on their own, the captain ratifies the crews' decision with a clear, audible "stop." Otherwise, the crew will begin deciding for itself when to stop, and this could be disastrous. By the way, when one command immediately follows another, it is not necessary to say "stop" before calling the next command.

TRAINING

A vital point for paddle boats (and oar boats when portegeeing): **BOAT ANGLE TO THE CURRENT**

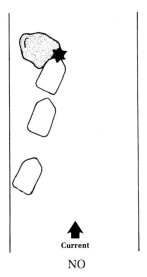

NO

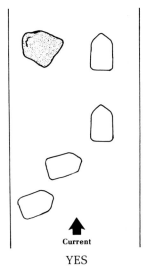

YES

Don't point the boat directly where you want to go. . .

Instead, aim far above the desired route. this allows you to cross the current and get into the water that is going where you want to go.

Just before teaching a whitewater school, all of the instructors should meet to share ideas and agree on techniques that will be emphasized. This tends to avoid the problem of instructors contradicting one another. It also provides an opportunity for the instructors to learn from each other. Even experts sometimes have very different ways of doing things.
WHITEWATER SCHOOLS: INSTRUCTORS' MEETING

Students should switch boats and instructors twice a day during long whitewater schools. Also, within each boat, occupants of the "hot seat," should be rotated frequently—tackling one or two rapids per stint.
ROTATE OFTEN

Whenever possible, a novice who is training on a regular trip should work with the most experienced guide on the trip.
TRAINING ON TRIPS: TRAIN WITH BEST GUIDE

On regular trips, before letting a trainee take over, the expert guide always asks for the guests' permission. The boaters will usually be more enthusiastic if they're told it will make the trip more exciting. But the guide should always assure them that he or she will immediately take over if their safety is endangered.
ASK IF OK WITH GUESTS

CONTINUE TO FOCUS ON GUESTS

Even during training, both the novice and the guide stay involved with the crew through continuing conversation and storytelling. Neither the guide nor the trainee should ever ignore the crew or focus only on each other.

GUESTS ARE FIRST PRIORITY

Sometimes, when the guide senses that the guests don't want the trainee to take control, or when other conditions suggest that the time's not right, the novice might not get as much practice as he or she wants. This will happen sometimes and should be cheerfully accepted. There will be other times. The first consideration is always the guests. On class IV and V rivers no clients may ride in boats guided by trainees.

A WORD ON HIRING GUIDES

If you are not being invited to train directly out of one of our whitewater schools, getting hired by Whitewater Voyages requires being interviewed and accepted by both our general manager _and_ an area manager. Our area managers are a core part of our management team, and play a vital role in selecting and <u>bringing out the best</u> in our guides. New guides—all guides—are expected to carefully heed the needs and concerns of our area managers—especially in regard to areas of performance needing improvement.

TRAINING STATUS

A trainee is an employee who is participating in a trip for the purposes of learning and improving their skill and who is not getting paid for being on the trip. There are a variety of ways in which one can be a trainee on a trip.

— You are an accomplished Whitewater Voyages guide who has worked other rivers and you are training on a new river with the intention of learning the run.
— You are an experienced guide who is new to Whitewater Voyages and you are training in order to learn how Whitewater Voyages runs trips.
— You are a class III guide moving into class IV or a class IV guide moving into class V. You are training with the purpose of improving your skill to meet the demands of a more difficult run.
— You are a Whitewater Voyages guide school graduate who has not yet done any commercial guiding. You are training with the purpose of gaining overall experience, improving a wide variety of skills, and learning the specific run.

These definitions aside, the term trainee more often that not refers to someone in the last category.

Sometimes trainees are in a separate boat with other trainees or are rowing a gear boat. However, when a trainee is going along in a boat with clients, and either doing some or all of the guiding, it is important for this arrangement to be okay with the passengers. Furthermore, it is important for our clients to know who is the paid guide, or guide in charge, and who is the trainee. This information can be conveyed with a simple introduction and is not meant to detract authority from the trainee. Rather, it's meant to assure our paying guests that they are in capable hands at all times and that the paid guide will step in and assume control at any time if necessary.

If you are a paid guide with a trainee who is guiding your boat, while still being sensitive to the perspective of the trainee, realize that you are ultimately responsible for what happens in your boat, safety-wise and enjoyment-wise. It is not okay for you to allow a trainee to trash paying clients for the purposes of learning.

Trainees should remember that their initial training period can be fairly extensive and that the actual length of training can vary greatly depending on individual skill and learning curve, high versus low water, difficulty of run, etc. Also, it's not at all uncommon for trainees to feel they are ready to work before trip leaders, senior guides, and the area manager feel they are ready. This often happens because trainees see a smaller "big picture" and within their more limited view, they may feel they are ready. Those with more experience, however, see a bigger picture and it is within that larger view that they often feel the trainee needs additional training.

STRUCTURED TRAINING

Some years there are only a few trainees and so these trainees get a lot of individual attention and instruction without needing a structured training program. However, in a season with lots of trainees, everyone can benefit from having a structured training program.

A designated training coordinator can be responsible for orienting trainees to a new area, explaining the training period to them, and getting them set up with a training instructor. The training instructors are experienced guides who teach and mentor the trainees. When there are an abundance of trainees, it may be best, for continuity's sake, to assign one training instructor to each trainee so that together they can work on developing certain skills and someone can keep track of the trainee's progress. This training instructor-trainee pair is not a fixed arrangement but rather can change on a weekly or periodic basis so that the trainee is exposed to a variety of styles and the training instructor gets a break and gets to actually guide their own boat.

On rare occasions, it may be necessary and appropriate to pay for an additional guide on a trip to accompany a full boat of trainees and act as a group instructor.

From time to time we plan a number of mentor events, mainly for the Kern and the South Fork American, in which we can fine tune our river, rescue, and land skills. Topics will include rescue scenarios, boat unwrapping techniques, the latest in foot entrapment rescue, signals, nature interpretation, etc., etc. Please make a point of attending as many of these events as possible. If you have expertise that you'd like to share in such an event, please talk with your area manager. There is compensation for experienced guides who can skillfully lead mentor events.

EMPHASIS ON TRAINING TRIPS

Try to make training trips as informative as possible. Give talks and have discussions on river logistics, special hazards and how they vary with water level, permit and operating plan, local history, geology, flora, fauna, etc.

TRAINING-TRIP FOOD COSTS

On any trip where the number of trainees and non-paying guests exceeds the number of paying clients, those trainees and guests contribute $4 per meal. This would include training trips where there are meals served—although the contribution could be reduced if a frugal chef is able to plan a simple, inexpensive menu on trips that are strictly training.

GUIDE SCHOOL EXAM QUESTIONS
FOR DISCUSSION

OAR TECHNIQUE

1. List two advantages of rowing a raft in the "Galloway position" (facing the bow, which is pointed down river).
    1) The rower has a clear view down river.
    2) Pulling back on the oars in an upstream ferry slows the boat in relation to the current, providing more time to maneuver.

2. A. Why is the portegee method of rowing (pushing on the oars) weaker than pulling back on the oars?
    –The portegee utilizes only the arms and stomach, while pulling back on the oars uses the arms, back, and legs.

    B. List two situations in which the portegee method should be used.
    1) Setting up for rapids.
    2) Pushing through holes.

3. A. When rowing around a river bend in a fast current, toward which bank do you point the bow?
    –Point the bow toward the outside bank.

    B. Toward which bank do you row?
    –Row toward the inside bank.

4. The "ferry angle" is the angle of the raft relative to the _____
    –Current! (*Not* the bank)

5. A. When do you use a ferry angle of 60 degrees or greater?
    –Use a 60 degree ferry angle (or greater–a 90 degree angle is often the best!) when the waves are too small to flip the raft.

    B. When do you use an angle of 30 degrees?
    –Use a 30 degree ferry angle when the waves are so large that the bow must be pointed into them lest you risk capsizing.

6. List the paddle strokes used in rafting.
    –Paddle strokes: Forward, backstroke, draw, pry, corner sweep.

7. Which stroke is used most often? Why?
    –The forward stroke is used most often because:
    –It is the strongest.
    –Crews tend to stay in sync better paddling forward as opposed to back paddling.
    –Crashing into waves with good forward speed maximizes the fun!

8. List the commands used in captaining a paddle raft. Which command (not a stroke) is used most often?
    –The commands: Forward; back paddle; right turn; left turn; stop; hold on, lean in and get down; and high side. Also, for somewhat slower but more precise, energy-efficient maneuvers, there are: right forward (this means only the right side paddles forward), right back (only the right side back paddles, etc.), left forward and left back. "Stop" is the command used most often.

9. Define "feathering a paddle."
    –On the return, knifing the blade through the air.

10. A. When padding around a river bend in a swift current, toward which bank (inside bank or outside bank) do you generally point the bow?
    –Point toward the inside bank.

    B. Toward which bank do you paddle?
    –Paddle toward the inside bank.

11. What do you do if your paddle crew is consistently stronger on one side?
    –Have people change positions until the crew is balanced from side to side. The biggest people are not always the strongest paddlers.

12. What do you tell your crew to make them want to paddle in unison?
    –Tell them that they achieve three things by paddling in unison:
    1) All of their efforts are more effective: The boat lunges forward with each stroke.
    2) They avoid banging paddles.
    3) And most important, they look sharp.

13. On class IV and V rivers, where on the raft do you place your strongest paddlers?
    –In the bow.

14. One of the members of your paddle crew (perhaps because they are older or very young) may need some extra help staying in the raft. Where should you place them in the boat?

–Have them sit near you in the stern, where you can keep a close eye on them, give them extra help, and even grab them if necessary to keep them from falling overboard. With such people, it is often helpful to quietly give them special, individual instructions before challenging rapids: For example, you might say in a quiet aside to such a soul, "In the next rapid, I want you to concentrate on just hanging on."

15. How can you as a guide create strong paddle crews? Answer: At put-in, in a clear, thorough, supportive paddle-boat talk flowing with positive strokes, good humor and attention to detail, cover the following:

–Teach everyone how to safely and securely brace their feet, and how to sit, not in on the cross thwarts, but out on the perimeter tube where they can more easily reach the water and deliver powerful paddle strokes.

–Show them how to hold their paddles with the inboard hand across the top of the t-grip and the outboard hand well down the shaft.

–Clearly and carefully explain and demonstrate all strokes and commands. Emphasize the importance and correct technique for making long, strong forward and back paddle strokes.

–Designate your two bow paddlers as the "strokes," and have them match strokes with each other, and have everyone else match strokes with them.

–Teach your crew to match the power and speed of their strokes to the tone, volume and urgency of your commands.

–Do paddling drills which practice all strokes and commands, including turns. Make sure everyone is paddling correctly. Whenever necessary, in an encouraging and also clear and firm way, provide extra attention and instruction to make sure everyone is paddling correctly, and staying in sync throughout even long series of strokes.

–Teach and practice having your bow paddlers dig powerfully through holes.

–Emphasize that all participants, including small people, are vital members of the crew, and even when crew members feel overwhelmed, they should keep trying to follow the commands. Make it clear that you depend on them.

–When you really need extra power, motivate your crew by forcefully repeating commands and with fun, energizing phrases, such as, "Forward! Forward! Forward! Gotta get there! Gotta get there! Forward!", and "Back paddle! Back paddle! Need ya now! Need ya now! Need ya now! Back paddle! Back paddle!"

–After and during bursts of good paddling on the part of your crew, give lots of praise and positive strokes for a job well done!

–Above all, build rapport with your crew and earn their trust. From the very beginning use their efforts with utmost economy. If a crew feels commands are left standing longer than necessary and their efforts are being wasted, they will paddle less hard and stop on their own. But if they sense you really need every stroke and that you are making every stroke count, they will paddle their hearts out for you!

–Also, a crew can throw themselves into paddling all the harder when they know that their captain will warn them by yelling "Lean in" or "Hold on" before the boat receives big jolts that could bounce people overboard.

16. List three hazards about which boaters should be forewarned before stepping ashore during a river trip? **ON SHORE**
    1) Slippery & sharp rocks
    2) Poison oak
    3) Rattlesnakes

17. When should your raft's "agile-bow person" step onto shore?
    –The agile-bow person should step or jump ashore just before the raft touches the bank—not after the raft bounces away.

18. What must be done to make the raft "ready" to shove off?
    –To make the raft ready:
      –Tie in all gear.
      –Give put-in safety talk to crew.
      –Untie the boat.
      –Coil/tuck away all lines.
      –Lift the boat off the beach—the boat should be floating and held in place only by someone standing at water's edge or holding onto a branch or rock.
      –Each crew member is in his or her place, with life jacket fastened and paddle in hand.
      –When truly "ready" a guide can sit with paddle blade up and vertical in the "I'm ready" signal and keeps an eye on the trip leader.

19. What is the most important factor to consider when you are purifying water with chlorine or "halazone?"
    –Time! Allow at least 30 minutes for the purifier to kill the bacteria and escape as gas.

20. What should professional guides do when everyone is eating a meal?
    –Mingle! Each guide should sit down near a boater or two and talk to them.

21. Where on a rafter's body should most of the flotation material in a life jacket be located?
    —On the chest, to float the unconscious victim face up.

22. List the four causes of rapids.
    1) Constriction of the river channel.
    2) Obstruction of the river channel.
    3) Gradient or steepness of the river bed.
    4) Water volume.

23. Why does water move upriver on the down river side of a large rock?
    —The downstream current rushing past creates a low-pressure zone immediately downstream from the rock, which is filled in by water flowing back upstream.

24. What single piece of data best indicates the difficulty of a river run?
    —The single piece of information which best indicates a river's difficulty is its rating of I to VI on the international scale.

25. Why do afternoon winds often blow upriver?
    —Warm air rises.

26. What should you do if you suspect the unknown river you are running contains an unrunnable rapid?
    —The safest course is to stop and scout the entire run before proceeding.

27. What do you (as captain/oarsperson) do when your raft is about to run sideways into a large boulder?
    —If feasible, power forward or back to miss the rock or give the raft a spin to cartwheel off the rock or at least hit the rock bow or stern on. If none of these actions are possible, call, "High side!"

28. A member of your crew wants to swim in the river as the raft drifts through a long calm. What should you tell them *before* they go overboard?
    —Before the swimmer goes overboard in a clam, advise him or her to never dive or jump, but instead ease in feet first, to stay close to the raft and to get back aboard at least 100 yards above the next rapid.

29. What are the rules of safe water fighting?
    —The rules of safe water fighting:
      —No water fighting when in or approaching rapids.
      —No boarding.
      —No pulling or pushing people overboard.
      —Use caution at close range.
      —No squirting water cannons or powerful squirt guns into people's faces. Instead squirt up and let the water rain down on the enemy.
      —Do not water fight when it is just too cold.

30. What do you (as captain/oarsperson) do when your raft gets stuck sideways in a hole?
    - Keep your crew low on the downstream side of the boat. Boats caught in holes often spin; people up on a tube tend to get sucked overboard. So keep the crew off the tubes and down on the floor on the downstream side. If the raft does spin, be ready to change sides quickly.
    - In a paddle boat, have your crew do draw strokes downstream with their armpits pasted to the downstream tube. When enough blades draw downstream, the boat tends to be freed from the hole.
    - In an oar boat, all the while keeping your crew low, use your oars to turn the boat end-on to the hole and try to row out downstream.

31. As a guide, what do you do if you flip?
    Answers:
    - Count heads. If people are missing, immediately begin a search, first checking any places they could be trapped underwater.
    - Unless it is unsafe to do so, stay with your boat (by grabbing a perimeter line just before or as the boat flips) and climb onto the up-side-down bottom.
    - Continue giving guidance/directions to your crew
        - Yell: - "Keep your feet up!"
            - "Swim for the boat!" (If appropriate.)
    - Sometimes leave the overturned boat to avoid a strainer, a class VI waterfall, or some other deathtrap.
    - Right your boat with your belt flip line or a bow or stern line through a side D-ring. Depending on the situation, this might be done in midriver right away or as soon as the upside down boat has been paddled into an eddy.

32. What do you do after you wrap?
    - Choose and signal direction of pull. (Toward which you will pull the raft off.)
    - Get crew to safety.
    - Set up continuous-loop load distribution system. (To attach rescue line to far end of raft.)
    - Post a person upstream above the rapid to warn approaching boats that a rescue is in progress.
    - If possible, post a boat downstream to pick up any swimmers and items that float loose.
    - Pull the boat off with a dampened rescue line and either a Z-rig, a pig rig or, if the boat is not wrapped tight and you have a big group, a direct pull.
    - During this process continue to care for the group as a whole.

33. What are the key elements of the strong, economical guiding style?

–Strong angles between 45 and 90 degree to the current.

–Quick changes of angle using one's strong turning option: Double-oar turn for oar boats and entire crew plus captain's paddle for paddle boats.

–Economy: Using as few strokes as possible to achieve the desired results.

34. What are the key elements of the "making-time-down-river" style of guiding?

–Use downstream angles.

–Avoid eddies.

–Stay in the strongest jet of current.

–Also, to maximize "making-time-down-river", use your crew to paddle downstream.

35. What are the key elements of the "rock-assist, low-water" guiding style used during extreme low water?

–Tight teamwork.

–Precision maneuvering.

–Low siding.

–Doing the "wild thing."

–Placing "the rock in the groove" to do a turn while passing over a wet rock.

–Sometimes deliberately bounce off high (non-undercut) rocks to get rid of momentum and change direction in tight places.

–Above all, exude and instill high energy!

36. What are the key elements of "high-water" or "big-water" guiding?

–Look and plan extra far ahead.

–Start moves well ahead of time.

–Square off (at 90 degrees) to big waves, holes and eddy fences, and hit them with momentum.

–To break through extremely big, violent waves, holes and eddy fences, power downstream using downstream angles to maximize momentum.

–Paddle boats: Generally use the forward stroke with bow angled downstream.

–Oar boats: Either go stern first with the pull stroke or power bow first with the portegee—which can be amazingly effective in big water.

–Very tight boat spacing to keep swims as short as possible, and minimize the chance of a swimmer getting away downstream—a big risk in high water.

–Emphasize to all trip members: If you swim, immediately self-rescue by swimming as hard as you can to the nearest right-side-up boat.

–In extreme high water, emphasize containment and downstream safety: Maintain a downstream safety net (to keep swimmers from flushing away downstream) with expertly guided cata-rafts, oar boats, stern mounts and kayaks.

–Another technique is to deliberately line up your long side tube with diagonal waves in order to surf along them— but use caution to avoid flipping.

37. What are the key elements of the "milking-the-river-for-excitement" style of guiding?
    –Use the strong, economical style to get your boat into the water flowing toward a big, exciting, but runnable hole.
    –In a paddle boat: Whooping and hollering to spur your crew to paddle hard to accelerate into the hole.
    –In an oar boat: Portegee into the hole.
    –A key consideration: Be sensitive to your crew. If they show they do not want to get wet (which might be the case on a cold day), do not milk the river.

38. Name two reasons to maintain tight boat spacing?
    1) Enables quick rescue support, keeping swims short.
    2) Allows you to "go to school" on the boats ahead.

39. What do you do if your entire crew falls out and flushes off downstream, leaving you alone in your paddle boat?
    Possible answers:
    –Throw toss bag downstream past most swimmers, and yell, "Grab the line! Swim for the line!" After they grab the line, reel them in.
    –If the toss bag option is not feasible, draw stroke off your stern or bow to catch swimmers.

40. What do you do if you find yourself alone in your paddle raft on river left and your crew has swum ashore on river right?
    Possible answers:
    –Toss bag, swing across.
    –R-one off stern or bow using draw strokes to paddle boat across. (This is surprisingly effective.)

41. What should you do if one of your crew members collapses into unconsciousness due to possible cardiac and/or respiratory arrest?
    –Immediately perform the ABCs (airway, breathing, circulation/pulse, etc.) of BLS (Basic Life Support).
    –Get medical help and evacuate your victim to a hospital via the fastest possible means. Depending on the situation, this might be by ambulance, company vehicle, private vehicle, raft, helicopter, etc.
    –Also: Take good care of the rest of your group, and, as soon as appropriate, begin the necessary paperwork, notify the management agencies and the Whitewater Voyages main office, plan a debriefing with Bill, consider post-traumatic stress counseling, etc.

42. What are some things a guide can do to reassure a client who can not swim? (Assume you are on a class III river.)
    –Have them float in their life jacket beside the raft in a calm. This reassures their "body/mind" that they will

float and be OK if they fall overboard.

—As with all clients, make sure their life jacket is secure.

—Tell them we routinely take non-swimmers on class III with no problem.

—Share with them that the key thing is that they be comfortable (or at least outwardly calm) with the idea/possibility that they might wind up floating in the water.

—Make sure they hear (or just heard) an extra-thorough safety talk. In some cases it might be helpful to review the key pertinent safety talk points as follow: If they fall overboard, they would most likely bob up right next to their raft, extend their paddle as a handle to safety, and be pulled right back into the boat. In the event they were separated from their raft, they keep their feet up, toes at the surface, and stroke as well as they can either toward the boat or shore, following their guide's directions, or, if they can't hear their guide, whichever seems best. If they are in a big rapid, they would float it out with feet on the surface pointed downstream (breathing in the troughs between the waves), and stroke as best they can for the boat or bank in the next relative calm. Throughout all this, of course, the boat would be doing it's best to pick them up.

43. What are some ways that a guide can create a positive, supportive atmosphere that enhances people's fun and brings them back for future trips?

—Greet and welcome people warmly.

—Learn people's names.

—Be helpful, kind and considerate.

—Give thorough, entertaining safety talks and in-boat trainings packed with humor, positive strokes and all of the essential info on how to cope with emergencies and be part of a strong crew.

—Keep your boat right side up, and in the rapids keep all of your people in your boat.

—Answer all questions with thoroughness, care and appreciation. Realize that your caring answers can turn any question into a good question and can send the message that here with Whitewater Voyages, it is OK and safe to know what you know, OK and safe to not know what you do not know, and OK and safe to be open and unguarded.

—Look for opportunities to give positive strokes.

—Be open, reach out, get to know people, be curious.

—Mingle at meal times.

—Listen! Listen so well you can repeat back in your own words what is said. Realize that caring listening may be the greatest, most healing gift any human being can give another.

–Avoid machismo, putdowns, criticism, judgements, competition, elitism, bragging and sarcasm.

–Draw from a big repertoire of activities, stories, jokes, games, nature lore, etc.

–Choose games and activities which help people feel included rather than excluded.

–Enter into the experience. Be present. If you find yourself thinking about something or somewhere else, invite your attention back into the moment by asking yourself, "How can I enhance my experience—and the experience of the people I am with—right now?"

–Keep folks informed of the plan for the day/plan for the trip.

–Acknowledge and thank people.

–In your inner most self talk, cultivate a sincere intention to create a positive, supportive atmosphere in which you and your companions, free from having to defend yourselves, can relax, open up, expand and grow. This, after all, is at the heart of real fun!

–Etc., etc.

44. How much flotation should a life jacket have for high water?
    –22 or more pounds flotation.

45. When R2ing (with just two people in a paddle raft) where do the paddlers sit?
    –Usually, across from each other in the center of the boat.
    –Another possible option is for them to sit diagonally opposite one another, that is, with one in the stern on one side and the other in the bow on the opposite side.

46. If you see that your boat is about to collide with a rock, what are some things you as a guide might do?
    –Try to get your boat into the water missing the rock by getting an angle and, in a paddle boat, calling "forward" or "back paddle," or, in an oar boat, pulling (or pushing) on the oars.
    –If you cannot avoid the rock? Depending on the situation:
        –Hit the rock straight bow or stern on. This reduces the chance of flipping against the rock.
        –If your boat is in a ferry angle, swing your bow in the direction of the rock. This will tend to spin you off the rock, place more of your boat in the water pillowing off the rock, and, if there is a collision, point your bow straight at the rock.
        –Call "High Side" and/or "Lean in. Get Down. Hold on."

47. If your boat is hung up on a rock, what are some things you might try to get it off?
    –Sometimes, if you shift weight to a part of the boat that is not on the rock, the boat will float off. This

technique is particularly successful when you can have people shift their weight onto an end of the boat that is floating in strong current that is moving past the rock.

–Dipping or stroking with an oar or paddles can sometimes spin the boat off.

–Get bumped off by another boat. This should only be attempted in mild conditions, and boats bumping off other boats need to take care not to wind up stuck themselves.

–Do the "wild thing," that is, everyone in the boat jumps around like a wild monkey to make the boat bounce and slither off the rock. Encourage enthusiastic jumping, but at the same time caution people to be careful not to bounce themselves out of the boat!

–An agile person, usually the guide, gets out, pushes the boat off the rock and jumps back in as the boat spins off.

–Get a line to shore and have enough people pull until the boat floats free.

–Only if it is safe to do so, first have most or all of the crew get out of the boat, next move the lightened boat off the rock, and then have everyone carefully re-board. Be aware that a hung up boat can act as an undercut, and can be a serious hazard. See below.

48. When a raft is hung up on rocks in swift current, in what way can the raft itself be a serious hazard?

–A stationary raft hung up on rocks with strong current going under the raft can act like an undercut rock! Swimmers, kayakers, etc. can be swept underneath and pinned underwater! This means that swimmers, kayakers, etc. must take great care to avoid swift current streaming into and under hung up rafts.

49. Your oar raft, which is heavily loaded with baggage and two big, overweight people, hangs up in a shallows in **slow current**. After trying every other means, you realize the only feasible way to free the boat is to have the people get out. (Note: In this case there is no strong current sweeping under the raft.) On what side of the raft should you have the people step out? What should you tell them beforehand?

–Have them step out on the upstream side while holding tightly onto the raft. Tell them beforehand to get braced because the raft is likely to float up and be pulled downstream by the current as soon as it is freed. In this situation absolutely do not have them get out on the downstream side: The raft could float up, be caught by the current, knock them down and float over them, pinning them underwater. Use good judgement. Every situation is different.

–Important note: As covered above, do **not** have clients climb out of the boat into **strong current!** A stuck raft, especially when there are deeper channels of water going under the raft, can act like a large undercut, and people stepping out on the upstream side can be swept under the boat and pinned underneath.

50. What can you do if, despite every possible effort to create a strong crew, your crew is weak?

–Redouble your use of the strong, economical style of guiding: Use what power you have with utmost economy. Whenever possible, try not to have any command last longer than two or three strokes. Plan far ahead and begin critical moves as early as possible.

–In extreme cases on challenging runs, after consulting with the other guides on the trip, consider redistributing paddlers so that all boats have adequate power.

51. Why is keeping bow and stern lines neatly coiled and stowed a matter of life and death?

–If the raft were to flip, wrap or be caught in a hole, a swimmer entangled in a bow or stern line could be entrapped and held underwater.

52. From a safety standpoint, what are the two most fundamental goals of river guiding?

–Keep the boat right side up and keep everyone in the boat.

53. What are some tips for keeping everyone in the boat?

–All of the tips above for keeping boats right side up also tend to keep people in the boat.

–Make clean runs: Don't flip, wrap or tube stand.

–Don't hit rocks or other obstacles sideways. This may be the most common cause of losing people overboard.

–Teach people where to sit and how to safely and securely brace their feet.

–Prepare your crew for jolts that could bounce people overboard by calling "Lean in!" or "Brace for a bounce!" or "Hold on!" beforehand.

–Consider rigging center-and-top-of-thwart handholds. These are especially useful when your boat is caroming through challenging rapids and drops under less than full control.

–Teach and, when necessary, use the "Lean in! Hold on! And get down!" command.

54. To rescue a foot entrapment victim, what are some things rescuers might do?

Depending on the situation:

–Give the oxygen supply endangered/entrapment signal to alert others of this time-critical emergency.

–Stabilize the victim's head above water with a tag line

across the river.

–Free the victim with a Carlson cinch or free the entrapped limb with a weighted drag line across river.

–Do a strong-swimmer rescue with a quick-release harness supported by a line either spanning the river or from one bank.

–If the rapid is shallow and you have enough big rescuers, form a swift water crossing "wedge" to rescue the victim.

–Use a Telfer Lower to lower a raft from the calm above the rapid down to rescue the victim.

–Early on, post someone upstream above the rapid to warn approaching boats that a rescue is in progress.

–Have a leader with a clear view of victim and all rescue team members coordinate efforts with signals.

–Note: Because time is so critical, it is a good idea to check your watch as soon as you know someone is entrapped. In addition to asphyxiation (lack of oxygen), hypothermia, fractures, and possible blood loss from fractures are critical concerns.

–As much as possible during this process, continue to care for the victim's family and friends and the group as a whole.

55. What are some tips for keeping your boat right side up?

–Use a big enough boat for the river. On California rivers, a 14- to 15-foot boat is generally suitable for any runnable high water level.

–Avoid obstacles, such as big waves, rocks, strainers and holes, that could flip your boat.

–Hit runnable holes and waves straight bow or stern on with momentum, and dig (with paddle or oars) through them.

56. What is/are the signal(s) for:

–Stop.

–Are you OK?

–Are you ready?

–I'll be ready in 3 minutes?

–Speed up.

–I'm coming to you.

–Scout.

–Entrapment! Someone's oxygen supply is endangered.

–Are you ... missing...how many?

–Your... missing... 2 people...are there.

–We have everyone. Our group is complete.

–We are searching for ...2 people.

–The missing person(s) was/were last seen where indicated.

–We need a first aid kit.

–May we pass...please.

–Your are welcome to pass. We'll eddy out.

–We're waiting on the group ahead of us. Sorry.

–Good run.

–Learning opportunity.

TEMPORARY HELP

A temporary guide is one who normally works for another rafting company.

DEFINITION

While working with us, temporary guides are asked to consider themselves 100 percent Whitewater Voyages staff and to do their best to guide in a manner compatible with our methods and philosophy, as expressed in this book.

OUR METHODS AND PHILOSOPHY

On our trips, temporary guides are asked not to use watertight bags, ammo boxes, equipment or clothing marked with another company's name. If something like this is inadvertently brought along, it should be packed away out of view so that the name won't show in photographs.

USE ONLY OUR GEAR

Guides who normally work for another company are asked not to mention this fact—or the other company's name—to our guests.

DO NOT SPEAK OF OTHER COMPANIES

Because regular Whitewater Voyages guides are most familiar with our philosophy and can most impart the feeling of truly being with Whitewater Voyages, contact between clients and our regular guides is to be maximized. Hence, our regular guides always give the put-in talk and, when possible, temporary guides are placed in charge of baggage boats.

REGULAR GUIDES TAKE GUESTS, TEMPORARY GUIDES TAKE BAGGAGE

MOTOR TOW

Make absolutely sure motorboats carrying take-out coolers arrive early at the point where the river meets the lake. Motor tow boats should be ready and waiting when our boats first hit the lake. While waiting, the drivers don't wander off or tow other groups.

ARRIVE AT RENDEZVOUS EARLY

When rigging the motor boat, insure against the loss of the motor by tying a short safety rope to both the motor and a nearby D-ring.

SAFETY LINE

Pilots of propeller-driven craft are very careful on the upper reaches of the lake—and whenever near shore—not to let the propeller hit rocks hidden just below the water surface.

CAREFUL IN SHALLOWS

When other groups of rafts are to be towed behind our rafts, do not tie the rafts together by their bow and stern D-rings. Instead, run a single main line under and/or between the rafts and tie the rafts to loops in it. This prevents the D-rings from being weakened or pulled off. See illustration on following page.

TYING RAFTS TOGETHER FOR TOWING

When using a motor-powered boat to tow a string of rafts across a lake, minimize strain on the D-rings by towing slowly and accelerating very, very slowly.

TOW SLOWLY

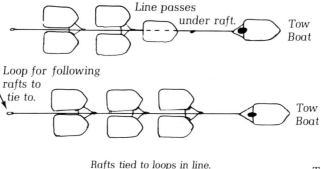

Line passes under raft.

Tow Boat

Loop for following rafts to tie to.

Tow Boat

Rafts tied to loops in line.

Tow Boat

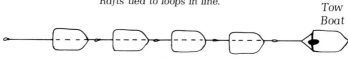

Line passes under rafts. Each raft is tied to loop in line. Use butterfly loops.

4-WHEEL DRIVE OPERATING INSTRUCTIONS
by Kevin Johnson

NEWER TRUCKS

With newer trucks, stop, put the gear selector in neutral, and move the 4-wheel drive selector until the 4-wheel-drive indicator light comes on.

PUTTING OLDER TRUCKS INTO 4-WHEEL DRIVE

Stop the truck. Get out and look at the front wheels. With old-style 4-wheel drives, encased in the end of the metal cylinder that sticks out of the center of each wheel is a small, red, plastic dial. There are two positions; "lock" and "free." Turn the dials of both wheels to "lock." You have just locked the wheels. Get back in the truck. Next to the gearshift lever is another, smaller lever with "4L-N-2H-4H" marked on the handle (4 Low-Neutral-2 High-4 High). Pull this lever into the 4-H position. You're in 4-wheel drive. Turn up the radio and go!

TROUBLE-SHOOTING

If the lever won't go into the 4-H position, then, with the hubs still locked, drive the truck forward several yards and try it again. Repeat this procedure until it goes in. It will. You may need the truck geared lower, shove the lever into the 4-L position. If the truck doesn't move when you let out the clutch, then you are stuck in the neutral position. *Turn the engine off!* Then move the lever into whichever position you want. Never drive over 45 miles an hour or on paved highway while in 4-wheel drive. Don't use it when you don't need it.

TAKING IT OUT OF 4-WHEEL DRIVE

Stop the truck. Push the lever back into 2-H position. If it won't go at first, drive the truck forward and try again until it does. It will. When it does, stop the truck, get out and return the hubs to the "free postion." It's back in 2-wheel drive. Turn up the radio and go!

During periods of extended non-use the 4-wheel drive system should be used at least once a month for several miles to lubricate the parts. **WHEN NOT USED OFTEN**

MEMORY AIDS FOR TUOLUMNE RAPIDS

Mnemonic for the first eleven rapids on the Toulumne:

Rivers (Rock Garden) **Need** (Nemesis) **Some** (Sunderland's Chute) **Help** (Hackamack Hole) **Running** (Ram's Head) **Individuals** (India) **Past** (Phil's Folly) **Strainers** (Stern or Squeeze). **Every** (Evangelist) **Breath** (Bent Thole Pin) **Counts** (Clavey Falls).
Created by Whitewater Voyages guide Joe Villasenor.

Mnemonic for the last nine rapids on the Toulumne:

Go (Gray's Grindstone) **Strongly** (Surf City) **Through** (Thread-the-Needle) **Drops** (Driftwood) **Straight** (Steamboat) **Cause** (Cabin) **Holes** (Hells Kitchen) **Are** (Alps) **Powerful** (Pinball).
Created by Whitewater Voyages guide Serina Tremayne.

BRIEFING: KERN RIVER

All Whitewater Voyages guides on the Kern River should carefully read—*and be totally familiar with*—the current Forest Service Kern River Operating Plan and Permit. The stipulations of both the permit and operating plan are to be followed to the letter. Absolutely no exceptions! **KNOW & FOLLOW PERMIT & OPERATING PLAN**

When conducting trips on the short sections of the Upper Kern, give each group as many runs as possible. Do at least three—and try for four or more if time permits. **UPPER KERN**

Never carry *anyone* in or on a trailer, on a roof, or in the *open* back of a pickup or truck! When more than 15 people are on the Upper Kern, use one of our busses or two vans. Please remember: our operation must not only *be* good, it must also look good! **NO PASSENGERS ON TRAILERS, ROOFS, OR IN THE BACK OF OPEN TRUCKS**

Trip leaders on the Kern make sure the trip gets packed properly and leaves for the river on time. This means making sure all guides on the trip get up in time to pack and leave on schedule. **LEADERS GET GUIDES MOVING ON TIME**

Emphasize the danger of trees in the river. No swimming allowed from the raft except at the swimming rapid. No water fighting near tree hazards or before rapids. **SAFETY TALK**

Bring rafts out of water and bleed to prevent chafing and over-inflation. Remind boaters that if they want to cool off in the river to wear life jackets and to stay out of the current. Tell them to stay in water shallow enough to wade in. **IN CAMP**

At White Maiden's Walkway, go left of the large rock at bottom if possible. If you can't and go right, try to stay away from the right wall. There have been some bad flips on the right wall. **WHITE MAIDEN'S**

PREP H   Just above Preparation H the trip leader should call a conference of all rafts to remind guides to run this rapid *far* left and tell boaters about the Royal Flush portage just downstream and to swim as fast as they can to the right bank if the raft flips.

PORTAGE   At the portage, make sure that those that help relaunch the rafts are wearing life jackets.

HORSESHOE   At Horseshoe, make sure boaters "hang on" in the upper drop on the far right so there are no swimmers there.

KERN HOUSE   Please take pride in and good care of our ideally situated Kern House. Keep the kitchen, bathroom and the rooms clean. Wash out coolers outside, and bring only the good food in to the refrigerator. When everyone is away, keep the doors and the front, back and side gates all locked. As a part of the warehouse work in lieu of rent, keep the house painted and in good repair and the grounds clean. Thanks.

BRIEFING: SOUTH FORK OF THE AMERICAN RIVER

WELCOME FOLKS TO RIVER PARK ADVENTURE CAMPGROUND   In keeping with our overall philosophy of warmly welcoming and caring for our clients, it is important that we cordially greet, welcome and host all of our guests at River Park Adventure Campground (which is also known as Beaver Point). Especially when folks first arrive, take some time to go up to them, welcome them, introduce yourself, give them a quick orientation regarding where to meet, camp, shower, etc., answer their initial questions, and, whenever time allows, give them a campground tour in the golf cart. A friendly reception like this can make a huge positive difference for folks, gets things off on the right foot and could even be a highlight of their trip!

QUIET ZONE   A quiet zone extends from Dutch Creek above Coloma to Greenwood Creek below Camp Lotus. To minimize their impact on the many people who live here, all rafting companies on the American have agreed not to yell or waterfight along this stretch. Both in their leaders' safety talks and the talks in each boat, this quiet zone should be mentioned in a positive manner.

After all, it is easy to understand the need for this quiet zone when one realizes that without it the residents would have to listen to hooting and screaming all day long every day of the summer. Our guests might be interested to learn that this quiet zone is the direct result of the California gold rush over 150 years ago. This very stretch of river is where gold was first discovered in California and, as a result, numerous permanent gold mining claims were established. This differs from most other Sierra rivers, where few claims were permanent and by now most of the land is controlled by the government as national forest or state park. When the gold played out, these claims became regular private property and over the years were bought and sold and passed from parents to offspring. Today the place is thick with a growing number of year-round inhabitants, although it now has only a fraction of its gold rush population.

It is important that we politely but firmly insist that our crews neither yell nor waterfight in this zone. Everyone should do their waterfighting upstream and downstream. Within this zone we have an excellent opportunity to interpret nature and tell our crews about the history of the gold rush and the surrounding region. (A good place to learn about this is the museum at Marshall Gold Discovery Historical State Park, and also by doing the River Park self-guided nature walk.)

Stop for lunch only at authorized sites. On the Upper run, it is alright to have lunch on the BLM land at the old miner's cabin site between Second and Third Threat Rapid. On the Gorge run, we are authorized to stop for lunch on any BLM land that is not the designated lunch site of another group. Generally, we use the Sandy beach on the "F" parcel near the toilets below Turtle Pond/Greenwood Creek. **USE ONLY AUTHORIZED LUNCH SPOTS**

On the American it is an El Dorado County requirement that we use coolers with readily visible thermometers mounted inside and that coolers containing perishable foods be 45 degrees F or below. So use plenty of ice. As on all trips, we use plastic cutting boards liquid hand soap/sanitizer, three piping-hot dishwater tubs, etc. The county will be doing spot checks. **USE COOLERS WITH THERMOMETERS.**

Whitewater Voyages and other companies have suffered terrible losses due to theft—mainly on the South Fork of the American—both during the night and in broad daylight. **PREVENT THEFTS**

Keep an alert eye on our gear at all times. If the group is going to leave the rafts for any amount of time, assign someone the job of staying behind and guarding the equipment. Impress upon everyone the importance of this task. **WATCH GEAR**

On the South Fork of the American, *all equipment* including rafts, life jackets, paddles, oars, ammo boxes, etc., is to be carried up into camp. If they are going to be used the next morning, the rafts may be left overnight on the River Park/Beaver Point beach. These should be bled (release air until slightly soft), stacked and chained. Also, whenever possible, guides should sleep near the rafts. **STACK, CHAIN, RAFTS**

William McGinnis'
Whitewater Voyages / River Exploration Ltd.

═══ EQUIPMENT PACKING LIST ═══

RIVER_____   # CLIENTS_____
TRIP DATE(S)_____   # GUIDES_____
                                    TOTAL_____

Check off each item as it is packed
and note quantities of each item.

SAMPLE: ✓ LIFEJACKETS: **20** Adult **6** X-large **4** Child

____RAFTS:_____
_____
_____
_____

____FRAMES: ____Pro, cooler type ____Pins ____Oarlocks ____Collapsible
           ____Pro, floor type ____Pins ____Oarlocks ____Collapsible
           ____Adv. floor type ____Pins ____Oarlocks ____Collapsible

____OARS: ____10-foot ____Wood ____Oarlock ____Collapsible
         ____9-foot ____Wood ____Oarlock ____Collapsible

____DECKS: ____Hanging Pro Poop Deck ____Straps
          ____Hanging Adv Poop Deck ____Straps

LUGGAGE
____RACKS: ____Alum. Rack for big 80 Pro ____Straps
          ____Metal Paddle Rack ____Straps ____Floor
          ____Wood Paddle Rack ____Straps

____PADDLES:_____

____PUMPS: ____Cylinder Pumps ____4" ____6"
          ____Foot Pumps

____ELECTRIC BLOWERS:

____LINE: ____Short Line Bags ____Toss Bags
         ____Long Line ____Extra-long Safety Line

____TARPS: ____Large ____Small ____Canvas ____Plastic

____BAILERS: ____Large Buckets ____Scoop Bailers

____LIFEJACKETS: ____Adult ____X-large ____Child

____WATERTIGHT BAGS: _____

____BLUE BAGS

____BLACK BAGS

____KLAMATH BAGS ____1 Strap type ____2 Strap type
                 ____Plastic Liner ____Elastic Bands

____REPAIR KIT (Check taped seal & contents)

____FIRST AID KIT (Check taped seal & contents)

____WATERTIGHT CONTAINERS:
                    ____Ammo boxes ____Rocket boxes ____20mm boxes

____WATER (Fill 'em all): ____Canteens
                    ____Five-gallon Igloo jugs (Add ice)
                    ____Five-gallon plastic bottles
                    ____Extra frozen bottles in coolers

____WET SUIT & BOOTIE RENTALS (Double check!!!) _____

____KITCHEN BOX (Check contents)

____DOs: ____12" ____14" ____16" ____Charcoal

____LIGHTER FLUID ____

____2 FRY PANS

____2 GRATES ____Extra grate(s) for giant group

____1 LARGE COFFEE POT

____1 MEDIUM COFFEE POT

____3-4 BILLY POTS W/LIDS

____DISHWASH: ____3 Chickie pails ____Dishwash unit ____Extra propane

____METAL BUCKETS: ____Large ____Medium ____Small

____STRAINER

____LUNCHBOARDS (Emergency backboards)

____SPECIAL CUTTING BOARDS ____Table cloths

____STOVES ____Extra stove fuel

____FOOD BOXES & BAGS

____COOLERS (with food) ____Extra ice ____Thermometers
                    ____First day's lunch in separate cooler
                    ____Top trays to keep food out of icemelt

____LUNCH UTENSIL BAG: ____Tomato slicer ____Paper towels
                      ____Cheese slicer ____5 paring Knives
                      ____3 spoons ____1 garbage bag w/fastener
                      ____3 forks ____1 bottle liquid hand soap
                      ____2 spreaders ____2 large knives
                      ____30 + cups ____Extra-long spoon
                                       (14" plus)

____SHOVEL

____WOOD ____Ax ____Wedge ____Splitting Maul

____DUFFEL BAGS (Empty, for garbage)

____POTTY: ____Potty can ____Toilet seat
          ____Lime ____Scoop ____Toilet paper (plenty, in plastic bags)
          ____Potty tent ____3 Plastic bags
          ____Instructions for holding-tank-type potty
          ____Chemical toilet ____Chemicals
          ____Funnel ____Extra holding tank
          ____Cleaning kit: brush, soap, Pinesol

____MOTOR TOW: ____Outboard motor ____Tow boat
              ____Gas Tank ____Extra gas ____Extra sheer pin
              ____Outboard motor oil ____Fuel line ____Motor mount
              ____Safety line to prevent loss of motor

____INFLATABLE KAYAKS ____Seats ____Pumps
                      ____Kayak paddles
                      ____Valve pump adaptors ____Extra paddles
                      ____Kayak repair kit

____SCHOOLS ____Exams ____Guide's Guide
           ____Chef's rosters/itinerary
           ____List of participants ____Maps

____LIBRARY BOXES

____SPARE CLOTHES (bags of extra sweaters & wind breakers)

____PEDDLER'S CASE ____T-shirts (full selection) ____Visors ____Decals
                   ____Bandanas ____Fabric patches

____TRIP LEADER: ____Trip file ____Leader's report ____Clip boards
                ____Extra release forms ____Envelope for receipts
                ____Pens ____Emergency cash ____Credit cards
                ____Gate key ____Shuttle driver key ____Check(s)
                ____Stash box keys ____Special books, maps
                ____Brochures (plenty) ____River permit ____Alarm clock
                ____Travel sheet ____Shuttle driver info
                ____Boatman's license BLM trip ticket
                ____Class II license & health certification

____TOOLS

____EXTRA SPARE TIRE

____EXTRA GAS

____TRAILER ____Extra hitch ball & bolt ____Make sure hitch is tight

____BLANKETS & PILLOWS

____TENT(S)

____GLOVES

____CAMERA(S)

____AMERICAN RIVER: ____Paddle & chain to lock up boats at night
                   ____Visitor tickets for Marshall Gold
                   Discovery State Historic Park
                   ____Thermometers in coolers (required)
                   ____Special cutting boards (required)

____KLAMATH RIVER: ____Curly Jack signs

____SPECIALS _____
_____
_____

FIRST AID KIT CONTENTS

FIRST AID KIT CONTENTS

Leave the first aid kits pre packed at all times. After completely packing and closing the kit, tape the kit shut with one piece of blue electrical tape. When the kit is used, break or remove the tape -- when it returns from the trip, it will only need to be re-done if the seal is broken or missing. Never replace the seal until the kit has been fully checked and re-stocked.

Trip Leader Packet		**Packet #5 - Sealed - "Trauma Rama" Kit**	
☐ 2 - **Emergency Procedure Sheets**.		☐ 2 -Triangle Bandages - for slings	
☐ 2 - *each* **Injury Forms** - Client & Guide.		☐ 2 - Roller Gauze	
☐ 3 - **Witness Forms**		☐ **1 - Eye pad**	
		☐ 2 - Large Compresses	
Packet #1 - Ziplock - Library		☐ 1 - CPR Shield Pocket Mask	
☐ **Permit Copies** - include all rivers in area.		☐ 4 - Pairs of Gloves	
☐ 2 - **Hospital Cards for Employees**		☐ 6 - 4 X 4's Gauze and 2 X 2's Gauze	
☐ 1 - **Red Cross First Aid Handbook.**		☐ 1 - Set oral airways (optional)	
☐ 1 - copy of. **"Mountaineering Medicine".**			
☐ 2 - Ballpoint **Pens**.			
Packet #2 - Ziplock - "Boo Boo" Kit		**Packet #6 - Sealed - Medicine Chest** (see extra notes next page)	
☐ 10 - Triple Antibiotic Ointments		☐ 5 - Sting Swabs	
☐ 6 - Gauze 4 x 4's,		☐ 3 - Ammonia Swabs/5 Hydrocortisone cream	
☐ 6 - Gauze 2 x 2's		☐ 10 - Peptol Bismol Tabs	
☐ 15 - Band-Aids		☐ 10 - Kaopectate Tabs or Immodium AD	
☐ 5 - Stretch Coverlets		(intestinal)	
☐ 15 - Butterfly or Steristrip Band-Aids		☐ 1 - Oil of Cloves or 4 - Ambusol	
☐ 5 - Swabs, Benzoin		☐ 8 - Antihistamine Tabs (Benadryl)	
☐ 4 - Pairs Protective Gloves		☐ 5 - Hydrocortisone Cream	
☐ 5 - Pads - Providone-Iodine Prep		☐ 2 - Pkg. Gatorade or Squincher	
☐ 6 - Alcohol Pads		☐ 1 - Glucose	
☐ 4 - moist towlettes		☐ 1 - Dispenser Primatene Mist	
☐ 10 - Tampons			
Packet #3 - Sealed - Tool Kit		**Packet #7 - Sealed - Hardware**	
☐ 1 - Tweezer		☐ 2 - Matches or Lighters	
☐ 1 - Scissors		☐ 10 - Safety Pins	
☐ 1 - Hypothermia & 1 regular Thermometer		☐ 3 - Needles (sewing)	
☐ 1 - Mini Flashlight		☐ 2 - Canteen Jug Lids	
☐ 1 - Eye Cup		☐ 1 - Water Purifier	
Packet #4 - Ziplock - Headache Bag		**Loose Items** ✳ 2 - Biohazard Bags (see over)	
☐ 10 -Tylenol Packets/Aspirin Free		☐ 1 - Mist inhaler	
☐ 10 - Ibuprofin Packets		☐ 1 - Sam Splint ☐ 1 - Emetrol	
☐ 10 - Aspirin Packets		☐ 1 - Benzoin Spray	
☐ 2 - Kids Tylenol (Angina)		☐ 1 - Insect Repellent ☐ 1 - C Collar	
		☐ 1 - 60cc Syringe ☐ 1 - Soap	
		☐ 1 - Hydrogen ☐ 1 - Road Flare	
		☐ 2 - Ace Bandages ☐ 1 - Aloe Vera	
		☐ 1 - Waterproof roll of 2" Tape and 1 roll 1" Tape	
		☐ 1 - 4 oz. Saline Bottle or 2 - ½ oz Bottles	
		☐ 2 - Ice & Hot Packs	
		☐ 2 - Sun Screens or Zinc Dioxide	

Extra notes for: PACKET #6 - SEALED MEDICINE CHEST

MEDICINE	DOSAGE	INDICATIONS FOR USE
BENADRYL	**Adults** ~ Take 1 to 2 capsules every 4 - 6 hours. ***Not to exceed 12 capsules in 24 hours.*** (***Children*** *Ages 6 - 12 years - take 1 capsule every 4 - 6 hours.*)	Temporarily relieves runny nose, sneezing; itchy, watery eyes; itchy nose or throat due to Hay Fever or other respiratory allergies and the common cold.
KAOPECTATE	**Adults** ~Take 2 caplets after the initial bowel movement and 2 caplets after each subsequent bowels movement, not to exceed 12 caplets in 24 hours. (***Children*** *Ages 6 - 12 years - take 1 caplet after initial bowel movement and 1 caplet after each subsequent bowel movement, not to exceed 6 caplets in 24 hours.*)	Relieves Diarrhea and Cramping. **Drink plenty of fluids to prevent dehydration!!**
PEPTO BISMOL	**Adults** - 2 tablets, **Children** - 9 - 12 years - 1 tablet. Repeat every ½ to 1 hour as needed. Maximum dosage - 8 doses in a 24-hour period.	Provides relief for Indigestion, Upset Stomach, Heartburn, Nausea and Diarrhea. **Drink plenty of fluids!!!**

✳   Biohazard bags ~ all instruments and treating items that come in contact with bodily fluids - including (but not limited to) needles, swabs, used gauze, band aids, etc.

✳   Mist inhalers ~ are one use (one person) items, replace with new inhaler after removal from lid.

REPAIR KIT CONTENTS

List of repair kit contents (taped inside kit lid)
Glue and catalyst
One-part cement
Waterproof sandpaper
Small paint brush
Mixing cup
Wide roller
Patching fabric
Scissors
Ballpoint pen
Glue solvent
Extra paint brush
Needle nose pliers
Needle & thread
Liquid rubber
Spare oarlock & rings
Hose clamps
Duct tape
Adjustable wrench or vice grips
Screwdriver
Spare frame set screws & allen wrench

In the context of a river trip, guides glow with charisma in the eyes of their crew. Some guides lose their perspective in the flow of this energizing adoration and start thinking in an "us versus them" manner summed up by the words, "I'm a cool river guide, and these people in my boat are not." The contextual adoration tends to be so strong, trip members will even let guides get away with this. The big problem with this is that everyone loses. Truly cool guides remain humble and reflect the energizing attention flowing toward them back out onto every individual present and the group as a whole. This way everyone, including the guide, gets to feel and truly be cool and appreciated.

Fully enter into the experience of each trip. Be present. If you find yourself thinking about something or somewhere else, invite your attention back into the moment by asking yourself, "How can I enhance my experience—and the experience of the people I am with—right now?".

7 : EXPEDITION FOOD PLANNING GUIDE

GENERAL ADVICE

Cooking on the river is similar to cooking at home. With a sprinkling of ingenuity, one can adapt any home recipe to the river. In fact, many guides feel more at ease cooking on the river than they do at home.

ANYTHING IS POSSIBLE

Our clients are impressed when the menu is varied, and, interestingly enough, variety often costs no more. So, while not forgetting the budget, bring out your favorite recipes. Be creative!

CREATIVITY & VARIETY

Consider purchasing lunches at a delicatessen. Deli's have a broad selection—including turkey breasts, ham, pastrami, summer sausage, etc.—and they will slice everything up.

THE DELI ROUTE

Some butchers will freeze meat orders—which is great for longer trips.

FROZEN MEAT FOR LONG TRIPS

Think about dinner preparation schedules ahead of time. If things must marinate, complete this before everyone crowds around the kitchen area smacking their lips for food. Arrange food items so they're easy to locate—otherwise you'll be frantically wondering where things are. Of course, enlist the aid of your fellow guides and the boaters to help prepare dinner. Meal preparation should be a community experience.

DINNER PREPARATION

Although I like it just fine, tuna casserole for dinner seems to be scorned by many as a low-budget, end-of-the-line meal. We avoid serving it.

AVOID TUNA CASSEROLE

On long trips with space for extra baggage, fill a cooler with a 15-pound block of dry ice and take along frozen yogurt or ice cream for dessert. This special, Christmas-like treat impresses everyone.

ICE CREAM

SHOPPING CHECKLIST FOR SHORT TRIPS

LUNCH 1	LUNCH 2	LUNCH 3
____bread (variety)	____bread	____bread
____mayonnaise	____mayonnaise	____mayonnaise
____mustard (hot/plain)	____mustard	____mustard
____cheese	____cheese	____cheese
____ham	____cold cuts	____cold cuts
____turkey	____tuna fish	____cream cheese
____onions	____relish	____green onions
____pickles	____green onions	____celery
____cucumbers	____cucumbers	____carrots
____avocados	____olives	____olives
____tomatoes	____hard boiled eggs	____tomatoes
____sprouts	____pickles	____avocados
____lettuce	____tomatoes	____pickles
____peanut butter	____avocados	____cucumbers
____jam	____sprouts	____sprouts
____fruit	____lettuce	____lettuce
____cookies	____peanut butter	____peanut butter
____drink	____jam	____jam
____gorp	____fruit	____fruit
	____cookies	____cookies
	____drink	____drink
	____gorp	____gorp

HAPPY HOUR	DINNER 1	DINNER 2
____potato chips	____steak	____chicken
____crackers	____potatoes	____rice
____dip	____green vegetables	____green vegetables
____cheese	____salad:	____bar-b-q sauce
____wine	____ lettuce	____salad:
____7-up	____ tomatoes	____ lettuce
____grapefruit juice	____ cucumbers	____ tomatoes
____oranges	____ green onions	____ cucumbers
____limes	____ avocados	____ green onions
____carrots	____ mushrooms	____ avocados
____celery	____ radishes	____ mushrooms
	____salad dressing	____ radishes
	____A-1 sauce	____milk
	____catsup	____drink
	____milk	____cake
	____drink	
	____cake	

MENU FOR SEVEN-DAY EXPEDITION

BREAKFAST 1

____eggs
____mushrooms
____green peppers
____cheese
____green onions
____milk
____hash browns
____bacon
____blueberry muffins
____juice

BREAKFAST 2

____french toast
____bread
____eggs
____milk
____syrup
____bacon
____yogurt
____O.J.
____fruit

MENU FOR SEVEN-DAY EXPEDITION

FIRST DAY

EVERY DAY	LUNCH	DINNER
Coffee	Ham Sandwiches	BBQ Chicken
Tea	Gorp	Rice
Cocoa	Drink	Vegetable
	Cookies	Cole Slaw
	Fruit	Devil's Food Cake

SECOND DAY

BREAKFAST	LUNCH	DINNER
French Toast	Egg Salad	Steak
Bacon	Sandwiches	Potatoes
O.J.	Gorp	Vegetables
Melon	Drink	Tossed Salad
	Cookies	Fruit Melange

THIRD DAY

BREAKFAST	LUNCH	DINNER
Scrambled Eggs	Cream Cheese	Pork Chops
Hash Browns	Spread	Apple Sauce
Blueberry Muffins	Bagels	Peas
Apple Juice	Gorp	Corn Bread
	Drink	Fruit Salad
	Cookies	
	Fruit	

FOURTH DAY

BREAKFAST	LUNCH	DINNER
Tomato & Cheese Omelettes	Chicken Salad Sandwiches	Hamburgers
Bacon	Gorp	Baked Beans
O.J.	Drink	Potato Salad
Melon	Cookies	Ice Cream
	Fruit	

FIFTH DAY

BREAKFAST	LUNCH	DINNER
One-Eyed Egyptians	Tuna Salad Sandwiches	Ham
Sausage	Gorp	Yams
Fruit	Drink	3-Bean Salad
Grape Juice	Cookies	Pineapple Upside Down Cake
	Fruit	

SIXTH DAY

BREAKFAST	LUNCH	DINNER
Granola	Bean Dip	Shish-Kabob
Coffee Cake	Guacamole	Rice
Yogurt	Tortillas	Tossed Salad
O.J.	Gorp	Pioneer Cobbler
	Drink	
	Cookies	
	Fruit	

SEVENTH DAY

BREAKFAST	LUNCH
Scrambled eggs	Cold Cuts
Muffins	Gorp
Bacon	Drink
Fruit	Cookies
O.J.	Fruit

MENU FOR EIGHTEEN-DAY EXPEDITION

DAY 1
B: Doughnuts, orange juice, milk, yogurt
L: Cheese, lunchmeat sandwiches, iced tea, cookies, fruit
D: Chinese beef & mushrooms, rice, sno-peas, cream cheese, chocolate cake, beer, wine

MENU FOR EIGHTEEN-DAY EXPEDITION

DAY 2
B: Bagels & cream cheese, strawberries, grapefruit, juice
L: Guacamole, pita bread, tomatoes, lettuce, cheese, lemonade, bananas, oranges
D: Hamburgers, homefried potatoes, BBQ chili beans, leaf lettuce salad, cookies

DAY 3
B: French toast, grapefruit slices, orange juice, syrup
L: Cream cheese spread, pita & regular bread, lettuce, tomatoes, orange drink, apples, cookies
D: BBQ chicken, corn on the cob, fruit salad, instant pudding, wine

DAY 4
B: Eggs, Jack cheese, green chilis, blueberry muffins, apple juice
L: Lunchmeat sandwiches, pb & j, instant drink, cheese, oranges, plums, etc.
D: Steaks, potatoes, green beans, brownies, beer

DAY 5
B: Cereal, powdered milk, blueberries, orange juice
L: Tuna, cheese, crackers, bread, apples, cookies, hard candy, iced tea
D: Meatless spaghetti, garlic bread, green bean salad, cookies

DAY 6
B: Grapefruit juice, pecan pancakes, syrup, butter, boiled eggs (extra for lunch)
L: Egg salad sandwiches, crackers, bread, pb & j, pickles, granola bars, gorp, lemonade, apples
D: Chinese fried rice w/ham, peas, shrimp, cashews, pineapple upside down cake

DAY 7
B: Granola, fruit, powdered milk, pineapple juice
L: Deviled ham, bread or seatoast, cheese, crackers, olives, fruit drink, pickles, cookies
D: Chicken curry, rice, peas, cashews, cookies, lemonade

DAY 8
B: Hot cereal, brown sugar, butter, powdered milk, Tang, grapefruit slices
L: Chicken salad, crackers, seatoast, tea, dried fruit, cookies
D: Tuna noodle casserole, green beans, biscuits, rum cake

DAY 9
B: Cinnamon coffee cake, peaches, grapefruit juice
L: Canned ham sandwiches, cheese, seatoast, pb & j, fruit drink, cookies, dried fruit
D: Lasagna, fruit salad, drink mix, gorp

DAY 10
B: Blueberry muffins, Tang, dried fruit, butter
L: Salami, seatoast, crackers, cheese, drink mix, gorp
D: Chicken soup, vegetables, snackin' cake

DAY 11
B: Applesauce pancakes, syrup, butter, Tang
L: Tuna salad, candy, dried fruit, cheese, crackers, tea
D: Chili w/cheese, Mexican cornbread, rum punch, pudding cups

DAY 12
B: Cinnamon-caramel rolls, grapefruit juice, dried fruit, cereal
L: Dried salami, raisins, dried fruit, cheese, fruit cups, crackers, seatoast
D: Clam spaghetti, corn, fruit, candy

DAY 13
B: Cereal, blueberries, powdered milk, apple juice
L: Chicken salad, pears, seatoast, gorp
D: Smothered burritos, tomatoes, snackin' cake, drink mix

DAY 14
B: Fruit salad, biscuits, honey, butter, Tang
L: Canned ham, cheese, cookies, triscuits, apricots
D: Tamale bake, soy burger, tomatoes, corn, cheese, cornmeal, black olives

DAY 15
B: Oatmeal, raisins, applesauce, Tang
L: Peanut butter & jelly, dried fruit, pickles, olives, cheese, crackers
D: Pepperoni pizza with mushrooms, instant pudding w/cherries

DAY 16
B: Muffins, butter, apricots, Tang
L: Tuna salad, gorp, Hawaiian punch, granola bars, pb & j, crackers, seatoast
D: Ham w/pineapple, mustard sauce, brown sugar, corn, green bean casserole, cookies

DAY 17
B: Coffee cake, applesauce, tomato & pineapple juice
L: Dried salami, pudding cups and cookies, tea, cheese, seatoast, crackers
D: Potluck-leftovers

DAY 18
B: Cereal, pears, peaches, apricots, Tang
L: Leftovers

KITCHEN BOX CONTENTS

Utensils
1 Bottle Opener
2 Can Openers
3 Paring Knives
1 Large Ladle
3 Large Spoons

KITCHEN BOX CONTENTS

1 Leaky Spoon
3 Large Forks
3 Large Tongs
Spoon/Fork Salad Tongs
4 Spatulas
Extra Spoons
Extra Forks
Extra Butter Knives
Extra Plates
Extra Cups
1 Measuring Cup
60 Skewer Sticks (optional)
1 Hand Mixer

Food Support
5-10 lbs Coffee
Instant Coffee (reserve)
25 Tea Bags
Herb Tea
1 Box Hot Chocolate
White Sugar
Brown Sugar
Non-Dairy Creamer
1 Quart Cooking Oil
Barbecue Sauce
Syrup (optional)
1 Can Frosting
Decorator Frosting
Vanilla Extract
Dry Milk (small box)
Flour (optional)
White Vinegar
Wine Vinegar
Extra Powdered Drink Mix
Soy Sauce
Catsup
Honey
Chicken & Beef Bouillon Cubes

Miscellaneous
Liquid Hand Soap
Dish Soap
Flashlight
Aluminum Foil
2 Boxes Wooden Matches (keep in plastic bag)
2 Rolls Paper Towels
10-20 Heavy Duty Plastic Garbage Bags
10-20 Garbage Bag Fasteners
1 Box Zip-Lock Bags
6 Hot Pad Gloves
1 Pair Channel Locks
3 Dish Scrubbing Brushes with Handles

SOS Pads
Extra Roll of Toilet Paper (keep in plastic bag)
1 Qt. Clorox with Eye-Dropper (for water purification)
1 Shovel
1 Saw
1 Pack Birthday Candles
2 Lighters

Spices
2 Salt
2 Pepper
Garlic Salt
Lawrey's Seasoning Salt
A-1 Sauce
Nutmeg
Cinnamon
Dill Weed
Parsley
Oregan
Mustard Powder

LUNCH UTENSIL BAG CONTENTS
1 Tomato Slicer
1 Extra Long Spoon (14″ or longer)
3 Forks
3 Spoons
1 Large Knife
4 Butter Knives
1 Can Opener
4 Paring Knives
1 Cheese Slicer
2 Spreaders
30 Cups
1 or 2 Garbage Bags w/Fasteners
1 Liquid Hand Soap/Sanitizer
1 Roll Paper Towels
1 Cheese Grater

OTHER COOKING GEAR
(not usually kept in box)
D.O.'s
Charcoal
3 Chickie Pails
2 Fry Pans
2 Grates
1 Large Coffee Pot
1 Medium Coffee Pot
3-4 Billie Pots w/Lids

QUANTITY/YIELD LIST
APPROXIMATES

GORP: 1 lb. Peanuts
1 lb. M & M's
1 lb. Raisins

Yield: 20-25 people

Also good: Yogurt peanuts, carob cashews, dried
dates, shelled sunflower seeds, etc.

MEATS: Steak: 1/4 - 1/2 lb. steak per person
Chicken: approx. 1/4 chicken (buy whole) per
person plus one or two extra chickens
Pork Chops: 2 per person
Ham: 1/4 - 1/2 lb. per person
Hamburger: 1/3 to 1/2 lb. per person
Tuna: (1 7 oz. can): approx. 3 persons
Chicken (1 5 - 6 oz. can): approx. 2 persons
Bacon: 3 slices per person
Sausage: 3 per person

BREAD: 1 loaf = approx. 8 sandwiches

EGGS: 2 per person

POTATOES: (red-small/med. size) 2 per person for dinner
1 per person for breakfast

JUICES: 2 large cans of concentrate for 20 people

RIVER RECIPES
TO SERVE 20-25 PERSONS

BUTTERED FRENCH BREAD APPETIZER
     11 Loaves French sourdough bread
     3 lbs. Butter
Slice loaves lengthwise, butter liberally. Wrap in tin foil and heat
over the fire. Bon appetit!

HAM AND PEACH SAUCE
     cooked canned ham (10 lb. size)
     peaches (about 20)
     2 cups brown sugar
     3 cups of frozen orange juice concentrate
     5 tablespoons butter
Mix the peach glaze sauce first. To do this combine about 20
peeled and finely chopped peaches with sugar and thawed juice
concentrate and butter in a pan. Let simmer 15 minutes. Cut up
the ham and fry it in a frying pan, spoon the sauce over each
piece. Serve when ham is hot.

CHICKEN WITH PINEAPPLE

        5 frying chickens-cut up
        5 cups of pineapple chunks
        1-1/4 cups of orange marmalade
        salt, pepper
        5 envelopes of chicken gravy mix
        1-1/4 cups of white wine
        paprika

Butter or grease the D.O. and fire it up. Stick in the chicken. Season with salt and pepper. Drain the pineapple and save the liquid. Scatter the pineapple over the chicken. Add water to the pineapple liquid to make five cups. Combine with gravy mix, marmalade and wine. Spoon over the chicken and sprinkle with paprika. Bake the chicken at about 400° for about one hour (have plenty of coals on hand), spooning sauce over chicken until tender and brown.

SOUTH SEAS SAUSAGE AND RICE

        6-1/2 pounds old country style smoked sausage
        4-1/2 cups of catsup
        5 tablespoons of prepared mustard
        6 cups of fresh pineapple chunks
        3 cups pineapple juice
        20 cups of hot cooked brown rice
        5 cups of chicken broth
        5 cups of chopped onion
        12 tablespoons soy sauce
        5 large green peppers, cut into 1″ pieces

Cook sausage in 3 cups of water for about 5 minutes. Remove from water and cut into thin slices. Combine sausage and onions in large skillet and cook until onions are tender/crisp. Stir in mustard, soy sauce, catsup, broth, pepper, pineapple, and pineapple juice. Simmer about 10 minutes. Add green peppers and cook 5 minutes longer, serve on rice.

BOATMAN'S CHILI AND RICE
An easy meal!

        3-1/2 pounds of lean ground beef
        3 tablespoons of salt
        5 (11 oz.) cans of vegetable beef soup
        6 cups of hot cooked brown rice
        2 cups of sliced onion
        10 tablespoons of chili powder
        1-1/4 cups water
        2 cups green pepper
        2 large cans pinto or kidney beans

Saute beef, peppers and onion until well browned. Add salt, chili powder, beans, soup, and water, simmer about 10-15 minutes and serve over rice.

RIVER PEPPER STEAK

    20 cups of hot cooked brown rice
    10 tablespoons of butter
    5 tablespoons of paprika
    5 cups of sliced green onions including the tops
    10 tablespoons of cornstarch
    1-1/2 cups of soy sauce
    5 pounds of lean steak cut into thin strips
    6-1/2 cups of beef broth
    10 green peppers cut into thin strips
    1-1/4 cups of water
    10 large tomatoes cut into eighths

Sprinkle steak with paprika. In large skillets brown meat in butter, add garlic and broth. Cover and simmer for 30 minutes. Stir in onions and green peppers. Cover and cook for five minutes. Blend cornstarch, water, soy sauce, and stir in meat mixture until clear (about 2 minutes). Add tomatoes and stir, serve over rice.

COLORADO SWEDISH MEATBALLS

    5 cups of dried bread crumbs
    1-1/4 cups evaporated milk
    5 pounds of ground beef
    5 eggs
    10 teaspoons of minced onions
    1-1/4 cups hot water
    3/4 teaspoon allspice
    1-1/4 teaspoons black pepper
    1-1/4 teaspoons garlic salt
    1-1/4 cups oil or shortening
    2-1/2 teaspoons of beef base
    brown rice or noodles

Soak crumbs in evaporated milk, then combine with beef, egg, onion, and seasonings. Shape into balls. Brown all sides in hot shortening, pour off excess fat. Dissolve beef base in hot water and add to meat balls, cover and simmer 20 minutes. Pour over rice or noodles.

MORE RECIPES

MAIN COURSES:

SAVORY SUPPER BAKE

    1 can (20 oz.) apple slices, drained
    3 cups cooked elbow macaroni
    1 cup diced boned chicken or turkey
    1 cup diced cooked ham
    2 Tbl. butter or margarine
    1 small onion, chopped
    2 cans (8 oz. each) tomato sauce
    1/2 tsp. basil leaves
    1/2 tsp. salt
    1 cup shredded cheddar cheese

Arrange 1-1/2 cups apple slices and all of macaroni, chicken and ham in alternate layers in D.O. Melt butter in skillet. Add onion. Saute until golden. Add tomato sauce, basil and salt. Pour into D.O. Top with cheese. Garnish with remaining apple slices. Cover. Bake for approximately 45 minutes. Serves 6-8.

SWEET AND SOUR CHICKEN

    3 cans chicken
    1 can pineapple chunks
    1 can sweet and sour sauce
    1 cup onions
    1 cup green peppers

Simmer together for 15 to 20 minutes. Serve over hot biscuits (made in D.O.) or brown rice. Serves 6.

CORNED BEEF WITH BISCUITS

    melt 1/4 tub margarine
    saute 1 onion (chopped) and 1 green pepper
      (chopped)
    sprinkle with approx. 1 cup Bisquick
    add slowly, stirring constantly—10 cups milk
    add 2 cans cream of mushroom soup (or instant)
    add 3 cans corned beef

Season to taste. Serve on hot biscuits (made in D.O.) or brown rice. Serves approx. 20.

BEEF WITH MUSHROOMS

    1 pound flank steak (cut in 1/4" slices)
    1/4 cup soy sauce
    1 Tbl. cornstarch
    1 Tbl. dry sherry (or dry white wine)
    1 tsp. sugar or honey
    1/2 cup sliced onion
    4 Tbl. vegetable oil
    1/2 tsp. salt

2 (4 oz.) cans mushrooms
or 6-8 oz. fresh mushrooms
1 slice ginger root

Mix 1st 6 ingredients and set aside. Put 2 Tbl. oil in hot skillet over high heat. Add salt & mushrooms. Cook, stirring, about 2 mins. Remove from skillet. Add remaining oil to skillet & add ginger root. Keeping skillet over high heat add beef mixture and cook, stirring, less than 2 minutes. Add mushrooms and mix well, serve with brown rice, noodles or potatoes. Serves 3 to 4.

CHINESE FRIED RICE

2 Tbl. oil
2 cups coarsely chopped onions
1 cup coarsely chopped green peppers
2 cups cooked brown rice — cold
2 eggs, slightly beaten
1 Tbl. soy sauce
1/2 tsp. salt

Heat pan, add oil, fry onions and peppers until brown. Add *cold* brown rice and saute. Add eggs, seasoned with soy sauce and salt, and saute until done. For variety, add 2 cups chopped cooked meat (bacon, ham, shrimp, chicken) or peanuts. Serves 4.

CHICKEN CURRY

1/2 cup butter or margarine
4 cups cooked chicken (canned chunk chicken,
   or fresh chicken)
1/4 lb. sliced mushrooms
1 cup sliced onions
1/2 cup chopped celery
1/2 cup sifted flour
4 tsp. curry powder
garlic (to taste)
salt (to taste)
2 cups chicken broth (bouillon)
2 cups canned milk
3 oz. toasted almonds
coconut (for garnishing)

Heat butter or margarine in a pan. Add onions & celery, saute a few minutes, then add mushrooms. Saute a couple more minutes and then remove the vegetables using a slotted spoon. Put them in a bowl and set aside. Now blend into the remaining butter: sifted flour, curry powder, garlic & salt. Heat the mixture, stirring constantly until the mixture bubbles. Remove it from heat, add gradually, stirring constantly: chicken broth & milk. Return to heat and bring to a rapid boil (always stirring). Cook 1 or 2 minutes longer, add chicken and vegetables, cook together until hot, serve over rice. Sprinkle coconut & almonds over the top. You can also sprinkle it with peanuts, bananas, raisins, chutney, etc. Serves 5.

BURRITOS
>flour tortillas (jumbo size)
>green chili pork sauce
>refried beans (1/3 can per burrito)
>hamburger (1/4 lb. per burrito)
>taco seasoning
>lettuce
>sharp cheddar cheese
>black olives (chopped)
>chopped tomatoes
>sour cream
>hot sauce

OLLA PODRIDA
>2 yellow onions
>4 pkgs. chicken breasts
>2 pkgs. chorizo (Mexican sausage)
>2 large can tomatoes
>4 cans garbanzo beans (chick peas)
>1 head cabbage — finely sliced
>1 lb. carrots — sliced
>oil

Brown onions and chicken in oil. Add chorizo. Stir. Add tomatoes, garbanzo beans & carrots. Simmer until carrots are almost tender. Add cabbage. Cover and cook approximately ½ hour or until carrots are done. Serves 12 - 16. Good with cornbread.

SALADS:

TUNA OR CHICKEN SALAD
>7 large cans tuna
>1 large jar mayonnaise
>2 chopped onions
>1/2 package celery (chopped)
>1 small jar sweet pickle relish

Season with lemon juice and mustard. Yield: approx. 21 servings.

EGG SALAD
>2 doz. eggs (hard boiled)
>1 jar mayonnaise
>1/2 package celery (chopped)
>season to taste

Yield: 12-15 servings.

GREEN SALAD
>2 heads iceberg lettuce
>4 heads red lettuce
>7 tomatoes
>4 cucumbers

3 green peppers
mushrooms
1 bunch green onions
1 box croutons
1 package sharp cheddar cheese (diced)
Yield: approx. 20 servings.

3-BEAN SALAD

4 cans kidney beans
4 cans green beans
2 cans garbanzo beans
1/2 head red cabbage (chopped)
2 cans artichoke hearts
1 bottle Italian dressing
Yield: approx. 21 servings.

FRUIT SALAD

7 cans fruit (fruit cocktail, peaches, etc., except
canned pineapple)
7 oranges
10 apples
fresh fruit when in season.
Yield: approx. 21 servings.

GUACAMOLE

3 avocados, peeled and pitted
1 medium onion, finely chopped
2 green chili peppers, chopped
1 Tbl. lemon juice
1 tsp. salt
1/2 tsp. coarsely ground pepper
1 med. tomato, peeled and chopped
mayonnaise
several dashes tobasco sauce
Beat avocados, onion, peppers, lemon juice, tobasco, salt and
pepper until creamy. Gently fold in tomato. Spread top with thin
layer of mayonnaise. Stir gently just before serving.
Yield: 4 servings.

COLE SLAW

1 head cabbage, grated
2 apples
1 bunch celery, diced
5 carrots, grated
raisins (yellow)
1 bottle cole slaw dressing.
Yield: 8-10 servings.

DESSERTS:

PINEAPPLE UPSIDE-DOWN CAKE
> line D.O. with aluminum foil
> grease with oil or butter
> line the D.O. with 1 can pineapple slices
> sprinkle over pineapple: 1/2 cup brown sugar, and
>   2-3 Tbl. pineapple juice
> prepare and pour over fruit: 1 white or yellow
>   cake mix (adjusted for altitude)

Cover and cook 25 to 40 minutes, depending on heat.
Yield: 8 to 10 servings.

PIONEER COBBLERS
> line D.O. with aluminum foil
> place in bottom of D.O.: 1 quart sliced peaches
> sprinkle on top (or add to batter): 1 tsp. nutmeg,
>   and 1-2 Tbl. sugar
> prepare and pour over top: 1 pkg. French vanilla
>   or white cake mix (adjusted for altitude)

Cover and cook 25 to 40 minutes, depending on heat, until brown.
Yield: 6 servings.

BAKED FRUIT MELANGE
> 1 can (1 lb.) apricot halves, drained, reserve
>   syrup
> 1 can (8 oz.) pitted bing cherries, drained, reserve
>   syrup
> 1 can (8 oz.) pineapple slices, drained, reserve
>   syrup
> 2 oranges, peeled, sliced, reserve rind
> 1/4 cup firmly packed brown sugar
> 1/4 tsp. ground nutmeg
> dairy sour cream

Pour reserve fruit syrups into saucepan. Grate 1 Tbl. rind. Add to syrup. Boil until syrup is reduced by half. Arrange orange slices with fruit in D.O. Pour syrup over fruit. Sprinkle with sugar and nutmeg. Cover and cook 20 to 30 minutes, depending on heat.
Yield: 6 servings.

BROWN BEARS IN APPLE ORCHARD
> line D.O. with aluminum foil
> grease with oil or butter
> line the bottom of the D.O. with 2 or 3 sliced
>   apples
> mix and pour over fruit: 1 pkg. gingerbread mix

Cover and cook 25 to 45 minutes, depending on heat.
Yield: 8 to 9 servings

CHOCOLATE PUDDING CAKE
>line D.O. with aluminum foil
>grease lightly with butter
>mix 1 cup brown sugar with 1/2 cup cocoa
>add 2 cups water and stir until blended
>add 1 cup miniature marshmallows over the
>mixture
>Prepare and mix 1 devil's food cake mix,
>(adjusted for altitude).

Place pudding mixture in D.O. and spoon cake mix over the top. Top with 1 cup chopped nuts. Cover and bake 40 to 45 minutes. Yield: 8 servings

APPLE CRUMB
>3 large cooking apples (or canned slices)
>6 heaping Tbl. flour
>3 oz. butter
>6 tsp. brown sugar
>3 Tbl. castor sugar
>mixed dried fruit
>raisins
>lemon juice
>nutmeg and cinammon

Skin, core and slice apples. Sieve flour into bowl, add butter, rub together into breadcrumbs. Stir in castor sugar. Put in slices of apple with mixed fruit and cover with moist brown sugar. Sprinkle crumble on top of apple, cook in D.O. for 30 minutes.

A RECIPE FOR CONTENTMENT
Do good unto others and it will return threefold.

In your innermost self talk, cultivate a sincere intention to create a positive, supportive atmosphere in which you and your companions, free from having to defend yourselves, can relax, open up, expand and grow. This, after all, is at the heart of real fun!

8: ENTERTAINMENT AND INTERPRETATION

It is not enough just to get people as safely as possible down the river, it is also paramount for guides to enhance the fun, camaraderie, learning and openness on river trips. As much as any other, the spirit and contents of this part of this book go to the very heart of what it is to be a truly great river guide.

Deep Fun: Moving People from Fear to Courage to Joy

For people new to rafting, the thought of floating down through the swirling currents and surging, cresting waves of an actual wild river—in an inflatable rubber boat composed mainly of thin air—can be a daunting prospect. Such fears are entirely normal. In fact, when most people contemplate outdoor adventure activities like whitewater rafting, it is entirely normal to experience fear, consciously or unconsciously, on a number of levels. There is physical fear: Am I going to get hurt? Am I going to die? There is social fear: Am I going to be accepted or rejected by this group? And biggest of all, for most of us, are fears around issues of self esteem: Can I do this? Am I OK?

First, we as guides can assuage these fears with some facts: Modern whitewater rafts are extremely rugged, stable, compartmented and unsinkable. All participants of guided river trips wear very buoyant high-float life jackets. Whatever guided river trip one picks in the world today, literally thousands—and in many cases hundreds of thousands—of people have safely rafted before you. While, just as with any outdoor adventure activity, there is inherent risk, rafting with professional guides is far safer than skiing and probably safer than driving on a modern freeway or walking on a city street.

Second—and this is the key point—skilled river guides can implicitly assuage all of these fears in the very way they prepare people and guide them down the river. Every trip begins with a thorough safety talk and in-boat training which teach everything trip members need to know to make it safely down the river— thereby addressing physical fear. And by doing this with warmth, caring, good humor and respect, professional guides create an atmosphere of acceptance and support and good fun in which social fears and fears around issues of self esteem melt away.

In fact, a river journey with well-trained guides is much more than just a physical movement from put-in to take-out, it is a journey from fear to confidence to joy, from being a stranger to being known and feeling bonded with one's boat mates, from feeling perhaps scattered and self-critical inside to feeling more self-accepting, more whole, more fully alive—and, as an extra plus, it is a journey from feeling cut off from the natural world to feeling connected with and truly amazed and delighted by the magic of our planet. In short, a well-guided river trip is a voyage into deep fun.

Comments on *Deep Fun*
by Longtime Whitewater Voyages Guide Toni Hall

Hi Bill: I enjoyed reading "Deep Fun" and think this is where you excel: making people feel comfortable on raft trips. This is the true talent of an expert guide. I will always remember and respect you for something you told us long ago when we, as raft guides, had nearly completed another long hot drought-ridden summer on the water. I think it was on an American trip, years ago, when you advised us to "go and mingle" with the guests. Of course we were all huddled together in one group far away from the nearest guest, talking and laughing. Being young and perhaps not without a little hubris, we were, at the end of a long season, dependent on and bonded to each other. We also tended to put the guests in the "them" category as in us versus them.

What I mean to say is, I guess, more of a caution to young guides about including their guests into the full experience of whitewater rafting. Over the years, and I am sure you have found this too, that sharing experiences on trips has become more important than technical expertise on whitewater. Guests are an integral part of a team and it's the guide's art to inspire, teach and encourage them to be part of the whole experience.
I will always remember a story Pat Crevelt told me about his river trip as a guest with a company in Alaska. He said he had gotten up a little later one morning and found that he had missed breakfast. He asked if there were any eggs left. At the point, one of the guides actually took a plate of eggs and threw it into the garbage bag, saying "You snooze, you lose." Pat didn't say anything because he was "in their territory." He said this attitude prevailed during the whole trip, making everyone uncomfortable.

I think the most valuable lesson to put into the Guide's Guide is not how to tie knots or read water, but how to make the guests feel like part of a team on the river. I have seen very few Voyages guides who have not been able to do this and there are, of course, some exceptional guides that come to mind who do this extraordinarily well. But, when you are very young, being on the water and getting the boat downstream are sometimes the primary foci. The "Deep Fun" section is an incredibly important bit of wisdom.

General Guidelines for Enhancing Fun, Camaraderie, Learning and Openness

–**Earn the Group's Trust and Support:** In the beginning of each trip you are laying a foundation of seriousness that must underlie heartfelt silliness. Give an extra thorough safety talk with humor and supportiveness, and extra thorough in-boat training with a blend of humor, lots of positive strokes, nurturing and firmness. Thoroughly teach your crew everything they need to know to paddle well, stay in the boat, and cope with emergencies. It is only when everyone feels reassured that they are in good hands and knows how to play their part that they can completely relax and really be silly—and, in a sense, build an edifice of silliness on this foundation of seriousness.

–Seize the Moment: Be present in the moment—don't wait for take-out, tomorrow, etc. Whenever you notice yourself thinking about or yearning for take-out or anywhere else, ask, "What can I do right now to make this trip, this moment in this boat, in this camp, more enjoyable, fun, and supportive for all of us?" This is it! There is only now. In a very important sense there is nothing else. Our best option is to be here now!

–Tune In to the Group: Care about and take an interest in people and their real concerns. Really listen. Sense their mood, their inclinations. Be sensitive to who's a little afraid, who's a little rowdy, etc. Rather than launch into a set routine, reach out to, tune in to and respond to the group you are with.

–Be In the Moment with Your Own Feelings Too: Like a river flowing through you, notice, take in and welcome your emotions and in due course let them go. Use your feelings to guide you and spur you on in reaching out, connecting, encouraging people to open up, and ever so gently in luring them into silliness. It is by staying in touch with yourself that you can best connect with others— inside yourself you can sense what is going on for others.

–Share Your Attention Evenly: Include everyone.

–Be Humble, that is, Include Everyone in Your Coolness: Perhaps the single most influential thing a guide can do to inspire openness, trust and true camaraderie–and, hence, deep fun–is to simply be humble and appreciate others. In the context of a river trip, guides glow with charisma in the eyes of their crew. Some guides lose their perspective in the flow of this energizing adoration and start thinking in an "us versus them" manner summed up by the words, "I'm a cool river guide, and these people in my boat are not." The contextual adoration tends to be so strong, trip members will even let guides get away with this. The big problem with this is that everyone loses. Truly cool guides remain humble and reflect the energizing attention flowing toward them back out onto every individual present and the group as a whole. This way everyone, including the guide, gets to feel and truly be cool and appreciated.

–Cultivate an Appreciation for the Possibilities of Human Groups: Human groups, such as the circle of human souls in a raft or around a campfire, are capable of amazing quantum-leap magnifications of energy and aliveness. When a charismatic guide receives the energy flowing from the group and channels it back out to everyone present with the implicit message, "Everyone is cool and appreciated," everyone, including the guide, tends to experience, to put it mildly, an improved sense of well being, a heightened awareness (colors become more vivid, etc.) and a greatly increased flow of energy and aliveness! An amazingly wonderful aspect of all this is that everyone, including the guide, gets to experience the god-like pleasure of hanging out with cool, god-like people.

–Give Lots of Positive Strokes: Show lots of acceptance, approval, and support. Above all, do not judge others (whether they are present or not) or put others down. Negativism, elitism, bragging, sarcasm, put-downs, teasing, serious competition or machismo on the guide's part tends to make people feel judged, cautious, afraid. An atmosphere of acceptance and support, on the other hand, helps people feel okay, safe, expansive, free, and at one with themselves, their companions, the river and their world.

–The Goal Is to Include, Accept and Appreciate—and to Send the Message that Everyone Is Truly OK, Great and Wonderful—Just as They are Right Now! This is one of the most healing of all messages—and puts the group on the path to deep fun!

–Make It Okay to Be Quiet or Loud or Silly or However People Are Feeling!

–Inspire Mutual Respect and Appreciation Among All of the Members of the Group: In their influential, charismatic role, guides can create an atmosphere of mutual respect and appreciation. At times you will get mixes of very different human souls on your boat and in your camp. In your own way, communicate acceptance and support, saying both implicitly and at times explicitly: "We each have our own truth, and still we can treat all questions, answers, and statements of every kind with appreciation and respect."

–Celebrate the Fact that the River of Each Human Soul Tends to Be Deep and Wide and Multi-Layered and Ever Flowing. It is normal for us to have multiple and even contradictory feelings about issues, ourselves and one another all at the same time. As guides we can model and inspire in others an acceptance and celebration of this ever unfolding, multifaceted, mysterious richness! It is totally OK that at times parts of us don't like certain things about others. As human souls, even with all of our differences, we have an infinite number of things in common. When you have people on a trip who outwardly are very different from one another, you as the guide can in fact use this to enhance the group's experience. First, set an example of finding and focusing on things everyone has in common (as humans in any setting but especially when working together to run a river, we have just about everything in common, fundamentally). Later, as the group's bonds and sense of unity strengthen, appreciate and celebrate the differences—which turn out not to be so different after all. When a group of us humans has a really good time together, our very differences, seen from the perspective of all we have in common, can greatly add to the fun we find in being together!

–Develop the Biggest Repertoire You Can of nature lore, stories, games, songs, spins, wholesome jokes and other techniques.

–Exercise Caution: Of course, carefully evaluate the appropriateness of each activity of each group and each setting. Avoid injury and other problems by always using caution and good judgement.

–Above All, Be Present and Look for the Good In People!
Depending on the group, rowdiness and silliness can be great and even magical—and so can more quiet ways of seizing the moment. Let's start with the former:

River Games: A Touch of the Silly and the Rowdy

Caution: Any game that increases the chances of people getting discombobulated or someone falling overboard, should only be done with 100% willing crews in places where it is reasonably safe to swim.

–Dance of the Plunging Torsos: Antics with a serious purpose, this bit of tomfoolery is both fun and teaches a crew to paddle together. Right at put in, when teaching your crew how to paddle during your in-boat training, have them sit in their paddling positions and have each crew member grip the outboard shoulder of the person in front of them with the hand of their inboard arm. All of these inboard arms are locked straight. This position somewhat simulates the paddling position of inboard hand on the paddle t-grip, and it locks the torsos of the entire crew together. You sit in the bow facing your crew and hold the inboard hands of your two bow paddlers. Reminding everyone, including your bow paddlers, to lock their inboard arms straight, you pull the torsos of your crew far forward and then push them far back over and over again. Locked together by their straight arms, plunging forward and back, the crew not only laughs with delight but also directly experiences body sensations similar to those of paddling together, taking long strong strokes, and using the full power and range of motion of their upper bodies.

–Tea Cups: First, the paddlers seated on one side of the boat turn around to face the stern. Then, everyone does forward strokes to spin the boat as it floats through a mild rapid.

–Point Down River: With the crew's eyes closed, do teacups or any spin and, when the boat has come to a complete stop, ask your crew members, all the while with eyes closed, to point their finger in the direction they think is down river—and while they hold this point, only then have them open their eyes.

–Bow-Stern Switch: The crew stands, turns around to face the stern, and sits down. You captain from what has suddenly become the bow. Get's a good laugh.

–Foreign Planet–also called Upside Down Backward Spin: In a big calm or very mild, wide-open section of river far from any major rapid, everyone in the boat except the captain: First, stows their paddle. Second, slides their fannies down into the boat a ways. Third, wedges their feet. And last, leans back and slide out and down so their lower backs are firmly supported by the perimeter tube with the tips of their heads nearly touching the water. With the crew looking out upside down, the captain then slowly spins the boat to give everyone an astonishing visual treat! The passing view of water above and sky below so amazes the senses that people feel almost like they are on a breathtakingly strange and beautiful foreign planet. Tends to awaken folks to the ethereal beauty of our ancestral home planet: Earth!

–Eddy Spins: Use eddy turns when running rapids. As always, caution people on the downstream side to lean in when entering eddies, and those on the upstream side to lean in when leaving.

–Bow Belly Ride: One at a time, members of the crew volunteer to ride in the bow, kneeling, with their chest against the rear side of the bow tube and their face just above and well behind the very front of the bow tube. This affords the bow belly rider the refreshing thrill of taking waves straight in the face, and, just as importantly, gives everyone else a great view of their tush. Even more than with other river games, the success of bow belly riding depends on the group's go-for-it-ness, sense of humor, willingness to be silly and look silly, and overall supportiveness of one another. Standing bow riding is definitely not recommended because it can all too easily result in injury with people falling back on others or pitching forward.

–Wild Thing: When stuck on a rock or just to get some silliness going or even in a mild rapid, everyone stands on floor of the raft and jumps and wiggles around like a maniac stomping their feet and shaking their anatomy with wild abandon. The wild thing, which was invented by Stephanie Stewart, is fantastic for freeing stuck boats, and helps folks realize just how hard it is to tip a raft over. The high-level art to inspiring enthusiastic participation in the wild thing has to do with tapping deep inner resources of silliness in oneself and others, and yelling, "Do the wild thing," or, "Let's make like a bunch of wild monkeys." When a guide has a knack, people giggle and wiggle and love it.

–Trust Lean: On a lake or a very long calm in very hot weather, first, tuck paddles out of harms' way in the bow. Then, have the entire crew stand, hold hands and step up on the perimeter tube. Forming a sort of circle around the top of the perimeter tube, everyone leans out in a trust lean. If the group does not fall in, have them all start taking steps to the right or left around the raft. Trust leans can build group supportiveness, trust, fun, etc. Make whatever happens okay.

–Blind Run: Above a rapid, everyone but the captain closes their eyes, and continues following the captain's commands down into and through the rapid. The crew keeps their eyes closed until given the all-clear to open them. When vision, our dominant sense, is suspended for a time, people experience the temperature, motion and roar of the rapid with a fresh, amazing intensity.

–Surfing Holes: In safe holes where a swim is okay, and only with 100% willing crews, paddle back upstream into "surfable" holes. Move people toward the bow to increase the hole's grip on the boat. Each surf may be short or long, and can result in the boat bucking and nose diving, filling with water and even flipping. Be prepared to high side quickly if the boat goes sideways in the hole. If you're not in a self-bailer, be prepared to do a lot of bailing. Important: Only surf holes which spit out swimmers, and not in holes which can entrap, hold and tumble swimmers!

–Stern Stuffing: Move the entire crew into the stern compartment for spins or very wild rides through rapids. Because flips are very likely, stern stuffs should be done only with loose, goofy, 100%-willing crews in rapids with clear, deep channels and good recovery pools where it is OK to swim.

–Boofing: Picking up speed to slide one's boat up onto smooth, ramp-like mid-river boulders and then sliding back down off.

–Aerobic Paddling: To cross long clams or lakes, explain the following paddling pattern to your crew: 10 hard strokes, 10 easy strokes, 9 hard, 9 easy, 8 hard, etc. Invented by Ann Pavel, aerobic paddling gets everyone counting strokes, takes their mind off the effort they are expending, and, before you know it, you have crossed the lake or calm!

–Paddle Chants: Another way to enhance the fun and at the same time distract your crew from the effort they are expending, paddle chants come in infinite variations and interweave chanting, stroking, paddle bumps to the raft, more stroking, paddles touching overhead, more stroking, paddles passing, twirling, and on and on. You can use suggestions from your crew to spontaneously create brand new chants, or you can use tried and true old favorites such as, "Row, row, row your boat, etc." A great chant is the Hepwa Babba chant in the "Chants and Songs" section below.

–A motivating phrase: "OK! This next rapid has a photographer. Let's go for the ultimate brochure shot! Smile, etc…"

–Flip Drill: Do flip drills only with a totally willing crew! In a lake or very long calm, first, hook flip lines to or run your bow and stern lines through the D-rings on one side of your boat. Next, the crew stands up on top of the perimeter tube on the opposite side, and, while holding their paddles out away from the boat out of harm's way, leans out pulling on the lines to tip the boat up, up and over. As the boat passes the equilibrium point and begins to come down upside down, everyone jumps out so the boat won't land directly on them. Next, everyone throws the flip lines over and across the boat's bottom, and puts paddles and any loose floating items up on the overturned bottom. Then the crew members swim across under the boat to the other side and, one at a time, pull themselves up onto the overturned boat with the help, if necessary, of the flip lines. Once everyone is up on top the upside down boat, the crew again stands on one side, holds paddles out of harm's way, leans back on the lines to bring the boat up, up and over, and again jumps out away just before the boat flips down right side up. Lastly, everyone helps boost and pull everyone else back into the boat! Complete the drill by coiling and securing all lines.

Some key notes on flip drills: Above all, do flip drills only in appropriate safe locations with crews which are completely, 100% enthusiastic about it. If anyone is not eager to do it, do not do it. Beforehand, put everyone's hats and eyeglasses in a safe place–otherwise, some are very likely to be lost. Thoroughly prepare people ahead of time by explaining all of the steps of the drill, and forewarn them that they will very likely experience a touch of pandemonium, especially when the boat goes over and when they swim across under the boat! This forewarning about the likely mild "pandemonium" feeling of panic, fear and emergency can transform a person's experience from feeling gripped by fear to simply noticing that something in them is touched by fear. A key part of this is knowing their feelings are normal, OK and shared by others. The best way to cross under a boat, is to face and grip the raft and reach, grab, push and kick yourself in the direction you want to go—as opposed to doing an underwater Tarzan swim. The steps described above are for a full-on guide school flip drill, where it is important that each prospective guide learns how to pull themselves unassisted up onto an overturned boat. When done just for fun, you could just have everyone help everyone else reboard the raft each time.

–**Squirt Rafting:** Use downstream ferries to pick up speed into eddies, and just as the boat crosses the eddy line, call "Over left" or "Over right" (same as high side left or right) so as to **increase** the amount of water taken in and the tipping of the boat. This generally swamps or flips the boat, and is definitely not recommended for commercial guiding, but is worth mentioning as an extreme example of sheer human inventiveness. If squirt rafting is done at all, it should only be attempted by teams of highly experienced, 100%-willing rafting friends in safe, deep eddies where swimming is okay.

–**Captaining by Committee:** To make a mild river more fun, especially for a group of guides or very experienced paddlers, captain by committee. That is, anyone can suggest a command by making a motion, but the motion must be seconded by someone else before the crew can act. To make things really exciting, require a motion, a second, and a vote for each command. Can be hilarious. Not recommended for regular commercial trips.

Adventure Swims

When supervised by professional guides, adventure swims not only add to the fun of river trips, they can directly enhance safety by preparing trip members for the occasional inadvertent flip or person overboard that is an inherent part of rafting.

–Adventure-swim rapids should have relatively clear, deep, straight channels, and good recovery pools or slower sections just downstream for pulling in swimmers. No rapid is completely hazard-free, but those with dangerous strainers, big class-V drops, powerful "keeper" reversals capable of recirculating swimmers, suck holes, undercut rocks or "rooms of doom" (places where swimmers are likely to be entrapped) should generally not be used as venues for voluntary swims.

–Every participant is different, and it is impossible to know ahead of time exactly how any given person will respond to an adventure swim. Still, guides should do their best to be on the lookout for anyone for whom an adventure swim would be too great a challenge (in particular watch for people who are mentally handicapped), and as diplomatically as possible avoid having unsuitable folks take the plunge. If the swim is presented as purely voluntary, and somewhat daring or even downright risky (of course, all swims should be presented as voluntary and "done at one's own risk") , quite often anyone with concerns about their readiness for the swim will opt not to do it. Another, and in some cases better, strategy, when the guides have concerns about someone's readiness, is to skip the adventure swim altogether and focus on other alternatives.

–Before adventure swims, especially the first such swim for a trip, it is often a good idea for guides to review the classic (non-self-rescue) technique for swimming rapids: Float on your back with feet downstream, toes on the surface, cushioning contact against any rocks with feet and bending knees, kicking off rocks, using arms to maintain and when necessary regain this feet-downstream orientation, and, at the guide's signal, rolling over to do a strong crawl stroke either to the raft or shore. Also, remind folks to hold their breath in the crests, and to breathe in the troughs between the waves.

–The walk-up-and-swim-down style: After pulling over below the swimming rapid, while some of the guides wait in rescue position with rescue boats and/or toss bags below the rapid, swimmers, led by a guide or two, walk back up to the top of the rapid, and one at a time, follow-the-leader-style wade out, get into the feet-downstream position, float through the rapid, and swim to shore in the eddy below the rapid.

–The wait-at-the-top-then-swim-down style: After dropping off the swimmers on the shore above the rapid, the guides float their boats down to the calm eddies below the rapid. The swimmers then wade out, get into the feet-downstream position, float through the rapid, swim to the rafts in the eddies below and are then pulled back aboard.

–The float-near-the-boat style: Just above the rapid, the participants jump or slide feet-first into the water on the downstream side or end of the boat, float through the rapid a few yards downstream from the boat, and, at rapid's end, are pulled back aboard. Beforehand guides teach participants that most likely they will float along a few yards from the boat, but if they should start to float further away, they should, as soon as the river clams, swim hard to stay near the boat. (Because surface tension slows water and boats on the surface, swimmers down deeper in the water generally move slightly faster than boats, making it best for swimmers to jump out on the downstream side.)

–A variation of this latter style is the float-near-the-boat-in-a-clam style: Swimmers slide feet-first into a deep, long calm, float along in the vicinity of the boat, and are pulled back aboard well above the next rapid. Before the swimmers go overboard, guides advise them to stay close to the boat—say, within 50 feet in long calms, closer if a rapid is looming in the distance.

Chant and Songs

–**Miwok Indian Song:** This authentic Miwok song was—and still is—sung by groups for extended periods to build up winning juju energy for their side in competitions:

Choo chiminee
Chō ōo chiminee
Waya winna
Waya ha

While there is no direct translation, this song roughly means, "We are going to win! We are REALLY going to win BIG! We are good! We are SO GOOD!"

–Hepwa Babba Chant:: An authentic African call and repeat chant having to do with feeling close to earth. O'Battala is an earth god.

Hey Babba
Hepwa Babba
Hey Hepwa
Hepwa Hepwa
Babba Babba

Sango
Sango Sango
Sango Yamawa
(And so on, on and on, in whatever order feels good to you.)

Conclude with:

O'Battala!

–Repetition Songs: One person sings out something, anything, and the group echoes. Works great with certain songs from the Pacific, Africa, etc., and just as well with made up songs. Also works great with anything: names, sign of zodiac, birthplace, first boyfriend/ girlfriend, favorite breakfast, hobbies, color of your underwear, etc.

–Song: To the tune of Doc Watson's "Deep River Blues":

I'm gonna paddle this ol' boat.
I don't care if she won't float.
Cause I got the deep river blues

Interpretation

Study and share the natural and human history of the canyon—including wild life, plants, geology, Indian culture, early explorers and settlers, Lewis & Clark, Major Powell, Mark Twain, the gold rush and more. Go beyond just teaching the names of things. Share the story—the more dramatically the better. With living things share the story of their struggle to survive. How they eat, protect themselves (keep themselves from being eaten, from getting too cold, too dry, etc.) and reproduce, that is, have sex. Done with energy, accurate detail and drama, this enables people to relate, feel the bond, the struggle to survive, the powerful life force that connects all living things. Later on, with interested groups, you may also want to talk about the whole political side—water politics, conservation, and how to protect our rivers. Here are some examples of "telling the story" to help people connect more deeply with our planet:

–Granite Boulders & Geologic Time: In the Sierra Nevada, give this talk at the riverside near some granite boulders: Once part of the vast granite batholith underlying the entire Sierra, these alluvial granite boulders have been rounded and smoothed by the river. Countless past floods and collisions with other rocks and boulders have slammed and hammered these boulders, pounding away sharp edges, revealing their present shapes.

A way to Grasp Geologic Time: Geologists estimate the earth was formed 4.5 billion years ago and the Sierra—and hence the granite in these boulders—was formed 10 million years ago. For perspective, we will also note that dinosaurs walked the earth from 150 to 65 million years ago and Cro-Magnon people, considered the first Homo-Sapiens, first appeared about 35,000 years ago.

One way to better understand these huge time spans, suggests celebrated geology professor Dr. Terry Wright, is to compare earth history to a human life span of 100 years: If earth's 4.5 billion year history is equivalent to 100 human years, one million earth years equal one human week. In these terms, the Sierra Nevada came into being, lifting up out of a level plane like a giant trap door, just 10 weeks ago. Dinosaurs first appeared 3 years ago, survived about 2 years, and died off about 1 year ago. Homo-Sapiens, by comparison, have been around for only 6 hours. And modern inflatable boats, an incredibly important development in the grand scheme of things, have been around for about 2 minutes.

–Mugwort: This perennial herb with silvery, downy leaves and stem grows to 1 to 5 feet high in moist, shaded areas of woods and along stream sides.

A well known herb since antiquity, mugwort is described on an Egyptian papyrus dated 1600 B.C. as a powerful medicinal herb. Medieval folklore held that sleeping with a mugwort leaf on one's pillow enables a person to dream into their future. The early Miwok people made small balls containing Mugwort and other medicinal plants and wore them strung on a necklace to prevent dreaming of the dead and to repel ghosts at night. Corpse handlers rubbed themselves with mugwort for the same reason. The leaves were also worn in the nostrils of mourners when crying because it was felt the pungent odor cleared the head. Mugwort has been used to alleviate rheumatism, and even in modern times has been taken to relieve obstructed menstruation and to reduce the itching and swelling from poison oak. Chinese doctors use mugwort in moxibustion, a technique in which the herb is made into incense, then burned and lightly applied to acupuncture points to stimulate them as an alternative to using needles. (From **The American River South, Middle & North Forks**.)

Note: When harvesting any wild plant, great care should be taken not to harm the plant or the greater plant community. A general rule of thumb is never to take more than one third of the plant's original leaves—and if one-third has already been harvested, leave the plant alone.

–Grey or Ghost Pine: This forlorn-looking conifer with its wispy crown and rather barren and often crooked, forking trunk and branches grows 90 feet high. Picturesque and delicate in appearance, the grey or ghost pine is the most common conifer in California. John Muir wrote: "No other tree of my acquaintance is so substantial in body and yet in foliage so thin and pervious to light. The sunbeams sift through even the densest needled trees with scarcely any interruption." John Muir allegedly also said that this pine is the only tree you can stand in the shade of and still get a sunburn.

At one time—but no longer—this tree was called a digger pine. "Digger" was a pejorative term used by early California pioneers for native American Indians, who ate the tree's rich pine nuts, and, in a stooped over posture somewhat similar to that of the tree, dug for roots, edible bulbs and rhisomes with digging sticks.

Ghost pines are said to have the best pine nuts—oily and rich—of the pine species. John Muir described a ghost pine nut harvest:: "The Indian men climb the tree like bears and beat off the cones with sticks while the women gather the big generous cones and roast them until the scales open sufficiently to allow the hard-shelled seeds to be beaten out. Then in the cool evenings men, women, and children form circles around campfires on the banks of the nearest stream and sit in easy independence cracking nuts and laughing like squirrels." The Miwok also boiled the twigs, needles, and bark into a strong tea to treat rheumatism. Seeds strung on thread made of wild iris fiber were used to decorate costumes worn in dance rituals. And the pitch of ghost pines was used for fastening arrowheads and feathers and for mending canoes.

White settlers considered this tree to be rather worthless except for fuel because its wood is lightweight and not very durable.

The 6 to 10 inch cones, which weigh up to 4 pounds when green, have sharp, claw-like cone scale tips—these are adapted to protect the large plump seeds from squirrels. None-the-less, ghost pine nuts are a staple squirrel food and also a favorite food of wood-peckers, jays, and other foothill birds. (From **The American River South, Middle & North Forks** and the writing of John Muir.)

–Poison Oak: Learn to recognize and avoid poison oak. This ubiquitous California native can grow as a shrub and sometimes as a vine; can have bright green, dark green or reddish green leaves; and always consists of three-leaf clusters.

"Poison oak is the most widespread California shrub and has one of the largest gene pools, allowing for great variation in its form, ranging from a small, woody plant to a massive vine or dense shrub. Many people have allergic reactions to poison oak ranging from a slight itch to a massive rash with blisters and severe swelling. Immunity to poison oak is erratic and may come and go. It is best to always exercise caution after coming in contact with this plant. Wash the skin with cool water and soap.

"There are a couple of plants that are found in close proximity to poison oak that can be used as remedies. A strong tea made from manzanita or yerba santa leaves helps dry up the rash. Also, the pulverized bulb of soap root, mixed with a little water to make a slight lather, applied to the rash, and left to dry may have good results. It is important to remember that the oils of the branches of poison oak are toxic even when the leaves have fallen.

Native Americans, in the manner of homeopathic medicine, used poison oak as lining in their fire pits when baking bread, and the trace amounts transferred to the bread provided some immunity from poison oak to the eaters. To this day, many full-blooded Native Americans seem to have a lasting immunity to the poison in this plant or are only slightly affected.

"Poison oak had many important uses for the Miwoks. The stems were sometimes used in baskets and the juice from the stems and leaves was used to cure warts. The juice was also used as a black dye after it had oxidized, and was employed in basket fibers and in tattooing the skin. It had yet another use as a cure for ringworm. The fresh leaves bound tightly over a rattlesnake bite were thought to counteract the poison, if applied immediately.

"Quail and many other birds devour the berries of poison oak and help in its propagation by scarring the seeds in digestion, making it easier for them to sprout after they come out. In fall its brilliant red foliage covers many slopes and roadsides.

Poison oak is sometimes called guardian oak or "white man's footprint." In a sense, it is nature's defense to trail blazing and fire. Because it typically grows where the earth has been damaged in some way, it can be seen as the earth's response to disturbance and as a "keep away" message. (From **The American River South, Middle & North Forks**.)

–Willows: While the roots of most trees need alternating cycles of wetness and dryness, willow roots, like those of alder, are able to thrive when continuously wet, even submerged. The name willow is derived from the Celtic "sal," meaning "near," and "lis," meaning "water." Willow species—of which there are five in the Sierra foothills—are fast growing with a short life span. Their thickly matted root systems prevent soil erosion along stream banks and hence play a vital role in stabilizing watersheds.

Native Americans wove strips of willow bark together to make twine, used the twigs in weaving baskets, and used willow branches to make fish traps. They also boiled the bark and used the strong tea as a treatment for sore throats and tuberculosis. In more modern times, powdered willow bark has been used as aspirin and as a poultice for burns. Its light, strong, flexible wood is favored for making cricket bats. Beavers eat little else, often eating willow for breakfast, lunch and dinner, day in, day out. Many small birds build their nests and live their lives largely in willows.

Willows produce seed capsules which open to release many minute seeds with cottony hairs—from 2 to 12 million seeds weigh one pound. (From **The American River South, Middle & North Forks**.)

–Fremont Cottonwood: The deciduous tree grows to 50 to 100 feet high. Discovered by and named for eponymous western explorer John Charles Fremont, this tree invariably signals the presence of water and as a result was a welcome sight to early explorers as they trekked the arid west. Indian women fashioned skirts from the twisted inner bark fibers. Spanish settlers planted their plazas with cottonwoods and referred to them as "Alamos." This tree produces fruit capsules which open to release countless small seeds with cottony hairs which float through the air like puffs of cotton, hence the "cotton" in the name. (From **The American River South, Middle & North Forks**.)

–Lupine: Lupine, the root of which—lupus—means wolf, often grows in rough, disturbed soil largely barren of other plants. It was long thought that lupine—like a "big bad wolf"—hence the name—took nitrogen from the soil, thereby harming other plants. But it was later found that lupine actually contributes nitrogen to the soils, making it an important colonizer plant and an important part of local ecosystems. In addition, lupine provide displays of dazzling, colorful flowers in spring, and provide habitat and cover to many animals.

–Wave Trains: Long rows of large waves, called wave trains, are caused by faster water colliding with slower water. Often, as faster water hits slower water, for example near the downstream end of rapids, it piles up temporarily in a "pile" or standing wave. But water does not like to sit in a pile, so the potential energy of its elevated position in the wave quickly transforms into speed, and once again you have faster water colliding with slower (usually deeper) water—and, hence, another wave—or pile of water is formed. As this process repeats itself again and again, long wave trains are formed. Interestingly enough, some early river runners mistakenly thought that standing waves were caused by a rock under each wave. Careful, unhurried observation and thought reveal the true explanation stated above.

–American Indians: Abundance and Leisure: This canyon was once the home of the Miwok Indians. The way of life of the Miwok and other native tribes was one of remarkable abundance and leisure. Generally, they were able to take care of their survival needs in about two hours of hunting and gathering per day.

The rest of the time, they passed, amazingly enough, largely playing games. Every Indian village had at its canter a large 90 or so foot in diameter game court where the villagers—and people from neighboring villages—would spend a big part of every day playing all manner of games. One such game involved rolling a wheel with a hole in its center. As the wheel rolled across the court, the players would gain points by shooting arrows and throwing spears through its rapidly moving center hole. (Also see Indian Football in the Land Games section below.)

An example of the successful hunting and gathering methods which afforded the California Indians so much leisure, is the following fish trapping technique: First, they would create with willow branches a fish cage about 20 feet in length and 18 inches in diameter with an opening with a trap door at the upstream end. They would position this cage downstream from two wing fences made of willow stakes driven into the river bed. The two wing fences formed a big "V" funnel that guided all fish coming downstream into the cage. With their cage and wing fences in place downstream, the Indians would go a mile or two upstream and tie willow poles together to make a pole long enough to span clear across the river from bank to bank. This river wide pole had branches protruding down from it extending clear to the river bottom all along its length. Two teams, one on either end of this long pole, would move the pole down river. With its branches brushing the river bottom, the pole drove all fish downstream, filling the cage with fish! The fish cage was kept in the river next to the village, providing an abundant supply of fresh fish. From time to time they would re-drag the pole to refill the cage.

A great book which describes the way of life the California Indians before the impact of European settlers, is Thomas Jefferson Mayfield's Indian Summer. Mayfield lived with the Indians on the banks of the Kings River from age 6 to 16, before the way of life of the Miwoks was devastated by contact with European settlers.

–Gaia Hypothesis: This wonderful theory is named for Gaia (pronounced "guy-ah"), the Earth Goddess. The Gaia Hypothesis theorizes that a part of the purpose of all living—and perhaps non-living—things on earth is to make the planet as a whole more livable for other living things. Countless phenomena throughout nature support this inspired theory.

For example: Countless trees and plants consume carbon dioxide, which is toxic to animals and humans, and emit oxygen, which is vital to life on earth. If it were not for this one simple fact, life as we know it on earth would be impossible.

An amazing example: The countless tiny algae throughout the world's oceans each have a microscopic speck of sulphur which is useless to the algae. But it is these countless bits of sulphur that, when sucked up into clouds through evaporation, create the rain that is so vital to life on this planet. Without the sulphur contributed by algae, the land surfaces of earth would be largely dry and barren.

A non-living example: Water, when it freezes, expands slightly. (Many liquids shrink when they freeze, but water expands!) If it were not for this simple phenomenon, life on earth might not have developed at all. For one thing, it is water freezing in the cracks of rocks—and expanding to break them apart—that has played a crucial role in transforming the original rocky ball that was primordial earth into the livable planet with soil and plants that it is today. For another thing: Because ice is less dense than water, it floats. This means that although ponds and streams and even parts of oceans ice over—life can still survive and evolve on the bottoms of ponds, streams and oceans—rather than be killed by freezing! It is on pond, stream and ocean bottoms that life on earth began!

When taken separately each of these examples inspires wonder and amazement, but perhaps is not conclusive. But when taken together with countless other examples, these phenomena can be seen as proof of a grand design and a grand designer. In this Gaia vision, the earth—our wonderful and wonder-filled planet—is in a sense a single living organism, all the parts of which—including humans—have as part of their true higher purpose making the overall planet into a more livable ball.

–Any Train or Railroad Track: Soon after—and as a result of—the California Gold Rush, came the building of the transcontinental railroad which was completed in 1869. A miraculous, monumental feat for its time, this railway was by far the longest railroad in the entire world at the time, and it transformed the journey from coast to coast from a perilous six-month ordeal by ship or horse-drawn wagon, to a journey of less than one week in relative safety and comfort.

Although this amazing creation led to the destruction of the way of life of Native American tribes, it promoted development and economic growth in a way never duplicated before or since, launched the United States on its path to becoming a world power, and was a powerful symbol of and impetus to the quintessential "we can overcome any problem" optimism and determination of the American spirit.

Built literally by hand largely by Chinese and Irish immigrants at the cost of incredible effort and hundreds of lives, the railroad set our country on the path of eventually accepting, integrating and appreciating the rich, hearty and diverse fabric of American life. This grand undertaking was envisioned and managed by men such as Charles Crocker, Collis Huntington, Leland Stanford and Mark Hopkins—men who risked everything they had and worked and obsessed for years to develop our nation and gain vast fortunes in the process!

This particular train/track is part of a vast rail network which evolved from the early railroads which built the transcontinental railroad. Its presence is directly related to—and a result of—this historic, American, human achievement. (For more on natural and human history interpretation, see the "Natural History Quiz" in the Bus Games section, and "Indian Football" and " Nature Diagram" in Land Games.)

Quiet Camaraderie

–Name Game Augmented: It has been said that a group feels large only until everyone learns everyone else's name, and then the group feels much closer and somehow "perfect." With the group in a well-formed circle in which everyone can see everyone else's face, go around the circle and have each person say their name plus make some sort of gesture while saying some additional word or phrase which rhymes or alliterates or somehow connects with them or their name. Anything and everything is welcome! The additional word or words can be purely descriptive, name something they might have brought with them on their trip, etc. Some examples: Diamond Dave (said while framing a diamond shape with forefingers and thumbs), Sue brought a SOTAR (said while moving a flat, open hand up and down like a boat going through waves), Ed brought an Elephant (said while swinging an arm as though it were an elephant's trunk), Hilary brought a Hungry Hippo, Frank the Crank, Miriam Divorce'em (said with an ever so slight toss of the head), and Barnacle Bill the Buccaneer (said with a hand over one eye like an eye patch and a guttural pirate's oath something like Aaaarrrrrrrggghhh). To heighten the fun and create repetition so people will remember the names, each person first repeats back all of the previously announced names, epithets and gestures starting with the leader. The leader begins and ends the game, finishing with a complete circuit around the circle repeating all names, epithets and gestures, beginning and ending with her or himself. One way to ease the pressure a bit is to announce that it is the obligation of everyone to help their neighbors when they get stuck. This game can make a large group feel intimate and comfortable fast.

–Mini-Whitewater School: A classic way to entertain and enhance your crew's experience on a river trip: Focus on the river and canyon. Teach them about haystacks, eddies, tongues, holes, etc. Talk about reading the river and why you're doing what you're doing. If appropriate, let them guide an easy stretch—make sure ahead of time that this is okay with everyone in the boat.

–Jokes and Stories: Share the jokes and stories which accompany each rapid. Always pick material that is appropriate for the group, especially when families with kids are present. Definitely no off color or risque stuff with kids!! A vital part of becoming a top notch guide is to devote time to developing your own repertoire of stories and jokes, especially those suitable for families and people of all ages.

–A Key to Quiet Camaraderie: Be curious about people, take an interest in them, draw them out, listen so well that you could repeat back in your own words what people share, make it your goal to learn something of genuine interest to you from as many people on the trip as possible.

–Some Old Reliables: Initiate conversations with openers that put people at ease and gently invite them to open up: How are you doing? How did you happen to come on this trip? Where do you live? Where do you work? What is your connection to this group? What are some of your favorite things to do? Where were you born? What are your goals? One way to initiate conversation and divide your attention evenly is, in the course of the day, to go around the boat and ask everyone a few questions. Another way is to address questions to the group as a whole, inviting anyone who wants to answer: Who has a goal? How is everyone doing? Anyone here have a job? Follow up on what people say. Share your experiences. Ask more questions. Draw people out. Let the conversation flow.

–Two Truths and A Lie: With the group in a circle on land or in a boat, each person in turn says three things about themselves, one of which is a lie. Everyone guesses which of the three statement is the lie, then the speaker reveals the lie. A great ice breaker for any trip.

–Get-Acquainted Questions: Go around your group and have each person share the following: (This can also be done as a call and repeat chant.)
• What is your favorite: Number? Color? Hobby? TV show? Place in your home or city? Kind of car? Sports team? Drink?
• What country would you most like to visit? Why?
• What would be an ideal vacation for you?

- What is a source of pride and joy in your life?
- Name something you like about your workplace?
- What skill could you teach others?
- What is the one value you treasure most?
- How would you describe your leadership style?
- What are the qualities of an effective team?
- What are the qualities of a good friend? Captain? Supervisor? Teacher? Parent? Crew member? Employee? Learner?
- What three adjectives would your colleagues/family/subordinates/friends use to describe you?
- What is the biggest achievement in your life?
- What crisis in life have you weathered successfully?

–**What Happens in the Canyon, Stays in the Canyon:** This "rule" may help some groups let their hair down more.

–**What Do You Do–In Depth:** Start with some sort of opener like: "What do you do when you're not rafting?" Often people respond with their title or profession—go beyond this—ask "What do you do each day?" In this mode, rather than tell your story, mainly be curious about them: What's going on in their life? What have they been obsessing about? Follow up on what they say. Draw them out. Let the conversation flow.

–**The "Bill Cross" Openers:** Conceived by Bill Cross, these openers are great for getting to know people, opening people up, reaching out. Go around the raft and have each person describe:
- When you were a child, how was the first house you remember heated?
- Recount your first recollection of a sense of family: Maybe an early Christmas, etc.
- Your peak mountaintop experience
- Your peak gourmet experience

–**Firsts:** Go around your boat and invite people to talk about:*

- The first time I went camping, rafting, on a multi-day hike, etc., was …
- The first time I accomplished something on my own was …
- The first time I deliberately disobeyed my parents was …
- The first time I felt responsible for some part of my well being or self care was…
- The first time I questioned my valued or did something that violated my sense of value was …
* From **Instant Icebreakers** by Sandy Christian and Nancy Tubesing

–**Some Questions to Ask to Get People to Talk about Themselves:** It makes things all the more interesting if you encourage them to talk about what they learned in the course of these experiences. Get them to talk about::
- What do you do to feel good?
- A time when he/she tried to help someone else change. What did he do? How did it turn out?
- The most challenging—and least challenging—thing he has ever done?
- A time when he had to overcome major obstacles to meet a challenge?
- The person he/ she admires most… and the person he admires least?
- A time when he tried to do something but failed?
- A time when something had happened to him?
- A mistake he/ she made in dealing with people?

- The best and worst educational course he's ever taken?
- A time when he made a major change? Why did he do it? How did it work?

–A Little Bit New Age: "If you want to link with another in your heart, appreciate him or her. By sending out your telepathic appreciation, you will automatically stop (ease) power struggles." Appreciate their nobility and power. (From Page 105 of **Living with Joy**.)

–Inner Glimpse: Go around the boat and ask each person to share something that is true for them at that moment: This could be a feeling…anything. Could be that they are feeling both excited and a little afraid. It could be they don't want to say anything, or something as simple as: They don't like the position they're sitting in. No rescuing needed. The goal here is to foster an atmosphere in which all feelings are okay—in which everyone is accepted as they are—and they can be themselves, as is. This atmosphere of acceptance—which helps each person accept himself and feel okay—is at the heart of a good trip! Try this only later in a trip after some trust has developed. Otherwise, "inner glimpse" can feel a bit forced to many people.

–Ooooommmmmm: As goofy as it may sound, having a group intone a series of Ooommmms together, especially on a quiet calm or in a cave or grotto, can really be fun—and even reverberate with something like magic.

–Encourage People to Reach Out to One Another: Ask, "Does anyone have any questions for me or anyone else in the boat?" In your own way, communicate acceptance and support, saying both implicitly and at times explicitly: "We each have our own truth, and still we can treat all questions, answers, and statements of every kind with appreciation and respect."

Bus Games

Make shuttles fun!

–Natural History Quiz: Call out questions about natural and human history, and reward answers with a group applause or a token gift such as a refrigerator magnet or piece of wrapped candy. On big buses use an amplifier up front or sit facing backwards in the second or third row of seats speaking loudly so everyone can hear you. Start with easy questions and create an atmosphere of celebration and success. The questions you ask will subtly influence people's perceptions. Create questions which inform, entertain and heighten people's curiosity about our world. Here are some sample questions (and answers) to get you started:

1) Who knows what force makes rivers flow downhill? (Gravity.)
2) Where does the water in this river come from? (From springs, rain, lakes and melting snow upstream, which come from clouds, which are created by evaporation from the oceans, which are fed by, yes, rivers!)
3) What do trees and plants do that is absolutely vital to the survival of animals and humans? (In addition to creating wood, food, shade, beauty, soil and habitat, and preventing soil erosion, they—and this is the indispensable part—absorb carbon dioxide and give off oxygen. Without trees and plants, there would be no oxygen and, hence, no animals or humans.)
4) Who knows why afternoon winds tend to blow up river? (Warm air rises.)
5) Here are four fundamental causes of rapids. Anyone want to guess what these are? (Steepness or gradient of the river bed. Roughness of the riverbed.

Constriction of the river channel. Sheer water volume. Each of these factors singly or in any combination can cause rapids.)

6) Rivers are rated on a difficulty scale that goes from 1 to 6. What is the difficulty rating of the river we will run/we ran today?

7) What is the difficulty rating of _____rapid?

8) What foods are enjoyed by both bears and humans? (Fish, berries, honey.)

9) Water which bubbles up out of the earth in natural hot springs has been underground how long? (2,000 to 4,000 years.)

10) Are there more bald eagles alive today than were alive 50 years ago? (Yes! Fifty years ago bald eagles were an endangered species, and today they are thriving!)

11) Is it safe to drink directly from the river? (No, protozoa giardia spread mainly by beaver have made all unfiltered surface water in North America unsafe to drink. When properly filtered, however, it is perfectly safe.)

12) What is the nautical name for the front of a boat? (The bow.) The back of a boat? (The stern.) The cross tubes in the middle of a boat? (Thwarts.) The little door-like device we open to inflate a boat, and close to keep it pumped up? (The valve.)

13) What do guides call it when they work their way around an under inflated boat pumping just enough air into each chamber to make the pressure drum tight? (Topping off.)

14) How many separate air chambers does a high quality inflatable boat have? (Counting the four perimeter tube chambers, the floor, and the thwarts, 8 or 9. Are these boats unsinkable or what?)

15) How can you tell if your life jacket is tight enough? (With all snaps fastened and straps pulled snug, it should be tight enough so that when you pull up on it, it stays put and will not slide up your chest—and you should still be able to breathe comfortably.)

16) Name the parts of a paddle? [The blade, the shaft, the throat (where the shaft meets the throat), and the grip (or T-grip).]

17) When you hold your paddle to take strokes, where should you grip it: (Inboard hand on the top of T-grip, outboard hand well down the shaft.)

18) If you guide yells, "High side!" what should you do? (Jump to the downstream side of the boat.)

19) What is the name of the rafting company you are rafting with today? (Whitewater Voyages—Insert your group's name here.)

20) What is the name of the best rafting company? (Of course, Whitewater Voyages! Of course, insert your group's name here.)

It can also be fun and at the same time educational to ask questions about the area you are in:

21) Who knows the name of the mountains this river drains?

22) What type of rock forms the foundation for the entire Sierra Nevada? (Granite.)

23) Who knows the names of an early explorer to visit this continent? This region? This state? This river canyon?

24) What is the name of the plant that, if you touch it, you are likely to get a skin rash? (Poison oak, poison ivy, poison sumac.)

25) What does this plant look like? How can you identify this plant so you know to avoid it? (Poison oak: Green or reddish three-leaf clusters, etc.)

26) If you were to inadvertently touch this plant, what could you do to reduce the chances of getting a rash? (Wash off with cold water.)

27) What actual part of this plant causes the rash? (The oil, which is present in the leaves and stems, and even in the barren twigs in winter.)
28) This is a really touchy one that will earn a really big applause: Who can guess the name of the Indian tribe that used to live in this area? (In California: Tubatulabal* on the Kern, Patwisha* and Wukchumni* on the Kaweah, Choinimni* on the Kings, and Miwok on the Merced, Toulumne, American and Yuba.)
   *The Tubatulabal, Patwisha, Wukchumni, and Choinimni were tribes of the Yokuts linguistic group.)
29) Who wants to take a guess how many hours per day on average it took the Indians in this area to hunt and gather enough food to live? (Amazingly enough, generally, about two hours per day.)
30) Who can guess what they did the rest of the time? (Mostly played games, did sweat lodges, chanted and told stories in their villages.)
31) When a young Indian brave killed his first dear, do you know who got it? (His grandparents.)
32) When a young Indian man fell in love and wanted to marry, his family would offer gifts to the proposed bride's family. If the gifts were accepted, a match was made. What happened then? (The man would eat meals with the bride's family for about a year.)
33) In Indian tribes the shaman performed healing ceremonies. These frequently consisted of having sick people lay by a fire while the shaman sang and did healing dances around the patient. Sometimes cuts were made on the patient and the sickness sucked out, and other times the sickness was removed by blowing over the body. Sometimes this worked and sometimes it didn't. Who can guess what occasionally was done to a shaman who could not cure someone? (Shaman who failed to cure people were occasionally killed.)
34) The most powerful shamans were called tripne, which means supernatural. These shamans not only had the power to heal but also could kill people, make it rain, and transform themselves into coyotes. Who can guess how the other Indians felt about these supernatural shamans? (They were afraid of them.)
35) In the spring when this canyon is blanketed in flowers, what do you suppose the Indians did with the flowers? (They covered themselves with flowers and made huge, colorful flower displays.)
36) What big event happened in California in 1848 and 1849? (The Gold Rush drew thousands of people from all over the world into California, thereby changing the history of the world.)
37) Before the completion of the transcontinental railroad in 1869, how long did it take by land to get from the east coast to California? (Six months.) How long by sea sailing around South America? (This also took six months.) After the completion of the railroad, how long did it take to travel from coast to coast? (One week!)
38) Did this railroad stimulate one of the biggest booms in economic development the world has ever known? (Yes!)
39) Which two groups of immigrants did most of the actual physical work building the railroad? (Chinese in the West, Irish in the East.)
40) What explosive liquid vastly speeded up construction of the railroad? (Nitroglycerin.)
41) Up until 1880, what was the largest lake in surface area west of the Mississippi? (Tulare Lake in the southern San Joaquin Valley. Like a vast, shallow inland

sea with an average depth of 8 feet, Tulare Lake covered a huge area west of the present day locations of Visalia and Fresno.)

42) Can anyone guess what happened to Tulare Lake? (The rivers which fed it were damned and diverted to irrigate crops, and the lake bed itself was turned into farmland.)

43) True to the American Way, did a bunch of people work very hard, take big risks, and get rich making this happen? (Of course!)

44) What large bird congregates by the tens of thousands in the Kern Valley each fall on its annual southward migration? (Turkey vultures—checkout the annual Turkey Vulture Festival.)

45) Where does the water in the Merced, Tuolumne, American and Yuba go? (The water from all four of these rivers is used to generate power, irrigate crops and provide water for cities and towns—and some flows out to sea through the Golden Gate.)

46) Where does the water in the Kern, Kaweah and Kings go? (Before 1880 or so, the water from these three rivers flowed into Tulare Lake, which only in very wet years overflowed a bit into the San Joaquin River which had an outlet to the ocean. Today, all of the water of the Kings, Kaweah and Kern is consumed by cities, towns and agriculture in Southern California.)

47) Who wants to guess how many major dams now stand in California? (Over 1400.)

48) How many top quality whitewater rafting runs remain in California? (Depending on how you count, about 15 to 30.)

Here are some questions designed to help people appreciate the power of the river:

49) Can anyone guess how much one gallon of water weighs? (About 8 pounds.)

50) What unit of measurement is used to measure a river's flow? (Cubic feet per second. In other words, the number of cubic feet of water flowing past one spot–or cross section–in the river in one second.)

51) Does anyone know how many gallons of water roughly equal one cubic foot? (8 gallons roughly equal one cubic foot.)

52) So, roughly how many pounds is one cubic foot of water? (About 64 pounds.)

53) If a river is flowing at 1,000 cubic feet per second (called cfs), this is equivalent to how many pounds per second? (64,000 pounds per second!) And how many tons of force? (32 tons of force per second!)

54) Our river today is flowing at about_____ cfs. This is equivalent to how many pounds per second? How many tons of force per second?

–**Self Revelation Quiz:** In a loud, clear voice audible throughout the bus, call out "safe" questions which invite people to reveal themselves in comfortable ways. Clearly explain to the group a way to signal "yes," "no," and a gauge-like range of responses from 0% to 100%. For instance, inclining one's head to the far left could mean 0% or "no" and inclining one's head far right could mean 100% or "yes," while holding one's head vertical could mean 50% and half way between 50% and 100% would mean 75% and so on. And rumbling one's feet on the floor with a sort of drum roll of the heals could put an exclamation point on what ever signal is being given. If everyone in the bus has a paddle, all paddles could be held vertically blades down and handles up. Handles touching or tapping the bus ceiling could mean 100% or "yes," and blades touching or tapping the floor could mean 0% or "no," and so on. To create a supportive, caring, deeply fun atmosphere, it is crucial that you ask only safe questions that will not embarrass anyone or push anyone too far out of their comfort zone. Here are some examples:

BUS GAMES

1) First of all, if you can hear me, signal yes.
2) How many people have never done this before? If this is your first time, signal yes. (A possible way to have some gentle fun with this is to pretend you think this is the first time they have even been in a bus, and say something like: "Well, for those of you who have never done this before, this is a bus. All you have to do is sit back and relax. Without us expending any effort, this entire, big, long, metal box with windows, controlled by_____, our intrepid driver, will move over the surface of the earth and take us to the river put-in. All we have to do is survive this goofy bus game.")
3) If you are hoping to survive this goofy bus game, signal yes.
4) On a scale from 0% to 100% (review how to signal 0%, 50%, 100%), what do you think are our chances of surviving this bus game?
5) If you would like not only to survive this bus game, but also somehow have fun playing it (as unlikely as this seems at this point), signal yes.
6) Going further, if you would like to learn something from this game—maybe even deepen your understanding of yourself or life itself, signal yes. (Leader signals yes.)
7) If you, maybe at work or in a dentist's office or anywhere, have ever yearned to be somewhere else other than where you were at that moment, signal yes.
8) If you have ever yearned to be in a beautiful natural setting with kindred souls with nothing to do but have fun, signal yes.
9) Of all the beautiful places you have ever imagined escaping to, what percentage had water? 0%? Half? Or all—100%?
10) If you have ever in your life had your mind wander and could not remember something that was just said, signal yes. (Leader signals yes as this is said.)
11) If you, like most people, including me (leader point to self), sometimes criticize yourself too harshly, signal yes. (As you say this, you the leader signal yes.)
12) If you would like to treat yourself really well, say yes. (Leader signals yes.)
13) The Golden Rule says "Treat other as you would like to be treated." If this makes sense to you, signal yes. (Leader signals yes.)
14) OK, on a scale of 0% to 100%, what is your energy level right now?
15) If you are up for being part of a strong team out on the river today, signal yes. (Leader signal yes.)
16) It is obvious to me that the universe has brought together the perfect people to share this river trip today. If you share this feeling—that we are the perfect people to share this adventure, signal yes! (Leader signal yes!)

–Now For a Variation: Explain to the group that now you are going to ask them to express their preference between a series of paired items. For instance, (A) coffee or (B) tea. If you prefer (A) coffee, (choose one) tap your paddle on the ceiling/tilt your head left/quack like a duck/rumble your feet in a drum roll on the floor, or if you prefer (B) tea, tap your paddle on the floor/tilt your head to the right/moo like a cow/clap your hands. So once again, (A) is tap your paddle on the ceiling/tilt your head left/quack like a duck/rumble your feet in a drum roll. And (B) is tap your paddle on the floor/tilt your head right/moo like a cow/clap your hands. So signal your preference between:
1) (A) Coffee or (B) Tea
2) (A) Chocolate ice cream, or (B) Vanilla ice cream
3) (A) Cats or (B) Dogs
4) (A) Macs, or (B) PCs
5) (A) Breakfast, or (B) Dinner
6) (A) Meat, or (B) Chicken

7) (A) Coke, or (B) Pepsi
8) (A) Buttered popcorn, or (B) Plain popcorn
9) (A) Wine, or (B) Beer
10) (A) Gourmet dining, or (B) Fast food
11) (A) Read books, or (B) See movies
12) (A) Run, or (B) Walk
13) (A) City, or (B) Country
14) (A) Winter sports, or (B) Summer sports
15) (A) Paddling in the bow, that is, up front where the waves tend to crash in, or (B) paddling further back in the boat
16) Around our campfire tonight, I would prefer: (A) More goofy games like this, or (B) a nature talk, jokes, stories and chanting

–Another Variation on Self Revelation Quiz: Change the 0% to 100% scale to a 1 to 10 rating scale, and, after a trip, have the group rate each of the major rapids the group ran that day. (This helps people remember the trip more vividly, and sends them home thinking about the fun they had.)

–Honey, I Love You: A great bus game for the final shuttle on trips where the group members have become thoroughly comfortable together. The leader says something like: "OK, we've got a great game called, 'Honey, I Love You.' The way it works is, the designated 'Honey'—and I'll be the first 'Honey' and start—sits right in the lap of someone special and says with lots of feeling— and nice and loud so everyone can hear—'Honey, you know I love you. Will you please just give me a smile?' If the recipient of these words can say back with a straight face without smiling, 'Honey, you know I love you, but I just can't give you a smile,' the 'Honey' must get someone else to smile. But if the recipient at any time cracks a smile, they become the 'Honey' and have to carry on the game by sitting in the lap of some new special person and getting them to smile. So the key words are, 'Honey, you know I love you. Will you please just give me a smile?' and the straight-faced reply is, 'Honey, you know I love you, but I just can't give you a smile.'" This game generally works best at the end of two-day or longer trips where the group has bonded and let their hair down enough to get silly together. Important note: If ever a "Honey" goes to two or three people in a row without getting a smile, the energy level in the group may not be right for this game and it is probably a good idea to quickly initiate a different game.

–Bus "Safety" Talk: Delivered tongue-in-cheek, this ironic parody of a trip leader's talk can get lots of laughs: "Welcome aboard for what will be the most dangerous part of our trip today: This perilous bus ride!"

"I'm sure you all understand the importance of showing appreciation for our driver___(driver's name)___ with a warm applause." (Lead applause for driver.)

"There is an inherent element of risk in riding on a bus. However, you can minimize this risk and increase your chances of surviving this bus ride by paying close attention to this bus safety talk."

"It is important to keep the bus right side up. So when the bus tips, lean toward the high side. The call for this is, 'High side!' So let's practice this important skill. Let's say the bus is tipping right (gesture right), so we need to lean left (gesture and lean left). So, on the call of 'High side left!,' everyone lean left. 'High side left!' (Leader leans left and motions for the group to do likewise.) Excellent! Now let's practice high siding right. So, get ready. High side right! (Leader leans right and motions for group to do likewise.) Excellent! Give yourselves a big round of applause!"

"If, despite our best high side, the bus start to roll down the cliff, you may be thrown out and find yourself sliding down the cliff. When this happens, slide facing downhill, with your feet out in front of you. As you slide, cross your legs at the ankle so you don't wind up straddling a tree. Speaking for myself, I always really hate it when I forget this point and wind up straddling a tree. All the while, listen to your guide, we will be watching for an opportunity to pull you back into the safety of the rolling bus. But if you see that you are not going to be pulled back into the bus, the landing you want to shoot for is a deep pool in the river at the base of the cliff."

"Well, that about covers it Thanks so much for joining us today. And thanks for your rapt attention to this talk, which I am sure has put everyone more at ease. Now all we have to do is sit back and enjoy the ride, or perhaps play some bus games to take our minds off the ride."

–"Not Very Punny" Puns for Bus Shuttles

1. A vulture boards an airplane, carrying two dead raccoons. The Stewardess looks at him and says, "I'm sorry, sir, only one carrion allowed per passenger."
2. Two fish swim into a concrete wall. The one turns to the other and says, "Dam!"
3. Two Eskimos sitting in a kayak were chilly, so they lit a fire in the craft. Unsurprisingly it sank, proving once again that; you can't have your Kayak and heat it too.
4. Two hydrogen atoms meet. One says "I've lost my electron." The other says. "Are you sure?" The first replies, "Yes, I'm positive."
5. Did you hear about the Buddhist who refused Novocain during a root canal? His goal: transcend dental medication.
6. A group of chess enthusiasts checked into a hotel and were standing in the lobby discussing their recent tournament victories. After about an hour, the manager came out of the office and asked them to disperse. "But why?" they asked, as they moved off. "Because", he said, "I can't stand chess-nuts boasting in an open foyer."
7. A woman has twins and gives them up for adoption. One of them goes to a family in Egypt and is named "Ahmal." The other goes to a family in Spain; they name him "Juan." Years later, Juan sends a picture of himself to his birth mother. Upon receiving the picture, she tells her husband that she wishes she also had a picture of Ahmal. Her husband responds, "They're twins! If you've seen Juan, you've seen Ahmal."
8. These friars were behind on their belfry payments, so they opened up a small florist shop to raise funds. Since everyone liked to buy flowers from the men of God, a rival florist across town thought the competition was unfair. He asked the good fathers to close down, but they would not. He went back and begged the friars to close. They ignored him. So, the rival florist hired Hugh Mac Taggart, the roughest and most vicious thug in town to "persuade" them to close. Hugh beat up the friars and trashed their store, saying he'd be back if they didn't close up shop. Terrified, they did so, thereby proving that only Hugh, can prevent florist friars.
9. Mahatma Gandhi, as you know, walked barefoot most of the time, which produced an impressive set of calluses on his feet. He also ate very little, which made him rather frail and with his odd diet, he suffered from bad breath. This made him ......A super calloused fragile mystic hexed by halitosis.
10. And finally, there was the person who shared ten different puns with his companions on a river trip, with the hope that at least one of the puns would

make them laugh. No pun in ten did!!!
(These puns were passed on to us by Bruce Lessels of Zoar Outdoor.)
What did the Zen Buddhist say to the hot dog vendor? "Make me One with everything."

–One Last Rapid: At take out on really hot days, just after reboarding the bus for
the final shuttle, a guide (after making sure there are no non-waterproof cameras
or other items which could be damaged by water exposed) says, "If you could,
would you like to run one last rapid?" When the group gives a big, "Yes", one,
two, or three guides run along the aisle of the bus vigorously shaking from side
to side big uncapped water bottles giving everyone one last refreshing splash.
Gets a big laugh and squeal of delight.

Land Games

Thoughts on Land Games and Entertainment:

–Enhance the Fun of Every Campfire with Games, etc.: Campfire games and
entertainment can be a trip highlight for many folks and should be a part of all
multi-day trips.

–Involve the Group: The best camp entertainment does not render the group a
passive audience—but instead gets them involved!

–Game Box: As well as jokes, stories, skits, interesting tales of human and natural
history, etc., a great way to spark participatory entertainment—is games! In
permanent camps and on multi-day trips, have a game box with participatory
games such as charades, Host a Murder, etc.

–Each Morning Announce an Evening Activity: A suggestion: Sometime on the
first morning of each multi-day trip either the trip leader or a guide designated
as the "Inspirer of Fun" or "Entertainment Master of Ceremonies" offers the group
some camp entertainment choices such as a Hosted Murder, charades, skits,
campfire stories, tales of human and natural history of the canyon you are in, a
joke fest, or some of the games described below, etc. Always pick games, jokes,
and stories appropriate for the group, especially when families with kids are
present. Definitely no off color or risque stuff with kids!! Later in camp in the
evening, go with the group's choice—with energy! Remember, much camp fun
will not happen on its own; we as the guides need to actively inspire it! The idea
is to find the right balance between gently nudging people toward fun while still
being respectful and taking care not to force them entirely out their comfort zone.

–Thoroughly Explain Each Game: When explaining how to play a game, always
assume there are people in the group who have never played it, and thoroughly,
patiently explain the rules and teach the skills—all the while placing the emphasis
not so much on winning, but on participating, supporting one another and having
fun.

–Be Careful: Carefully evaluate the appropriateness of each game for each group
and each setting. Avoid injury and other problems by always using caution and
good judgement.

Land Game:

–Indian Football: A favorite and authentic Miwok pastime, Indian football can
be played in any clear space 50 or more feet in diameter with 10-foot-wide goals
at either end. The "football" can be any soft, durable object about the size of a big
grapefruit such as a very small firm pillow, a nerf ball, or a towel knotted into a

tight ball. One thing that makes this game so much fun is that it pits the men against the women, the adults versus the kids, or just the big people versus the small people, with different rules for each side. As in soccer, the bigger, taller team can directly contact the ball only with their feet, legs, head and chest, but never with their hands or arms. The smaller team (usually the women or kids) on the other hand, can touch the ball any and every way they like, including picking it up, throwing it, catching it and running with it. The bigger team may, however, pick up their opponents, enveloping them in such a way as to pin the pillow-like ball between the opponent's arm and chest, and carry them body, ball and all across the goal line, thereby scoring a point. This is generally done with one big team member enveloping the smaller player's arms and torso to pin the ball (being careful not to touch the ball directly) while other big team members pick up and carry the smaller player's legs and middle body. Meanwhile members of the smaller team can grab, pull and sit on the legs and feet of the bigger team, to prevent them from gaining their goal and get them to put down their teammate. This game can be a ton of fun, but to keep people from getting hurt must be played with a sense of fair play and a balance of enthusiasm and restraint. The most important thing is not so much to score more points, but to enjoy the whole process, which with this game is very easy to do!

–**River Shaman:** A great game to play in the course of a river trip! First, select the shaman in such a way that no one knows the shaman's identity: For instance, count out a stack of cards (including a joker) with the same number of cards as the total number of people in the group, and go around showing a different card to each person without anyone else seeing them. The person who gets the joker is the shaman.

Then, the shaman, unobtrusively, one at a time, as opportunities present themselves in the natural course of the trip, reveals him or herself to the other trip members and assigns them a "totem." Totems can be anything at all including a bear, eagle, salmon, book, rock, bus, mountain, great Indian chief, or any natural, man-made or imaginary object or concept what-so-ever. After waiting enough time to conceal the identity of the shaman—and at a time when pretty much the whole group is present—each person acts out their totem (and gives subtle hints if necessary) until the others guess what it is.

Meanwhile, everyone who has not yet been assigned their totem tries to figure out who the shaman is. To give the shaman a fair chance, no one can say out loud or hint who they think the shaman is. Instead they may simply say, without indicating whom, that they think they know the shaman's identity. Whenever two trip members are ready to guess the shaman's identity, with the entire group present, they each first count to three, and then, on the count of four, silently, simultaneously point at who they think the shaman is. If both point at the true shaman, they both win. If the guessers point at different people, or at someone who is not the shaman, they stay in the game, and in due course get assigned and act out their totems, but they can no longer guess or hint at the shaman's identity. The shaman wins if she or he can assign totems to everyone without being revealed. And, of course, in the big picture, everyone wins by having the experience of participating in this multifaceted game of group improvisation and suspense. (River Shaman was invented by Peter Grubb on a Raftnet ROW Family Focus trip on Idaho's Salmon River,)

–Flipped Raft: Everyone first stands on a tarp on the ground, imagining it to be a flipped raft. The group then turns the "flipped raft" over without touching the surrounding ground. Everyone must be in contact with the tarp at all times.

–Whitewater Hilarium: A variation of the popular board game produced by Mattel Games, Whitewater Hilarium is a source of ongoing fun at Zoar Outdoor in Massachusetts, and is described here by Janet Burnett Cowie, Zoar's Director of Instruction Programs:

Goal: To find someone else who has the matching card, by acting out (speaking is allowed) the statement on the card. When you find the person, you can discard that card and choose another card until all the cards are gone in the pick-up pile and out of your hand. You will need 26 pairs of cards with words or statements associated with paddle sports.

Each pair of cards has the same message. Here are some of the examples that we use:

- "You just put on your drysuit and you need to pee"
- "Practicing your river signals…All of them"
- "Yard Sale"
- "You lost your bottoms swimming in a rapid"
- "All of your customers are swimming at once"
- "You are an undercut rock"
- "Fly fishing"
- "Squirt boater"
- "While driving the van, you look in the rear view mirror and see the boats in the middle of the road"

Before you start: Place all the cards upside down on a table or flat area where all participants can get to the pile. Decide on a place to discard the matched cards. Each player will draw 5 cards. Look at the cards. If the player draws duplicate cards, return one of each duplicate and choose replacement cards.

To play: All at the same time, everyone acts out the action or statement that is on their card. This is when the chaos begins. Everyone is acting and making noise at the same time. When you find someone who is acting the same way, see if they hold the matching card. If they are indeed holding the matching card, put the cards in the discard pile and draw another card. If they are not acting out the match card, continue to act and look for your match. You can act on one card at a time or act out one right after another. The strategy is up to you. Each player must maintain 5 cards in their hand, unless there are no more cards to choose from the drawing pile. Continue the chaos until the draw pile has no cards left. The first person to get rid (match) all the cards in their hand, once the draw pile is gone, wins. This game is good for 4 to 20 players. If you have more players, make the game last longer by reducing the number of cards in each hand. For a smaller group you can change the number of pairs of cards. Usually this game is interrupted by fits of laughter and hilarious behavior.

–Nature Diagram: A truly great game that can be played in any outdoor setting by people of any age, nature diagram greatly heightens people's awareness of the natural world. Beforehand, gather a dozen or so items such as leaves, stones, twigs and flowers from the immediate area and arrange them in some sort of diagram or pattern about six inches by six inches. It is important that all of the items be fairly common within, say, a 100 foot radius of the diagram. The diagram is then covered by a shirt or handkerchief. Then divide the group into teams of 3 to 5 people each and gather the teams close around the concealed diagram. Explain that the diagram will be uncovered for just 20 seconds, and then will be hidden again under the cloth. Also explain that all of the items in the diagram can be found within a 100 foot radius, and that each team will have a total of 5 minutes (with a 3-minute and a 4-minute whistle blast warning) to gather as many of the diagram items as possible and to arrange them into a similar diagram near the original. After making these announcements, give the teams a minute to plan strategies before unveiling the diagram for 20 seconds and sending them off to build their own. The team whose diagram most closely matches the original, which is uncovered at the end for comparison, wins.

–Pruee: Beforehand, secretly tell one person that they are the Pruee. Then gather the group into a circle and explain that they will be shutting their eyes and moving slowly around searching for the Pruee. When they touch someone, they say, "Pruee? Pruee?" If the person says back, "Pruee? Pruee?" they are not the Pruee, so both keep searching. If the person is silent, they are the Pruee, and you find their hand, hold it, become part of the Pruee and open your eyes. The game ends when everyone has found and become one with the Pruee. Play Pruee on smooth, open ground and have spotters who keep their eyes open and make sure no one gets injured by blundering into something.

–Jamaquack: Start with the group holding hands in a circle. A quarter of the group then go into the middle of the circle, hold their ankles, close their eyes and walk backwards trying to find the gap in the circle. The rest of the group can move to make the gap harder to find. Once a duck gets out, it can open its eyes and quack loudly to help and encourage others to find the gap.

–Hearts, Clubs, Spades and Diamonds: With the group sitting in a circle, each person cuts a deck to be identified as heart, club, spade or diamond. Someone shuffles the deck and shouts out the top card. Those whose suit is called, such as diamonds, must move one seat to the left. People can get stacked two and three high in someone's lap. If someone is sitting on them, they can not move. The first person to get back to their original seat wins.

–Amoeba Race: On cold days create tight amoebas to warm people up: Starting with everyone holding hands in a circle, the leader lets go of the hand of the person on their left, telling that person, who will become the nucleus, to plant their feet and not budge an inch as the group winds up around them. The leader then, with everyone continuing to hold hands, starts walking or trotting in circles around the nucleus, spiraling the group around and around, until the group winds up in a tight ball of human bodies. Form two amoebas and race.

On hot days, form looser amoebas by putting groups of ten to fifteen people inside racoon circles (fifteen-foot lengths of one-inch tubular webbing tied in a loop with a water knot) held waist high. Again, form multiple amoebas and race.

–People to People: Form your group into two concentric circles of paired people, with each person in the outer circle facing someone in the inner circle and vice versa. Shout out body parts to touch without falling down. For example, elbow to elbow, hand to foot. When people to people is called, the inner circle takes one step to the right, changing all partners.

–Evolution Tag: Everyone starts as an egg, waddling around in a crouch until they meet another egg. Upon meeting, they ro-sham-bo. The winner evolves into a chicken, who flaps folded arm wings and cackles around, searching for another chicken to ro-sham-bo with. The winner of this match evolves into a dinosaur. Ro-sham-bo losers devolve one level. The next evolutionary step is to an Elvis, and the final step is to become an enlightened being—a river rafter.

–**Eyes—Mouth—Body:** With everyone sitting in a big circle, go around the circle having people count off; the first person counts, "One," the second person counts, "Two," the third person, "Three," and the fourth person starts again with, "One," and so on—one, two, three, one, two, three, etc.—on around the circle. Each team is composed of a One, a Two and a Three. Ones become the EYES, who can see but cannot talk or move their body, except their hands. Twos become the MOUTH, who are blindfolded and can talk but cannot see or move their body. Threes are the BODY, who are blindfolded and cannot see or talk, but can move freely. The goal for the EYES and MOUTH is to guide the BODY to pick up an item placed by the leader about 10 to 20 feet away. Each team has a separate object to pick up. All of the teams go after their objects at the same time. Each team reaches their goal when their BODY has successfully picked up their object and placed it in the center of the circle.

Before beginning, give the teams a minute to figure out communication strategies. Make sure the EYES of each team see the specific object their team will pick up. Play this game a couple of times to allow the teams to hone their communication skills, then switch roles or put the object in a more difficult spot. After several times, shake things up by switching each teams' BODY at the last second. Important note: Do this game only in open, fairly smooth spaces, and have extra spotters so the blindfolded BODIES do not hurt themselves. This game can really bring people together and creates great debriefing possibilities.

–**Human Puzzle:** Standing in a circle, everyone grasps hands with two different people on the opposite side of the circle. While keeping all hands continuously clasped, untangle the puzzle.

–**Hunker Hawser:** Each person begins by holding a rope end while standing in or on their balance zone, which could be a low tree round, carpet square, plywood square, or a 12- to 18-inch circle defined by a loop of webbing laying on the ground. To win, a player must get the entire rope or cause their opponent(s) to step off their perch and touch the ground. Can be played by 2, 3 or 4 players.

–**Group Map:** The group imagines a U.S./world map spread out over an area 50 to 100 feet or so in diameter roughly designating with scratches in the dirt the location of the east and west coast of North America—and the other major continents. Point out North, South, East and West. The leader then asks a series of questions, each of which asks the participants to stand on the place on the map where: their family is from, they were born, they lived as a small child, they lived as a teenager, they live now, they had their best vacation, they would like to travel, and so on. After each question and resultant location shuffle, the leader asks a few people to tell where they are on the map and why they are standing there.

–**Ducks in a Row:** Have everyone line up and, without talking, place themselves in order of youngest to oldest, or shortest to tallest, or the person who has read the fewest books in the past year to the person who has read the most books in the past year, etc.

–**Group Count:** The group counts up to the total number of people in the group, in random sequence, one person at a time, with each person saying just one number. If two people say a number at the same time, the group starts over. If a group masters this, they can try doing the whole alphabet: Each person, depending on the group size, says one or two letters at random. Best played later on in a trip after the group has come together a bit, this game can be fun when waiting for other group members to show up, etc.

–Points of Contact: In groups of five, how few points of contact can each group make with the ground? Try six, then five, four, and so on.

–Horses and Riders: Musical chairs but with people taking the place of chairs.

–Find the Princess: A good mixing, ice-breaking game. Have everyone write down on a slip of paper three adjectives that they would use to describe their favorite feature, without giving away what that feature is. The pieces of paper are all placed in a pot. Once all of the slips of paper are in the pot, each participant picks one at random, and then sets out to find the person whose slip they selected and the feature the adjectives describe.

–Dividing One Group into Two, Three, etc: With all eyes closed, everyone whose birthday is from January to June makes the sound of a duck, while everyone whose birthday is from July to December makes the sound of a cow. Keeping eyes closed the whole time, ducks and cows gradually group up with their species guided by the booming "Mooo mooos" and "Quack quack quacks." To divide into thirds, fourths, etc., add dogs, chickens, cats, roosters, etc. and divide up the months accordingly. Of course, when you have people milling around with their eyes closed, you as leader keep yours open to make sure no one gets hurt.

–A Variation on Dividing a Group:* The rock, paper, scissor game can be used to divide up a group. On the count of three, everyone makes the symbol of rock (clenched fist), paper (flat hand), or scissors (two fingers extended in a V). Then, depending on the size of the sub-groups being formed, ask participants to find X others who have chosen the same symbol. (* From **Instant Icebreakers** by Sandy Christian and Nancy Tubesing.)

–Ninja—Bear—Hunter: An alternative to rock-paper-scissors ro-sham-bo: The Ninja dodges the bullet to win over the hunter but gets eaten by the bear; the bear gets shot by the hunter but eats the ninja; and, obviously, the hunter shoots the bear but is killed by the ninja. The two opponents, who could be two individuals or two whole teams, start by standing back to back, and, on the count of three, jump, spin and land facing their opponent while boldly making the sound and gestures of their character: Ninjas assume a karate attack position and yell "Hiiiiieeeeeeee!" Bears raise their paws like an upright attacking grizzly and roar. And hunters aim their rifle and shout, "Bang! Bang!" When done by opposing teams in two facing lines, the winning team must rush forward to tag the losing team before they retreat back over a safety line, say, 15 feet to the rear. Everyone who is tagged joins the tagging team. The game ends when everyone has merged into one team.

–Sunrise Roulette: Solidly embed the blade of a paddle in the ground about a foot deep with the shaft vertical in a place that will catch the direct rays of the rising sun. In the evening sometime after sunset, each person predicts where the sun will come up the next morning by making their mark or placing their token where they think the paddle's shadow will fall at the moment of sunrise. A similar game can be played by guessing the high water line each night.

–Dizzy Izzy: A funny game for go-for-it, rough-and-tumble people who are OK will falling down. Participants, one at a time, with their forehead touching a paddle handle whose blade is "planted" on the ground, run around and around in a tight circle 10 times as the group counts out the revolutions. Then the participant attempts to drop the paddle on the ground and step over it. Because people inevitably fall down, dizzy izzy should be done only in the middle of smooth, wide-open, sandy beaches or grassy areas, and never near obstacles or rough or hard ground.

–Spoons and Strings: Two or more teams, each with an equal number of players and a 2- to 20-foot string with spoons tied on at both ends, race to be the first to completely pass their spoons and string under the clothing—ankle to neck—of every team member. As the spoons pass under each player's clothing, that player may not touch them with their hands. Instead, their team mates must help them.

–Toss Bag Target Practice: People compete to hit a target with toss bags. Tied up boats make confidence-building first targets. Then graduate to smaller targets such as buckets or empty coolers, and move them further and further away to increase the challenge.

–Master/Servant:* Using the dynamics of power to create a positive group climate can create results that are surprising, delightful and energizing. Have people form quartets by finding three other people who are close to their height. The person in each group whose birthday is latest in the year, is the master, and the other three group members are servants. Masters have absolute power over their servants, but they must use their power only to promote joy, celebration and positive spirit among them and with the other groups. Masters take up to three minutes to think of something positive their servants can do that would promote joy, laughter, celebration, well-being, vitality, peace, calm and/or confidence for people on the trip. Once they have their idea, they give their servants instructions. Servants must carry out their master's instructions quickly and eagerly. As soon as they receive their instructions, servants circulate throughout the entire group for three minutes fulfilling their role. When they approach another person or group, the servant explains their master's instructions and carries them out as ordered. For example, master might order servants to smile at people, give big hugs, give compliments, rub people's shoulders, sing a lullaby, etc. Conclude by acknowledging everyone's creativity and energized participation with some words of praise and big group applause. (*From **Instant Icebreakers** by Sandy Christian and Nancy Tubesing.)

–Chubby Bunny: Four or five people at a time go up in front of the group and compete to see who can hold the most marshmallows or grapes in their mouth without swallowing any and still say "Chubby Bunny." Each time a grape or marshmallow is inserted into their mouth, each competitor must audibly say "Chubby Bunny."

–Grapefruit Pass: Teams race to pass grapefruits or fresh toilet paper rolls chin to chin without using any hands.

–Group Back Rub: Sitting or standing in a circle, everyone makes a quarter turn to the right and gives a back/shoulder rub to the person in front of them while receiving same from the person behind them. After a while, everyone switches and gives a back/shoulder rub to the person who just did this for them. (See "Rain" in the "Endings" section below.)

–It's Catching:* In groups of 8 to 16, go around the circle and have everyone introduce themselves by giving their name and demonstrating some imaginary ailment that they pass on to everyone else. Ailments can be anything and everything including whooping cough, eye twitching, involuntary leg kicking, paralyzation, etc. As each ailment is demonstrated, everyone else in the group "catches" it by mimicking the symptom. As each new symptom is added, everyone continues to suffer from all of the previously "caught" symptoms. By the end, everyone is jumping, twitching, coughing, sneezing and having a wonderful time. If possible, have someone film this and play it back to the group later. (*From **Instant Icebreakers** by Sandy Christian and Nancy Tubesing.)

–British Bulldog 1-2-3: A great warm-up game for cold days when you have a big, open sandy beach or grassy area. Designate safety zones at either "end" of the 60- to 80-foot diameter game area. The no-man's-land in between the safety zones is the realm of the bulldog, which to start is composed of the two biggest people in a group. At each sound of a loud signal from the leader, the rest of the group must run from one safety zone to the other, crossing through the realm of the bulldog. The job of the bulldog team is to way lay these other participants and "bulldog" them, that is hold them up in the air out of contact with the ground long enough to shout out, "British Bulldog 1-2-3!" Bulldogged people merge with the bulldog, until everyone becomes one big bulldog. Encourage people to play this game with a balance of enthusiasm and restraint, so people don't get hurt.

Racoon Circles

Promoted worldwide by Dr. Jim Cain, author of **Teamwork and Teamplay** and **The Book of Racoon Circles**, racoon circle games are played with 15-foot lengths of one-inch tubular webbing tied into a loop with a water knot. The games below are from **The Book of Racoon Circles**:

–Pass the Loop: Knot the racoon circle to create two smaller loops 24–30 inches in diameter. With the group holding hands in a circle, put a webbing circle around someone's arm, letting the other loop dangle. The goal is to pass the loop completely around the circle without disconnecting hands. The idea is for people to learn to help each other pass through the loop.

–Figure-8 Pass: Similar to pass the loop, this game starts with someone's arm through both loops. The goal is to pass the loops around the circle in different directions simultaneously. Half way around, the loops pass over one another on their way around the full circle.

–Inside Out: Start with the racoon circle laying on the ground, and the group standing inside it. The goal is for the entire group to move outside the circle without anyone using their hands, arms or shoulders. Mention to the group that this game calls for team problem solving and planning.

–Over the Fence: Start with two participants holding the racoon circle about 6 inches above the ground, with the two long sides of the circle about 12 inches apart (making the fence 12" thick). From here the fence is raised in 6-inch increments to 18 inches, 24 inches, and so on up to a maximum safe height of 4 feet. With the group divided evenly on both sides of the fence, at each height increment two people, one from each side, cross over. Important: While crossing, each person <u>must</u> be in contact with people on both sides of the fence.

–Grand Prix Racing: With equal-sized "racing" teams of 5 to 10 people each, each team stands around a racoon circle facing in with everyone holding the webbing with both hands in front of them. While making engine revving sounds, the teams wait for the leader's start signal, which could be a whistle blast or a loud, bold, "Ready, Set, Go." At this signal, the teams slide the racoon circles through their hands around in a circle as fast as they can. When the knot returns to the team member who represents the starting and finish line, the team lets out a big cheer.

–All Aboard: The entire group must stand inside a racoon circle spread on the ground long enough to sing a verse of "Row, row, row your boat." Start with a full size circle, and gradually make the circle smaller and smaller.

–This Tent is Too Small: A horizontal version of all aboard. Begin with either a huge racoon circle made with three 15-foot lengths of webbing tied end to end or a big circle made with a bow line or a toss-bag line. Start with this large circle spread out on the ground, and have everyone lie down and get comfortable inside it. If this went fairly quickly, from here, gradually shrink the circle by, say, four foot increments each time, and at each increment have the group again lie down and get comfortable inside the circle. Light snoring signals that each person has gotten comfortable. Only when everyone is snoring has the task been completed. All the while, talk about and imagine everyone being in one tent, sleeping together on a narrow ledge, or sleeping overnight in the nest of a prehistoric pterodactyl. Once everyone is comfortable and sufficiently compact, have everyone turn over— which, typically, people do four times each night. Also, the leader can ask some people to change places without disturbing others. With everyone comfortable and close together, this can be a good time to debrief, tell a story or play high point (see below).

Endings

–River of Appreciation: Toward the end of a trip, go around the boat and have each person thank or appreciate the next person for something heartfelt, for example, for helping paddle and thus contributing to the survival of the crew, for pulling you into the raft, for being stroke, for following their stroke, for being agile bow, for smiling at you when we got into the boat. The idea is to appreciate or express thanks for something, anything, big or tiny. After everyone has done this, go around the boat and ask each person to appreciate/acknowledge something in themselves.

–High Point: A great game to play toward the end of a trip. Go around the group and have each person talk briefly about their favorite part of the trip.

–Gold Nugget: Go around the group and have each person share something they will take away with them from the trip, such as something they learned, understood better or want to remember. Variations of this include "Bullet" in which everyone shares one positive word that sums up their experience on the trip, and "Snapshot" in which people think of a snapshot they wish they could have taken during the trip to take home with them.

–Lap Sit: Standing in a circle hip to hip, the entire group first does a quarter turn to the left, then takes one side step right to tighten the circle. The toes of each person should be directly behind the heels of the person in front of them. Then, all together, with everyone's hands on the shoulders of the person in front of them, everyone slowly sits down on the lap of the person behind them. With everyone seated, applaud the accomplishment, and then say, "OK, we're going to stand up on the count of three. OK, one, two, three, up."

–Chanting: If you did a chant earlier in the trip, the end of the trip is a great time to repeat it.

–Rain: In a tight hip-to-hip circle, everyone turns to their right and places their hands on the shoulders in front of them. Ask the person if they would like a shoulder massage. Then switch and do this again for the person who gave you one. Next, the leader describes and demonstrates the sequence of four motions which simulate rain, and explains that as each motion is performed on each set of shoulders, that person should likewise do this motion on the shoulders in front of them. The leader then begins the first motion on the shoulders in front of them, and this motion spreads around the circle. When the first motion completes the circle and reaches the leader's shoulders, the leader begins the second motion, and so on. When the fourth motion reaches the leader's shoulders, they start back down, doing the third motion, then the second motion, then the first motion. If people are quiet, everyone can hear the coming and going of the rain.

> Motion #1: Flat palm rubbing
> Motion #2: Finger tips tapping
> Motion #3: Flat hand gently hitting
> Motion #4: Fists gently beating

–Ooooommmmmm: One of my favorite times to do an Oooooommmm is in a group hug at the end of trips with willing, resonant souls.

Give lots of positive strokes: Show lots of acceptance, approval, and support. Above all, do not judge others (whether they are present or not) or put others down. Negativism, elitism, bragging, sarcasm, put-downs, teasing, serious competition or machismo on the guide's part tends to make people feel judged, cautious, afraid. An atmosphere of acceptance and support, on the other hand, helps people feel okay, safe, expansive, free, and at one with themselves, their companions, the river and their world.

9: KNOTS

A Word about Knots

Knots useful in rafting are generally quick to tie, strong under pull, and relatively quick to untie even after having been subjected to a heavy load. Presented here is a selection of knots with which one can handle virtually any rafting situation.

Knot nomenclature: In general parlance, any method of tying a rope is called a knot. But to insiders of the art there is a more precise language: A **knot** ties up a bundle, joins the ends of two very small cords and makes a loop, a noose, or a knob in a rope. A **bend** ties the ends of two ropes together. And a **hitch** ties a rope to a ring, tree trunk, or any other object. Also, the **running end** is the free, moving end of a rope; the **standing part** is the fixed, stationary end; and a **bight** is a doubled or folded over section of rope.

For more about knots—and swiftwater rescue in general—I strongly recommend the Whitewater Rescue Manual by Charles Walbridge and Wayne Sundmacher Sr. (Ragged Mountain Press, Camden, Maine), from which I have borrowed extensively in creating the drawings and descriptions below. Thank you Charley and Wayne!

COILING A LINE

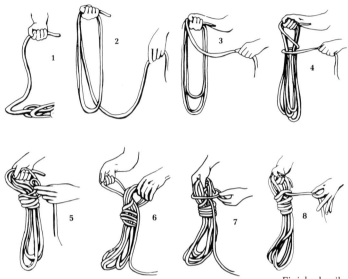

*Finished coil.
This coil is easier
to undo if you don't pull
it too tight.*

THE QUICK COIL

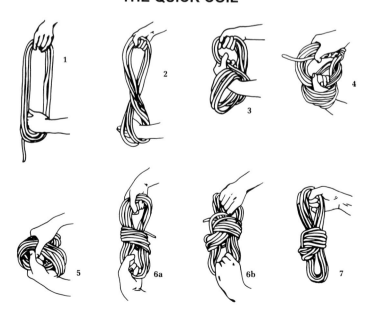

TWO HALF HITCHES ON A BIGHT

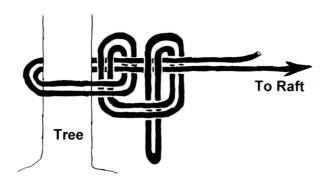

This is the preferred method for tying a bow or stern line to a tree or rock. When tying to a rock, make sure the back side is undercut so the rope can grip the rock.

WATER KNOT

Used to make racoon circles and webbing loops, and to join two lengths of webbing, the water knot is basically a follow-through granny or overhand knot. Because water knots are difficult to untie after being subjected to heavy loads, they are not recommended for rescue work. A stronger alternative which is easier to untie after heavy loading is the follow-through figure 8 described below.

BOWLINE

The bowline (pronounced "BO-lin"–with the "BO" sounding like the bow in bow and arrow) puts a loop of a fixed size in a line and remains the favored way to secure bow and stern lines to bow and stern D-rings. One way to tie a bowline is to first form a loop, then run the free end through, around the standing part, and back through the loop as shown.

TYING THE BOWLINE: THE TWO-FINGER METHOD

A fast way to tie the bowline:

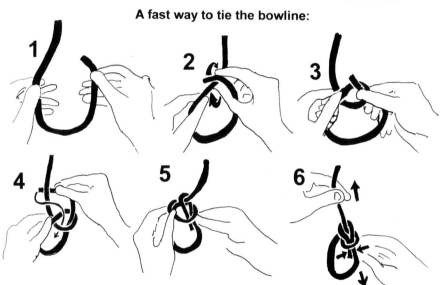

The crucial step in the "Two-Finger Method" is shown in # 2, where the thumb and fore finger pinch the running end to the rope, and twist (in this case clockwise) to instantly create the loop–which already has the running end coming out of it–as in # 3! Then, in # 4, run the free end around the standing part and back through the loop. To tighten a bowline, as shown in # 6, pinch the running end to the side of the loop with one hand, and pull on the standing part with the other hand.

THE RAFTER'S HITCH
& QUICK-RELEASE HALF HITCH WITH INSURANCE

The rafter's hitch creates a mechanical advantage system which is very useful in tightening down rowing frames, baggage loads, stacks of rafts on trailers, etc. and is a very stable hitch well suited to rafting. To some this is known as a trucker's or modified trucker's hitch, but a true trucker's hitch, unlike this hitch, can upset and come loose in the underwater wrenching which can occur after a flip. Besides, every trucker I've asked about it has declared, "That ain't no trucker's hitch!" So let it be known henceforth as the rafter's hitch!

← Anchor

1. With several twists, make a loop in the rope. (The more twists, the easier it will be to later remove the loop made in step # 2 when the hitch is untied.)

2. From the rope on the running-end side of the loop, pull a bight through the loop.

3. Pull end of rope through loop and cinch down tight.

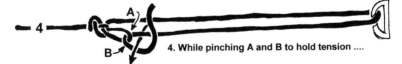

4. While pinching A and B to hold tension ....

Quick-Release Half Hitch →

5. .... make a quick-release half hitch as shown.

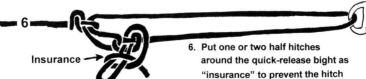

Insurance →

6. Put one or two half hitches around the quick-release bight as "insurance" to prevent the hitch from accidentally untying.

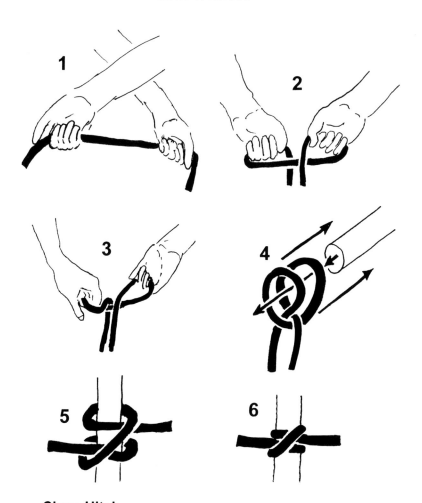

Clove Hitch

An excellent hitch for tying a line tight to an oar or pole. Steps 1 through 4 illustrate a quick way to tie a clove hitch onto the end of an oar. When tied at the end of a line or in the middle of a pole, tie a half hitch with the free end around the standing part–see 5 & 6. Notice that a tightened clove hitch looks like a "not equal" sign.

BASIC FIGURE 8

The basic figure 8 makes a good stopper at the end of a rope.

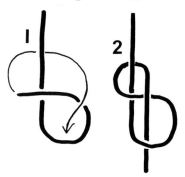

FIGURE 8 IN A BIGHT

The figure 8 in a bight makes a strong loop in the end of a line—or in the middle of a line if the two ends will be pulled in the same direction.

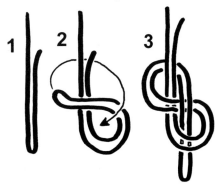

FIGURE 8 FOLLOW-THROUGH

Also called the figure 8 tracer, the figure 8 follow-through is the preferred knot for making webbing anchors and continuous-loop load distribution systems. It also can be used to join any two lines of equal diameter and to make a loop in the end of a line. Like all figure 8s, it is strong and still relatively easy to untie even after having been subjected to a heavy load. To tie it, first tie a loose figure 8 in one line, then with the second line follow the path of the first through the knot.

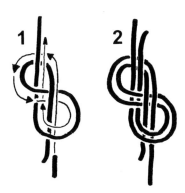

FIGURE 8 BIGHT IN A BIGHT

Also called a double-eyed or rabbit-eared figure 8, the figure 8 bight in a bight makes two loops in the end of a rope. Two loops instead of one clipped into a carabiner, for instance, can double the strength of this part of a rope and pulley system.

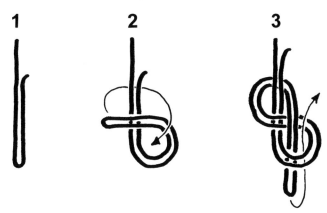

see next page

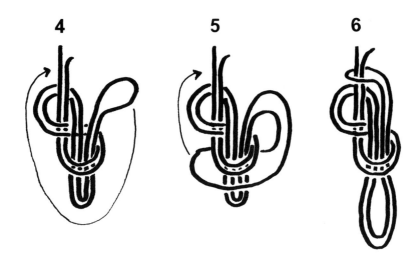

PRUSIK

Because it slides when loose and grips when tight, the prusik knot creates a movable connection point on a rescue haul line. Position the double fisherman's knot off to one side away from both the prusik knot and the point where the carabiner clips onto the prusik loop.

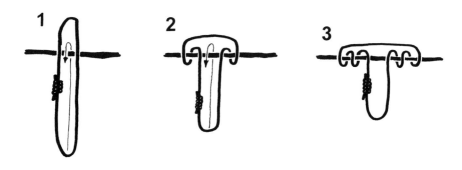

KLEMHEIST AND FRENCH PRUSIK

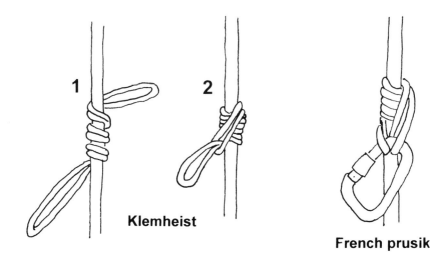

Klemheist

French prusik

Strong alternatives to the prusik knot, the klemheist and French prusik do not jam. The Klemheist is tied by spiraling a cord or webbing loop around the haul line at least three times and passing the bottom loop through the shorter top loop. When tied with webbing, the webbing must be laid flat against the haul line.

The French prusik is very similar to the klemheist, but uses a shorter sling with both ends clipped into a locking carabiner. The French prusik can be released under load by placing one's hand around the top of the knot and sliding the whole knot down. *Caution:* When using two prusik knots, a French prusik should not be used as the lower knot, because if the upper knot slips down onto a French prusik, the French prusik will release and both knots can slip. Because of this fact, climbers often use a French prusik as the top knot and a klemheist as the bottom knot.

DOUBLE FISHERMAN'S

The double fisherman's, which is also known as a barrel knot, securely joins two rope ends, and is the preferred knot for making prusik loops. Once subjected to heavy load, this knot is pretty much impossible to untie. When using this knot to join two different ropes, small differences in diameter are OK.

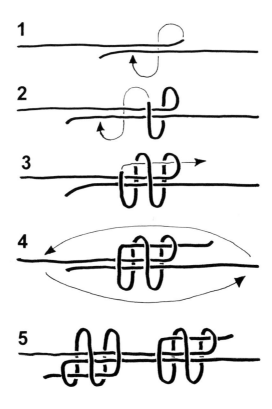

FRICTION RELEASE

When built into a Tyrolean or similar system between the anchor and the break, a friction release allows the system to be taken down by one person. Instead of having to reassemble the entire group to pull on the line to release the break, the tension–and hence the break–can be released gradually (and much more quickly) by one person. With a loop at one end clipped into one carabiner, run the 1" tubular webbing back and forth between the two locking carabiners five or more times. Then tightly spiral the webbing around and around the webbing between the carabiners, and clip a loop at the end of the webbing through one of the carabiners.

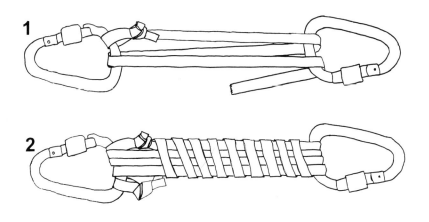

Three-Point Hitch for Boat Towing

This hitch removes the strain from bow and stern D-rings for boat tows, and is strongly recommended when towing long strings of rafts. A warm thanks to Jonathan McClelland of Friends of the River for passing along this great hitch!

Step 1

Attach 3 carabiners to the D-rings at one end of the raft.

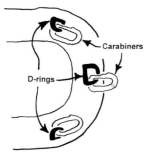

Carabiners

D-rings

Step 2

Either use a very long bow or stern line, or attach the free end of a throw rope to the bow or stern carabiner, and clip into a large locking carabiner.

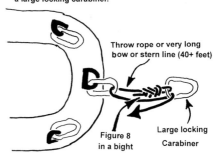

Throw rope or very long bow or stern line (40+ feet)

Figure 8 in a bight

Large locking Carabiner

Step 3

Clip rope through one side carabiner and back through locking carabiner.

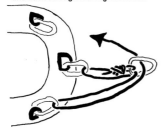

Step 4

Repeat step 3 on the other stide, but this time connect to the locking carabiner with a figure 8 in a bight.

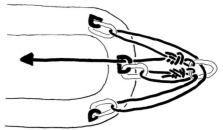

Step 5

Run the line down the center of the raft, and make a long bight on it to either pass thru or clip with another carabiner to the opposite-end D-ring. Make this bight long enough to clip to the next raft's three-point hitch. Tie a figure 8 in a bight. Clip the toss bag itself with the remaining line onto the line just inside the raft, and clip a water bottle, dry bag or some similar object on the other end as well to absorb kickback in case some part of the system fails.

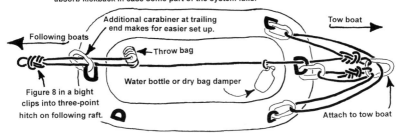

Following boats

Additional carabiner at trailing end makes for easier set up.

Throw bag

Tow boat

Water bottle or dry bag damper

Figure 8 in a bight clips into three-point hitch on following raft.

Attach to tow boat

The Inner Question

At put ins and early on trips, the inner question within most questions asked by clients is: "Is this a safe place to be me?" By answering all questions with thoroughness and caring, and by turning all questions into good questions by using them as an opportunity to share genuinely interesting information, aware guides send the message: "Yes, this is indeed a safe place to be just as you are. Everyone here will be treated with respect; you will not be made fun of or put down; here you can relax, be yourself, let your hair down, expand, grow, and even be silly, and still be accepted and appreciated!"

For example, to the common question, "How deep is the river?" a mindful guide might answer: "Thanks for that question! Well, here in this calm at put in the river might be about 15 feet deep, while downriver in that first rapid--and in other rapids further downriver--the depth in many places is much less, maybe as shallow as 6 feet. So, interestingly enough, often there is an inverse relationship between depth and level of challenge. In this 15-foot-deep calm the challenge is low, while in the much shallower rapids the challenge or difficulty (or ease with which one can make mistakes) is much greater."

Another example: A client asks, "So does the river flow back around to this point, so we end up back here?" A thoughtful answer: "Thanks for your question. Many people ask the same thing because all of the water rides they've done have been theme park rides like Disney's Flume ride which do flow back to their starting point. Well, this is an actual, natural river powered by gravity. The water moves because it is flowing downhill, so this water cannot flow back to this point, but can only flow down and down, down out of these mountains--and eventually down to the ocean, which, of course, is at sea level. Still, in a sense, in the big picture, this river actually does flow back to this point. Because rivers flow into the ocean, where water evaporates to form clouds, and clouds float on high in over the land to release rain and snow, and that rain and snow is what feeds this very river. So, yes, the water in this river does in fact flow back to this point! Thanks again for your question, which was fun to answer!"

Bear in mind that to some degree all trip members, either consciously or unconsciously, have this same question--i.e., "Is this a safe place to be me?"–and will register the message implicit in your answer! So if you want to be with people who are relaxed, loose, expanding and really having fun, answer all questions with thoroughness, patience, acceptance and appreciation!

Glossary with Commentary

ABC's: Airway, Breathing, Circulation. The first three things one checks when providing first aid.

Above: Upriver from.

Agile bow: A member of the paddle crew who is assigned the role of jumping out on shore and holding the boat. It is often helpful to carefully teach agile bow people to, first, stow their paddle, second, grab the bow line, and, third, jump onto the bank, preferably just as or before the boat touches the bank, not after it has bounced away. As obvious as this seems, many people, without instruction, will jump out without the line—or with both the line and their paddle, with can get in the way and trip them up.

Alluvial: Pertaining to material carried or laid down by running water. Alluvium is the material deposited by streams. It includes gravel, sand, silt, and clay.

Alluvial listening: Listening to someone without judgment or criticism and attending so closely that you can repeat back in your own words what is said. Attentive, caring listening is a living, guiding and leadership skill of fundamental importance, and this sort of focused, non-judgmental listening may be the greatest, most healing gift any human being can give another. Sometimes also called *river listening.*

Back pivot: Turning the raft from a ferry angle to a stern-downstream orientation. Used in tight places to recover from an extreme ferry angle, this maneuver narrows the passing width of the boat and allows it to slide closely past obstructions.

Back roller: A broad reversal such as that formed below a dam or ledge.

Back row: The pull stroke on an oar boat. Because it uses the legs, arms and back, the back row tends to be stronger than the push stroke, which uses mainly the arms and stomach. Also see Galloway position.

Baffle: A diaphragm which divides the interior of a raft's perimeter tube into separate air chambers.

Bar: An accumulation of sand, gravel, or rock in the river channel or along the banks.

Basket boat: A military-surplus raft constructed of an upper and a lower buoyancy tube; the upper tube flares outward, giving the boat a bowl- or basket-like appearance.

Beam: The width of a raft at its widest point.

Belay: To wrap a line around a rock, tree, carabiner or figure eight to slow or stop slippage. This technique allows one person to hold a line under great pull. A 360 degree wrap around a tree with bark, by the way, can provide a 100% belay.

Below: Downriver from.

Bend: A type of knot used to join two lines. Also, a curve in a river.

Bight: A doubled or folded over section of rope.

Big water: Large volume, fast current, big waves, often accompanied by huge reversals and extreme general turbulence. Also see "high water."

Biner: Short for carabiner, which means "clip" in Italian. In rafting, biners are used in rope and pulley rescue systems, to secure things to a raft and as items of adornment in river guide apparel. Also see carabiner.

Blade: The wide, flat part of an oar or paddle.

Boat: Raft. These words are interchangeable.

Boater: Rafter. Also, anyone in a kayak, canoe, etc.

Boat angle: The angle of the boat relative to the current.

Boil: A water current upwelling into a convex mound.

Boil line: The line below vertical-drop reversals above which the surface current moves back upriver into the falls and below which the surface current moves off down river. Also called a "boil zone" because often this "line" is a broad zone of white, bubbling, upwelling water much of which is merely "boiling" in place while some is moving upriver and some downriver.

Boof: To slide over rocks and off drops in such a way that the boat does not nose dive, but instead lands more level with the bottom down. Landing level keeps the boat more up on the surface compared with landing nose down and diving deep. Kayakers, as they go over drops, can boof by leaning back to lift the bow. In rafts this is generally done by emptying the bow compartment and moving everyone toward the rear of the boat. Boofing also refers to deliberately sliding up on to and then easing back off of, big, smooth, sloped, ramp-like rocks rising up out of the river.

Booties: Neoprene wet suit foot wear to keep your feet warm.

Boulder fan: A sloping, fan-shaped mass of boulders deposited by a tributary stream where it enters into the main canyon. These often constrict the river, causing rapids.

Boulder garden: A rapid densely peppered with boulders that necessitate intricate maneuvering.

Bow: Front or nose of a boat. See Galloway position.

Bow In: Same as bow on. With bow pointed forward and the overall boat perpendicular, squared off or "Tee'd" off to holes and waves.

Bowline: A line tied to the row of a raft. Also, a type of knot.

Bow on: See bow in.

Brace: Using one's paddle to stay in a raft or prevent a flip.

Breaking wave: A wave which falls back on its upstream face.

Broach: To turn a boat broadside to the current. Usually spells certain upset in heavy water.

Capsize: Said of a knot which collapses, changes form, weakens and slips. Also used to describe a raft flip.

Carabiner: Also called a "biner." A "D" or oval-shaped clip used to secure items into a boat and to construct safety and rescue systems. For rescue systems use only high quality mountaineering carabiners, and avoid the low-quality, hardware-store variety, which can break and cause rescue systems to fly through the air with potentially lethal force.

Cartwheeling: Technique of spinning a raft just before a collision with a rock so as to rotate the raft off and around the rock.

Cataraft: A catamaran-like inflatable boat with two parallel tubes or pontoons.

Cat's paw: A ruffling of the water's surface caused by a gust of wind. Can appear from a distance as a darkening of the river's surface.

Cfs: See cubic feet per second.

Channel: A deeper route through a section of river.

Chute: A channel between obstructions, usually steeper and faster than the surrounding water.

Classification: Difficulty rafting. Also see river rating.

Clean: Clear of obstructions. Said of a route or line through a rapid.

Confluence: The point where two or more rivers meet. North American Indians were onto something in honoring these places of powerful natural energy.

Cubic feet per second: Also called cubes, cfs and second feet. A unit of water flow used to indicate the volume of water flowing per second past any given point along a river. This number takes on far more meaning when used as a basis for comparison after one has become familiar with a variety of flows on a number of rivers.

Curler: A high, steep wave that curls or falls back onto its own upstream face. Considered by most to be a form of reversal. Also see reversal.

Current: Moving water.

Cushion: See eddy cushion or pillow.

Cushion off of: To use an eddy cushion to prevent a boat from hitting an object, often by initiating a pivot.

Day bag: A dry bag that is kept accessible during the day.

Diaphragm: See baffle.

Dig: Plunge paddle blades deep to grab the stronger downstream current well below the surface. Often initiated by the captain calling something like, "Dig! Dig!! Hard Forward! Dig!!! Dig!!!!". This technique can be effective in powering rafts through large holes especially when used by the two bow paddlers just as the boat hits the holes.

Double-oar turn: Rowing technique used to turn (or to prevent the turning of) a raft. Consists of simultaneously pulling on one oar while pushing on the other.

Downstream: In the direction of a river's flow, downriver.

Downstream angle: A boat's angle to the current when it is being rowed or paddled downstream faster than the current.

Downstream ferry: Rowing or paddling downstream at an angle to and faster than the current, often to punch across an eddy line.

Draw stroke: Paddling technique of moving a boat sideways toward the paddle. To do a draw stroke, reach straight out pendicular from the raft, and with the blade parallel to the boat and plunged deep, pull the paddle straight in to the raft.

D-ring: Metal, D-shaped ring attached to a raft and used to secure frames, lines, rope thwarts, etc.

Drop: An abrupt descent in a river. A pitch.

Dry bag: A bag for keeping gear dry on the river. To keep contents 100% dry, a tightly sealed inner liner bag is usually needed.

Dry suit: A suit designed to keep all water out, under which any amount of layered, insulating clothing can be worn.

Duckie: Also referred to as an inflatable kayak, funyak, and splashyak. A one or two person inflatable boat, usually paddled with double bladed paddles.

Easy-rower washer: Large plastic, rubber, or metal washer placed between the oar and frame to reduce friction.

Eddy: A place where the current either stops or turns to head upstream. Found below obstructions which rise above the river's surface, outjuttings of bank, and on the inside of bends.

Eddy cushion: The layer of slack or billowing water that pads the upstream face of rocks and other obstructions. See pillow.

Eddy fence: The often sharp boundary at the edge of an eddy between two currents of different velocity or direction. Usually marked by swirling water and bubbles. Also called an eddy line and an eddy wall.

Eddy out: To catch an eddy.

Falls: A drop over which the water falls free at least part of the way.

Fan rock: A rock in a river which throws up a fan-shaped plume of water. See *rooster tail.*

Farmer John: A wet suit which, like bib overalls, extends from ankles to shoulders. See *wet suit.*

Feathering a blade: On the return, knifing an oar or paddle blade through the air. This can make a significant difference when dealing with headwinds.

Ferry: A maneuver for moving a boat laterally across a current. Usually accomplished by rowing or paddling upstream at an angle to the current. See also *reverse ferry.*

Figure eight: A figure-eight-shaped device used in climbing and rescue work to belay, that is, slow or stop, the paying out of a line. Also, a wonderful, beloved, very functional family of knots.

Flat webbing: Single ply webbing too weak for rescue work.

Flip: When a boat is turned upside down by an encounter with a wave, a rock, or other mishap.

Flip line: A line used to turn a flipped boat right side up. These may be tied across a boat's bottom, worn as a belt around a guide's waist or stuffed toss-bag-style in small bags and hung at a boat's sides.

Flood Plain: That portion of a river valley, adjacent to the river channel, which is built of sediments deposited by the river and which is covered with water when the river overflows its banks at flood stages.

Flotilla: A group of boats together on a trip.

Foot cup: Shaped somewhat like the front half of a shoe and attached to the floor of a raft, these fabric/rubber "cups" can help rafters stay in the boat. Also called toe cups and foot cones.

Freeboard: The distance from the water line to the top of the buoyancy tube.

Galloway Position: Basic orientation for oar boats: the rower faces the bow, which is pointed downstream. This allows the guide to look directly and continuously at the rapid, and to back ferry left or right by first "facing the danger", that is, angling the bow toward the side he or she wants to pull away from, and then using the powerful pull stroke (which utilizes the arms, back and legs) to both move the boat laterally away from the danger and slow the boat relative to the current, thereby providing more time to make the move.

Gate: Narrow, short passage between two obstacles.

Ghost Boat: To push a boat out into the current and let it float through a rapid empty. Do this only in rapids in which the boat will not hang up mid way through, and which have a good boat recovery point below—such as a narrow passage where the current drives all boats close to the bank.

Gorp: A trail mix, often including M&M's, raisins and nuts, used as a high energy snack food on the river.

Gradient: The slope or steepness of a river expressed in the number of feet the river drops per mile.

G-Rig: Three pontoons lashed together side by side. Invented by and named for Georgie White, this floating island is suitable only for big rivers like the Frazer River in British Columbia or the Colorado of Cataract Canyon and the Grand Canyon.

Grip: The extreme upper end of a single-bladed paddle, shaped for holding with the palm over the top. T-grips are best because they can also be used as hooks.

Guide: The person who steers the boat down the river, giving paddle commands to the crew as paddle captain or rowing as oars person.

Hair: Fast, extremely turbulent water covered with white, aerated foam.

Hanging Tributary: A tributary stream that enters a main canyon over a waterfall. The tributary canyon mouth is on the wall of the main canyon rather than at river level.

Haystack: A large standing wave caused by deceleration of current.

Heightened Awareness: The shift toward a more vivid, alive and energized way of seeing and experiencing that tends to happen on river trips, especially trips infused with an atmosphere of acceptance and appreciation. A sort of "predictable miracle" on good trips.

Head Chef: A guide who plans the menu for the trip, purchases the food, and helps prepare the meals with the other guides.

High Float Life Jacket: A life jacket with 22 or more pounds floatation. Always a good idea and essential on high water.

High Side: The necessary act of jumping to the "high side" when coming up against an obstacle sideways. Always jump downstream, towards the rock or obstacle. When executed properly, this can help prevent a wrap or a flip.

High Water: River flow well above normal. Makes currents faster and some waves and holes bigger. Obstacles, such as rocks and holes, although fewer in number, tend to be more dangerous if hit. Some rapids get easier, others become more difficult. In extreme high water, the current can sweep through strainers on either bank, enormous holes can appear and one rapid can blend into the next.

Hitch: A type of knot which ties a rope to a ring, pole, tree, rock or other object.

Hole: A reversal. This term is generally applied to reversals of less than river-wide width. Also see souse hole.

Hoopi: Half-inch or 5/8th-inch diameter tubular nylon webbing put to a thousand and one uses in rafting. As far as we know, no one knows for sure the origin of this name, although it may refer to the use of similar webbing to make hoops in mountain climbing. Most often used in the phrase, "Got any hoopi?" Important note: Hoopi is valuable, important, even vital river gear. Take care not to leave it behind on river beaches, or let it blow away out of rafts on roof racks and trailers, or otherwise lose it or let it "walk away."

House boulder: A house-sized boulder.

Hung up: Said of a raft that is caught on but not wrapped around a rock or other obstacle.

Hydraulics: A general term for reversals, eddies, and powerful waves which can slow, change or accelerate a boat's speed and route through a rapid.

Hypothermia: A serious physical condition caused by a lowering of the core body temperature. Symptoms include lack of coordination, slurred speech, blueness of skin, dilation of pupils, decrease in heart and respiratory rate, extreme weakness, uncontrolled shivering, irrationality, apathy, and/or belligerence. Victims often become unconscious and sometimes die. When the air plus water temperature add up to less than 100 degrees Fahrenheit, take full precautions to prevent hypothermia including wearing wet or dry suits plus warm hats and lots of extra warm clothing, doing lots of warm-up games, providing a big hot fire and high energy food, and administering hot soup or juice. First aid for river hypothermia: Quickly strip off wet clothes, put in warm, dry clothes, and apply heat by building a fire, surrounding victim skin-to-skin in a bare-body sandwich; administering hot drink, etc.

J-rig: A pontoon-sized raft formed by joining several giant snout-nosed sponsons.

Keeper: A reversal capable of trapping a raft for long periods. Similar to, but more powerful than, a stopper.

Kernmantle: A type of line consisting of a central core of continuous parallel fibers covered by a woven sheath. Considered the best type of line for rescue work.

Knot-passing pulley: A pulley with oversized interior clearance to allow knots to pass through it.

Krusing "with a K": Spurring a paddle crew on with vigorously repeated commands mixed in with fun energizing phrases as in "Forward! Forward!! Gotta get there! Gotta get there!!" and "Back paddle!! Back paddle!! Need ya now!! Need ya NOW!!" This captaining style is so named because it was honed to a fine art by legendary Whitewater Voyages and Zoar class V guide, Barry Kruse (pronounced just like "cruise").

Laterals: A wave or hole peeling off an obstacle (such as a boulder or out jutting of bank) at an angle. In high or big water these can become major obstacles which sometimes flip boats or shunt, deflect or surf them into inconvenient places such as holes and strainers. One strategy for navigating big laterals is to use a downstream ferry to accelerate into and slice squarely through the uppermost end.

Lawn-chair position: Sometimes the safest way to ride out a rapid: Swimmers face downstream with feet out in front, toes visible on the surface, buttocks as high as possible, and arms out to the sides for stability and to scull to move across the current. As soon as it is safe to do so, swimmers should self rescue, that is, swim hard for the boat or shore, whichever seems best. Also see self rescue.

Lead boat: The first boat in the flotilla, often captained by the trip leader. Generally, no boat in the group passes the lead boat.

Lean In: At the sound of this call, crew members shift their weight in over the boat so that if they lose their balance, they will fall into, rather than out of, the boat.

Learning opportunity: A positive aspect of mishaps and mistakes (in rafting and in life in general) is that they can be valuable learning opportunities.

Ledge: The exposed edge of a rock stratum that acts as a low natural dam or as a series of such dams.

Left bank: Left side of the river when facing downstream. See river left.

Life jacket: A personal floatation device worn like a vest. All jackets should be coast guard approved. Also, for whitewater boating, high floatation of 22 or more lbs. buoyancy and bright colors like yellow or orange visible under water in the event of an entrapment and recommended.

Line: A route through a rapid. Also, in another context, a rope.

Low siding: Moving people to the low side of a boat, usually to squeeze through a narrow channel.

Low water: Flows well below an expected average. Low water is generally characterized by slower current and more rocks, often with tight chutes and channels. The good news is obstacles come at you more slowly, giving you more time to maneuver and, if hit, are less devastating than in higher flows. With strong teamwork, precision timing, skillful maneuvering and upbeat, high-energy guiding, low-water rafting can be a ton of fun.

Major axis: The long, strong dimension of a carabiner. Major loads placed on carabiners should be in line with this long dimension.

Making time downriver: A method of increasing downstream speed by using downstream angles, avoiding eddies and staying in the strongest jet of the current. Also see *downstream angle.*

Meander: A loop-like bend in the course of a river.

Minor axis: The short, weaker dimension of a carabiner. Major loads should not be applied in this direction.

"Nice looking rubber": One of the higher compliments that can be paid a raft.

Oar: A long, stout pole with blade on the end, attached to the boat with an oarlock or thole pin, and used to row. Note: An oar is not a paddle.

Oar clip: A piece of resilient metal in the shape of a pinched U that is used to hold an oar to the thole pin.

Oar frame: Same as a rowing frame.

Oar rig: A boat rigged with oars, and controlled by one person sitting on a rowing frame.

Oar rubber: A piece of thick rubber used to hold an oar to a thole pin.

Outfit: The articles and methods used to fit out, or rig, a raft for river running. For example, the outfit of an oar raft includes a rowing frame, oars, the method of securing the frame to the raft, the method of securing the gear to the frame, etc. The outfit of a paddle raft include paddles, perhaps a thwart ditty bag, and so on. The term may also be used to refer to any commercial rafting company.

Paddle: A canoe-type paddle held in the hands, not attached to the boat, used to paddle. Can be single-bladed (for rafting and canoeing) or double-bladed (for kayaking, solo cats, inflatable kayaks). Note: A paddle is not an oar.

Paddle boat: A raft with a crew of paddlers and guide.

Paddle captain: The guide in a paddle boat. Although they do use commands, more gifted practioners of this multifaceted art, rather than be called captains, might be more aptly thought of as nurturing teachers and motivational, cheerleading, inspirational, outreaching mentors.

Paddle commands: Calls used by a paddle captain to maneuver a paddle boat: Forward, back paddle, right turn, left turn, draw left, draw right, stop. "Right turn" means the right side back paddles as the left side paddles forward; and "left turn" means vice versa. Note: A huge advantage of using "right turn" and "left turn" in this way is that "right back" , "right forward" , "left back" and "left forward" can then be used to mean <u>only the side indicated does the stroke indicated</u>, allowing finesse and precision of maneuver!

Painter: A line, usually about 20 feet long, attached to the bow of paddle rafts and the stern of oar rafts. Not to be confused with the much longer bow and stern lines.

Pan caking: In a triple-rig or threesome raft, when the bow boat flips back onto the middle boat. Also, any inadvertent stacking of one boat on top of another.

Park: In a generally steep walled canyon, a wide, level place adjacent to the river with grass and trees, often found at the mouths of tributaries.

Piggyback Rig: A rope and pulley rescue system which quadruples a group's strength. Used to unwrap boats off of mid river rocks, etc. Also called a pig rig.

Pillow: The layer of slack water that pads the upstream face of rocks and other obstructions. The broader the upstream face, the more ample the pillow. Also called an eddy cushion or, simply, a cushion.

Pitch: A section of a rapid steeper than the surrounding portions; a drop.

Pivot: Turning the raft from a ferry angle to a bow-downstream orientation to the current. This narrows the passing width of the boat, allowing it to slide closely past obstructions. Sometimes called a front pivot.

Point positive: The custom when using river signals to always point in the direction you want someone to go, and never in the direction you don't want them to go.

Pontoon: An inflatable boat 22 feet long or larger. These big rafts usually have 3-foot tubes and 9 foot beams and range in length from 22 to 37 feet.

Pool: A deep and quiet stretch of river.

Pool-drop: A type of river in which rapids are separated by calmer pools of water, sometimes more forgiving than continuous gradient rivers.

Portage: To carry the boats around a rapid. This is necessary to circumvent Class VI rapids and other obstacles.

Portagee: A style of rowing once used by Portuguese fishermen, moving a boat forward by pushing on the oars.

"The position": In an oar boat, assuming "the position" means the guide braces the oar handles high and somewhat forward at arm's length to hold the blades down as deep as possible. Like digging in a paddle boat, this action can grab the downstream current below the surface to pull a boat through big holes and reversals.

Power face: The surface of an oar or paddle blade which normally pulls against the current.

Prusik: A knot which slides along a rescue line when loose, but grips when tight. Also, a loop dedicated to tying prusiks.

Prusik-minding pulley: See *self-tending pulley*.

Pry stroke: Paddling technique of moving a boat sideways away from the paddle. Effective only with small, light rafts.

Put-in: River access where a trip begins.

R1, R2, etc. A raft with one paddler, two paddles, etc.

Rapid: A fast, turbulent stretch of river, often with obstructions, but usually without an actual waterfall. The four causes of rapids are steepness, roughness and constriction of the riverbed and sheer water volume. Any one or any combination of these four factors can cause a rapid. Contrary to common misconception, only the plural takes an "s."

Ready: As in the phrase, "my boat is ready," this is a technical term with a precise meaning: the boat is untied and all lines are coiled and up off the floor; the training talk is complete; all gear is clipped or tied on; each crew member is in his or her place with life jacket fastened and paddle in hand; in short, the boat is truly ready to pull out at a moment's notice.

Rescue position: Getting into "rescue position" is the same as "*setting up safety.*"

Reversal: A place where the current swings upward and revolves back on itself, forming a treacherous meeting of currents that can drown swimmers and slow, swamp, trap, or flip rafts. Some reversals take the form of flat, foamy, surface back flows immediately below large obstructions just under the surface, while others consist of steep waves that curl heavily back onto their own upstream faces. Reversals are also called hydraulics, stoppers, keepers, white eddies, roller waves, back rollers, curlers, side curlers, souse holes, and, most frequently, holes. Although some of these terms are used loosely to refer to any sort of reversal, others carry more precise shades of meaning and refer to certain types of reversals. Each of these terms is discussed separately in this glossary.

Reverse ferry: A rowing technique whereby the oarsman rows diagonally downstream for a short distance so as to power stern first, often into an eddy. With a heavy raft, this technique sometimes provides the only means of entering an eddy. Also called a downstream ferry.

Riffle: A shallow rapid with very small waves, often over a sand or gravel bottom. Does not rate a grade on either the Western or the International scale of difficulty.

Right bank: Right side of the river when facing downstream. See also River Right.

River left: Left side of the river when facing downstream.

River listening: A skill of fundamental importance in guiding and life. Also see *alluvial listening.*

River rating: A measure of the difficulty of a rapid or a river.

River right: Right side of the river when facing downstream.

Rock garden: A rapid thickly strewn with exposed or partially covered rocks that demand intricate maneuvering.

Roller wave: A reversal. This term is used variously to mean curler and back roller.

Rooster tail: A fan-shaped plume of water exploding off of a submerged obstacle.

Rowing frame: A rigid frame that provides a seat for the oars person and allows the raft to be controlled by long oars. Also called oar frames, rowing frames often also serve as racks for gear.

Run: A section of river that can be boated.

Runout: One or more jets of current shooting off downstream from the bottom of a rapid or drop, often found where the water speed gradually peters out. These jets of runout are key features to consider in reading a rapid or drop from above. Because drops and steep rapids tend to be hidden from above by an intermediate horizon line, boaters approaching from upstream learn to look beyond the horizon line at the jets of surface runout. The deepest, clearest channels through the rapid or drop will generally be found directly upstream from the biggest jets of runout.

Safety boat: In high water, highly maneuverable lead boats such as stern-rigs, big c"= cÀ À catarafts and kayaks with very experienced guides which provide a downstream safety net for a group of boats. Also, boats waiting midway and at the base of rapids to provide rescue support for boats coming through. Also see *set up safety.*

Safety talk: A talk which precedes every trip, in which trip members learn about safety on the river.

Sandpaper: Small choppy waves over shallows.

Scout: To examine a rapid from shore.

Section: A portion of river located between two points; a stretch.

Set up safety: Position toss bag throwers and/or rescue boats at key points along and/or below a rapid to provide rescue support for boats coming through.

Self rescue: Instead of merely floating along in "lawn-chair position," actively participating in one's own rescue by swimming hard for the boat or shore, whichever seems best.

Self-tending pulley: A pulley with square corners which prevent prusik knots from getting jammed against it. Particularly handy when used as the anchor pulley in Z-rigs.

Shaft: The pole which connects the blade and the handle of an oar or paddle.

Shorty pontoon: A 22- to 25-foot pontoon. Also see *pontoon.*

Shuttle: The process of moving vehicles from the put-in to the take-out or trip members in the reverse direction. This can be accomplished by driving at least two vehicles to the take-out and one back to the put-in, by hiring drivers, or by using a charter flight service. Or you can hitchhike with a sign reading: RIVER RAFTING—NEED RIDE UPRIVER.

Side curler: A reversal parallel to the main current, formed by a side current passing over a rock as it enters the main channel.

Skills board: Teaching aids used in guide schools which provide hands on practice in various knot tying and swiftwater rescue skills.

Sleeper: Submerged rock or boulder just below the surface, usually marked by little or no surface disturbance.

Smoker: An extremely violent rapid; hair.

Sneak: To take an easy route around a difficult spot. Often takes the form of maneuvering down one side of a big rapid in order to avoid the turbulence in the center.

Solo cat: A one-person cataraft paddled with a double-bladed paddle.

Souse hole: A hole found below an underwater obstruction, such as a boulder. This term usually refers to holes of narrow or moderate width that have water pouring in not only from the upstream and downstream directions but also from the sides.

Sponsons: Enormous inflatable tubes mounted alongside pontoons for added stability.

Sportyak: A one-man, 7-foot rowboat of rigid plastic with spray shields jutting up from bow and stem.

Squirt rafting: Accelerating into (safe) eddies and just before crossing the eddy line, jumping onto the boat's low, leading side or end to make it dive and take in water. Even when performed in deep, clear eddies where it is OK to swim, squirt rafting is inherently risky and generally not recommended.

Stabilizing surface blow through: In some big holes, the white, aerated surface flow which blasts in at an incline and blasts on through. In many big holes where the water is entering at an incline (and not plunging in vertically) some of the water explodes in place and rotates back on itself, while some blasts on through. In many cases, the more surface water blasting on through, the more runnable the hole.

Stage marker: A gauge placed along a river shoreline that is calibrated in feet or fractions thereof starting from an arbitrary zero point. With appropriate conversion information, these readings may be converted into cfs or, more important, raft-ability ratings.

Staircase: A stretch of river where the water pours over a series of drops that resemble a staircase.

Standing wave: A wave caused by the deceleration of current that occurs when faster-moving water slams into slower-moving water, creating a pile of water, a standing wave. Unlike ocean waves, which sweep forward while the water in them remains relatively still, merely rising and falling in place, these waves stand in a fixed position while the water washes through them. The height of these waves is measured vertically from the trough to the crest.

Static line: A line designed to have minimum stretch under load. Only static "minimum-sketch" line (and not "dynamic" climbing line) should be used in rescue pulley systems, because static line reduces the potential, if some part of the system were to fail, of the entire system snapping back through the air with lethal force like a giant rubber band. Even static line, however, stretches somewhat and can snap back, so systems should be dampened with full water bottles, and other precautions should be taken—also see Part 5: *Rescue.*

Stern: Rear of a boat.

Stern rig: Also called a stern rig/paddle assist. An oar/paddle boat, in which the guide has oars and a frame in the stern, and the crew, sitting forward, has paddles. Often used for extra maneuverability on high water.

Stopper: A reversal powerful enough to stop a raft momentarily—or longer. Also called a stopper wave. Also see Keeper.

Strainer: Brush, fallen trees, bridge pilings, or anything else that allows the current to sweep through but pins boats and boaters. One of the most dangerous river features. Also called a sieve.

Stretch: A portion of river located between two points; a section.

The Strokes: The two bow paddlers who, following the captain's calls, match strokes with one another and set a paddling pace that is followed by the rest of the crew. When the entire crew paddles together, they avoid banging paddles, the boat lunges with each stroke, and, most important, everyone looks sharp. This term can also refer to the various paddle strokes used in rafting such as "forward", "back paddle", "draw" and "pry".

Strong, economical guiding style: A widely-used core method of guiding characterized by strong angles (between 45 and 90 degrees to the current), quick turns and using as few strokes as possible to achieve the desired results.

Sweep boat: A boat rigged with first aid, safety and rescue gear which usually runs last in the flotilla.

Sweep oar: A large oar extending over the bow or stern, commonly with the blade angled at the throat.

Sweep stroke: A turn stroke in which the blade is swept in an arc, often around a "corner" of the stern or bow.

Swimmer: In rafting, a person who has fallen out of a boat.

Tail waves: Standing waves at the bottom of a rapid.

Take-out: River access where a trip ends.

Technical: A term used to describe rapids which contain many obstacles and require a great deal of maneuvering.

T-grip: A T-shaped paddle handle. Placing the inboard palm over the top of a T-grip allows a paddler to easily control the blade angle. Also, T-grips make handy hooks.

Thole pin: An upright steel pin on a rowing frame that serves as a fulcrum, or pivot point, for the oar. Uncapped pins are used with oar rubbers, while capped pins, which are far safer, are used with oar clips.

Threesome raft: Three rafts lashed together side by side. Also see C-rig.

Throat: On an oar or paddle, the point where the shaft meets the blade.

Thwarts: Tubes which run across, or "athwart", the middle of a raft.

Tongue: The smooth "V" of fast water found at the head of rapids.

Toss bag: Also called a throw bag and rescue bag. A toss bag is a football-sized bag stuffed with floating line. The thrower, or rescuer, holds one end of the line and, usually with an underhand throw, tosses the bag, generally, to swimmers in a rapid. As the bag sails through the air, the line plays out, so that the bag lands light and empty—hopefully with the line within arms reach of the swimmer on the downstream side. Because a swimmer in the water will tend to move faster than a line floating on the surface, throw toss bags downstream, rather than upstream, of swimmers.

Trim: The angle to the water at which a boat rides. The crew and gear should be positioned so that the boat is level from side to side, and slightly heavier in the bow than in the stem.

Trip leader: A guide designated to oversee the smooth running of a trip.

Triple-rig: Same as Threesome Raft.

Tube stand: When an inflatable raft stands up vertically on one tube and then drops back down right side up.

Tubular webbing: Nylon webbing tightly woven in a tube shape. Generally used flat, it is in effect a hollow, two-ply weave, with great strength for its size.

Undercut: An overhanging rock or ledge with current flowing under it. Swimmers and boats should avoid these dangerous obstacles.

Upstream: The direction whence a river flows. The direction opposite that of the current.

Upstream angle: The angle of a boat which is being paddled or rowed in an upstream direction, and, hence, is moving more slowly than the current.

Upstream ferry: A regular ferry, in which a boat's upstream end is angled toward the bank it wants to approach, and the boat is paddled or rowed in an upstream direction, slowing the boat in relation to the current and moving it sideways in relation to the river.

Wave: A hump or bump in flowing water.

Wave train: A row of standing waves. Big, long wave trains provide wonderful roller-coaster-like rides, a rafting highlight!

Wet suit: A close-fitting garment of neoprene foam that provides thermal insulation in cold water. A popular style for rafting is the "Farmer John," which extends from ankles to shoulders and in cold weather is worn with a paddle jacket and extra layers of fleece, pile, capilene or wool. Shorties, which extend from thighs to shoulders, are sometimes used in warmer weather. Many guides wear a pair of shorts over their wet suit to protect the wet suit and reduce the tendency to slide around on the raft. I recommend shorts with a no-slip butt patch.

White eddy: A reversal below a ledge or other underwater obstruction characterized by a foamy back flow at the surface.

Whitewater: The white, bubbly, aerated water of rapids, hence, rapids in general–and *fun!*

Wild thing: A technique for freeing a boat hung up on a rock which involves the entire crew jumping around like wild monkeys.

Wrapped: Said of a raft pinned around the upstream face of a rock or other obstruction by the current. Boats so pinned are often held in place by tons of force.

Z-rig: A rope and pulley system which triples a group's strength. Used for unwrapping boats off mid-river rocks, etc. Also called a Z-drag. See "piggyback rig".

Bibliography and Books of Interest

Armstead, Lloyd D. *Whitewater Rafting in North America* (Globe Pequot). A guide to commercial rafting outfitters.

Bechdel, Les and Slim Ray. *River Rescue* (AMC Books).

Bennett, Jeff. *The Complete Whitewater Rafter* (Ragged Mountain Press).

Bigon, Mario and Guido Regazzoni. *The Morrow Guide to Knots* (Quill/William Morrow).

Bolling, David. *How to Save a River: A Guide to Citizen Action* (Island Press/The River Network).

Cain, Jim and Tom Smith. *The Book on Racoon Circles* (Learning Unlimited Corporation, 5155 East 51st, Suite 108., Tulsa OK 74135. Phone 918) 622 3292, Fax (918) 622 4203.

Cain, Jim and Barry Jolliff, *Teamwork & Teamplay*. Kendall Hunt Publishers, 1998. 1-800-228-0810.

Canari Press Editors. *Random Acts of Kindness* (Canari Press).

Carson, Richard D. *Never Get A Tattoo: Simple Advice on the Art of Enjoying Yourself* (Perennial Library/Harper & Row).

Carson, Richard D. *Taming Your Gremlin: A Guide to Enjoying Yourself* (Perennial Library/Harper & Row).

Cassady, Jim and Fryar Calhoun. *California Whitewater* (North Fork Press).

Cassady, Jim; Bill Cross; and Fryer Calhoun. *Western Whitewater: From the Rockies to the Pacific* (North Fork Press).

Cassady, Jim and Dan Dunlap. *World Whitewater* (Ragged Mountain Press).

Cassidy, John. Ed. *A Guide to Three Rivers: The Stanislaus, Tuolumne and South Fork of the American* (Friends of the River Books).

Chambers, Patricia. *River Runners' Recipes* (Pacific Search Press).

Christian, Sandy, MSW, and Nancy Loving Tubesing, EdD. *Instant Icebreakers: 50 Powerful Catalysts for Group Interaction and High-impact Learning* (Whole Person Associates, 210 West Michigan, Duluth, MN 55802, Phone 800-247-6789).

Cornell, Ann Weiser. *The power of Focusing* (New Harbinger).

Cornell, Ann Weiser. The Radical Acceptance of Everything: A Focusing Life (Calluna Press). An amazing life-enhancing book available from Calluna Press, 2625 Alcatraz Ave., #202, Berkeley. CA 94705-2720, USA. 510-666-9948.

Dalai Lama. *A Policy of Kindness* (Snow Lion Publications).

Darvill, Fred T., M.D. *Mountaineering Medicine* (Wilderness Press).

Eschen, Maria. *River Otter: Handbook for Trip Planning* (Another Press).

Ellison, Jib. *Basic Essentials of Rafting* (ICS Books).

Farquhar, Francis P. *History of the Sierra Nevada* (University of California Press).

Fluegelman, A. editor. *The New Games Book* (Dolphin Books).

Forgey, William W., MD. *The Basic Essentials of Hypothermia* (ICS Books).

Gawain, Shakti. *Creative Visualization* (Whatever Publishing).

Hillmer, Timothy. *The Hookmen* (University Press of Colorado).

Hodgson, Michael. *No Shit There I Was...* (ICS Books).

Houston, Pam. *Cowboys Are My Weakness* (Washington Square Press/Pocket Books).

Johnson, Jimmie. *Whitewater Rafting Manual* (Stackpole).

Johnson, Robert P. *Thirteen Moons: A Year in the Wilderness* (Capra Press).

Kientz, Marvin L. *Indians of the Sierra Foothills* (Three Forests Interpretive Association.

Lessels, Bruce. *AMC Whitewater Handbook* (Appalachian Mountain Club).

Lessels, Bruce & Karen Blom. *Paddling with Kids* (Appalachian Mountain Club).

Lipke, Rick. *Technical Rescue Rigger's Guide* (Conterra Technical Systems, www.conterra-inc.com).

Martinet, Jeanne. *The Art of Mingling* (St. Martin's Press).

Mayfield, Thomas Jefferson. *Indian Summer.* Mayfield's account of living in an Indian village on the banks of the Kings River from age 6 to 16.

McGinnis, William. *Class V Briefing* (Whitewater Voyages Press).

McGinnis, William. *River Signals* (Whitewater Voyages Press).

McGinnis, William. *Whitewater Rafting* (Quadrangle/New York Times Book Company).

Palmer, Tim. *America by Rivers* (Available directly from Tim Palmer, 396 3rd St., Beaver, PA 15009. timothytpalmer@yahoo.com).

Palmer, Tim. *The Heart of America* (Shearwater).

Peck, M. Scott. *The Road Less Traveled* (A Touchstone Book/Simon & Shuster).

Reisner, Mark. *Cadillac Desert: The American West and Its Disappearing Water* (Viking Penguin).

Richards, Dick. *Artful Work: Awakening Joy, Meaning, and Commitment in the Workplace* (Berkley Books).

Rohnke, K. *Silver Bullets* (Kendall/Hunt).

Ruiz, Don Miguel. *The Four Agreements* (Amber-Allen Publishing).

Stone, Justin F. *T'ai Chi Chih!* (Sun Publishing Company).

Treschsel, Jane Goad. *A Morning Cup of Yoga: One 15-Minute Routine for a Lifetime of Health & Wellness* (Crane Hill Publishers). Great stretches/yoga to begin any day!

Walbridge, Charlie and Jody Tinsley. *River Safety Anthology* (Menasha Ridge Press/American Canoe Association).

Walbridge, Charles and Wayne A. Sundmacher Sr. *Whitewater Rescue Manual (Ragged Mountain Press).*

Walters, J. Donald. *The Art of Supportive Leadership* (Crystal Clarity, Publishers).

Wilderness Conservancy. *The American River: North, Middle & South Forks* (Protect American River Canyons–PARC).

Wright, Terry. *Introduction to the Geology of the Sierra Foothills* (Wilderness Interpretation, P.O. Box 1194, Pollock Pines, CA 95726).

Wright, Terry. *Guide to Geology and Rapids, South Fork American River* (Wilderness Interpretation).

Wright, Terry. *Rocks and Rapids of the Toulumne River: A Guide to Natural and Human History* (Wilderness Interpretation).

Magazines of Interest

American Whitewater (The Journal of the American Whitewater Affiliation), P.O. Box 85, Phoenicia, NY 12464.

Adventure Sports Journal, P.O. Box 35, Santa Cruz, CA 95063.

Canoe & Kayak Magazine, P.O. Box 3146, Kirkland, WA 98083. www.canoekayak.about.com

Currents Magazine, National Organization for Rivers, P.O. Box 6847, 212 West Cheyenne Mountain Blvd., Colorado Springs, CO 80906. www.nationalrivers.org

Headwaters, The Newsletter of Friends of the River, 128 J St., Sacramento, CA 95814.

Men's Journal, 1290 Avenue of the Americas, New York, MY 10104.
www.mensjournal.com
Outside Magazine, 400 Market St., Santa Fe. NM 87501. 505-989-7100
www.outside.away.com
Paddler Magazine, 4061 Oceanside Blvd., Suite M, Oceanside, CA 92056.
Paddler's New Bulletin, Sierra Club River Touring Section, 6014 College
Ave., Oakland, CA 94618.

Websites of Interest

The websites below are offered as a sampling, a quick glimpse, of what is available.
For a list tailored to you and your area, type your key words into Google.

www.aca-camps.org/knowledge   The American Camping Association Knowledge
Center. An excellent source for books on adventure games.
www.AdventureSportsOnline.com Great website covering every type of
adventure sport.
www.AmericaOutdoors.com www.AdventureVacation.com Websites of America
Outdoors, the national outfitter organization.
Comprehensive listing of outfitters and river gear suppliers.
www.AmericanRivers.org The national organization dedicated to protecting
and restoring American Rivers.
www.cbrfc.noaa.gov Colorado and Green River Flow Report
www.Clavey.com Clavey River Equipment.
www.CoolWorks.com Jobs in great places.
www.DownRiverEquip.com Down River Equipment.
www.DreamFlows.com Excellent resource for river flows throughout the
Western United States.
www.drought.unl.edu/dm/monitor.html United States Drought Monitor.
www.FriendsoftheRiver,org California's leading river conservation
organization.
www.FunDoing.com Games for teachers and more, from Chris Cavert.
www.gcrg.org Grand Canyon Guides Association.
www.gcriverrunner.org Grand Canyon River Runners Association
(passengers association).
www.gcroa.org Grand Canyon River Outfitters.
www.GuideSchools.com A website dedicated to guide training.
www.LearningUnlimited.com A great team building resource.
www.LivingRivers.org Colorado Plateau River Guides Association.
www.nrsweb.com Northwest River Supplies.
www.Outside.Away.com Outside Magazine online.
www.PacificRiverSupply.com Pacific River Supply.
www.RaftingAmerica.com A listing of leading outfitters.
www.RiverGear.com Man of Rubber.
www.RescueRigger.com Special software for practicing rescue skills.
www.SpecialRescue.com For more on swift water rescue.
www.TeamworkandTeamplay.com Teamwork & Teamplay.
www.TheAdventureGroup.com The Adventure Group.
www.UtahGuidesandOutfitter.com Utah Guides and Outfitters.

http://waterdata.usgs.gov/nwis/rt.   River flows.

www.WhitewaterVoyages.com   The "River Skills" button on the Whitewater Voyages homepage takes you to special sections on whitewater wisdom, guiding and leadership skills, etc.

www.WildMed.com   The website for Wilderness Medical Associates, a leader in teaching wilderness medicine and rescue.

www.wrcc.dri.edu/snotelanom/basinswen.html   River Basin Snow Water Content.

INDEX

wave train, 242
websites for rafters, 295–96
   the wedge, 157
wet suits, 57, 178, 282, 291
WFR's (Wilderness First Responders),
      2, 177
"While Driving Home from the Kings
      River to El Sobrante"
      (McGinnis), 312
White, Georgie, 283
whitewater, 185–90, 255, 291.
      see also rapids
Whitewater Hilarium game, 255
Whitewater Rescue Manual (Walbridge
      and Sundmacher), 265
Wilderness Conservancy, *The American
      River: North, Middle & South
      Forks,* 241, 242
Wild Thing game, 235, 292
willow trees, 241–42
Witness Statement forms, 79–80, 169

Z

Zoar Outdoor, 254, 256
Z-rig, 147

While Driving Home from the Kings River to El Sobrante

I was born, I am here.
Rolling, now at 68, now at 75, in my big river van north on 1-5 headed home.
Bouncing from lane to lane over Altamont Pass, rolling home.
Forests of ridge top windmills cranking full tilt.
Browning hills, gusting head wind, and a setting sun marvel me.
Some say we're headed for the End.
As I bob and roll through undulating hills, the sun winks up, down, up.
The juice of life surges up my legs, roaring up my spine.
Hurtling toward the pale western glow, I feel the cool ocean air.
A surging river of red tail lights snaking, streaming, lunging
before me, around me, behind me.
And brilliant white head lights fleeing the other way.
A gathering subtlety of colors, darkening shapes.
Some say it's not good.
I say I'm here, I'm leaping and bouncing and dancing—
I say go for the good, find the good, make it good.

Two sets of tail lights just ahead bounce too close, my eyes bulge—
The lights squeeze past one another—I ease–
I say we're here, this is it—
I say go for the good, find the good, make it good—
Crest of cool hills with a river of cottony fog piling up and spilling over.
A mosquito dances by my ear—splat—I get him—
Now 64 mph on 680 North.
Silhouettes of darkening purples—
It's good—here—and, equally, where you are!
Me and the mosquito flat on my side window
bouncing into the twilight headed home—

Misting fog, like a slow-motion Yosemite waterfall, swirls and tumbles toward
me down the backside of the East Bay hills.
Me and the flat mosquito bounce and flow toward it, into it, with it.
Roiling, dissipating, tumbling through the twilight all around—
My big river van leaping and diving—headlight beams rising and falling—like a
dolphin on a wave—
Steering wheel in my left hand, pen in my right—
Watch out mosquitos, watch out ideas,
Purple silhouettes tumbling, flowing, leaping and diving overhead—
A smooth flow to van, clouds and body—
Big engine beautiful—Big wind, big fog, big flow beautiful—
I say it's good—here—and equally where you are!
Oh divine good god—you—me—all this!

—Bill McGinnis, June 5th, 2003.

Simply by practicing the philosophy and methods described in this book, caring guides can help themselves and others move from fear to confidence to joy; from feeling less known and connected to feeling more known, more bonded with others; from being maybe scattered and self-critical within, to feeling more self-accepting, more connected, more whole, more energized and intensely alive; from being somewhat oblivious, to experiencing one's body and the natural world with a heightened awareness in which everything---including the blue of the sky, the myriad greens of the plants and trees, the colors, shapes and textures of the rocks, the clear, elemental, cascading water, and the vital flow of energy within oneself---takes on a glorious, beautiful vividness.

Inspire mutual respect and appreciation among all of the members of the group: In their influential, charismatic role, guides can create an atmosphere of mutual respect and appreciation. At times you will get mixes of very different human souls on your boat and in your camp. In your own way, communicate acceptance and support, saying both implicitly and at times explicitly: "We each have our own truth, and still we can treat all questions, answers, and statements of every kind with appreciation and respect."

Greet and welcome people warmly.

Learn people's names.

Be helpful, kind and considerate.

Be open, reach out, get to know people, be curious.

Keep folks informed of the plan for the day/plan for the trip.

Mingle at meal times.

Acknowledge and thank people.

Look for opportunities to give positive strokes.

Alluvial Listening: Listening to someone without judgment or criticism and attending so closely that you can repeat back in your own words what is said. Attentive, caring listening is a living, guiding and leadership skill of fundamental importance, and this sort of focused, non-judgmental listening may be one of the greatest, most healing gifts any human being can give another.

About the Author

Born and raised in Richmond, California, Bill McGinnis started training as a river guide in 1963 at age 16 with one of California's first river rafting outfitters, and has since rafted rivers all over the world. After earning a Masters degree in English Literature from San Francisco State University, Bill founded Whitewater Voyages in 1975 with two rafts and a $500 gift from his grandmother.

One of the pioneers of California whitewater rafting, Bill has successfully built his company, Whitewater Voyages, to be the largest California rafting company guiding more people on California rivers than any other outfitter. In numerous bid-prospectus competitions (for rafting permits) throughout its history, Whitewater Voyages has been selected by the U. S. Forest Service and Bureau of Land Management on the basis of its guide training standards, history of outstanding performance and the overall quality of its camps, schools and trips.

An internationally known mentor for whitewater enthusiasts, Bill has written numerous books and articles about rafting. These include **Whitewater Rafting, The Class V Briefing, River Signals, The Guide's Guide** and this current volume **The Guide's Guide *Augmented***, which are used by guides, outfitters, boaters of all sorts and recreation resource managers throughout the world. This latest book **The Guide's Guide *Augmented*** is designed to help guides and outfitters increase the fun, safety and overall quality of their trips, and presents a comprehensive philosophy and detailed methods for creating what Bill calls "Deep Fun": Life enhancing trips which entertain, inspire, educate, thrill, heal and delight!

While he has a number of first descents and pioneering raft runs in California to his credit, McGinnis says it is his influence on guiding that he is most proud of. "I have helped foster an inclusive, nurturing style of guiding that helps people move from fear to confidence to joy," he says. "This way of guiding inspires openness, trust and true camaraderie." In recognition of his many contributions to the sport of rafting, in 2000, Bill was named one of the top 100 paddlers of the century by **Paddler Magazine**, the leading national paddle-sport publication.

As well as teaching guide schools, occasionally leading trips and managing Whitewater Voyages (with the help of many wonderful people), Bill does yoga, swims while listening to recorded books on his iPod, and is working on his next big book, which has the working title: *You Are A River: Thriving on Planet Earth*. Drawing on a lifetime of running rivers and leading people in all kinds of situations, this book will be the fullest expression yet of Bill's philosophy of and methods for making the most of–and creating joy in–the ever unfolding, often challenging adventure of life on this planet.